EMPLOYER-ASSISTED HOUSING

A Benefit for the 1990s

EMPLOYER ASSISTED HOUSING

A Benefit for the 1990s

David C. Schwartz
Daniel N. Hoffman
Richard C. Ferlauto

The Bureau of National Affairs, Inc., Washington, D.C. 20037

Copyright © 1992
The Bureau of National Affairs, Inc.
Washington, D.C., 20037

Library of Congress Cataloging-in-Publication Data

Schwartz, David C.
    Employer-assisted housing : a benefit for the 1990s / David C.
Schwartz, Daniel N. Hoffman, Richard C. Ferlauto.
        p.   cm.
    Includes index.
    ISBN 0-87179-729-1
    1. Industrial housing—United States.   I. Hoffman, Daniel N.
II. Ferlauto, Richard C.   III. Title.
HD7289.5.A3U67   1992
331.25'5—dc20   91-46544
                                                                          CIP

Printed in the United States of America
International Standard Book Number: 0-87179-729-1

Acknowledgments

This book could not have been written without the support, help, advice, encouragement, assistance, and love of a very large number of people. We are pleased to acknowledge the contributions these people have made to this book, and to our lives.

This book derives from a three-year study of employer-assisted housing at the American Affordable Housing Institute at Rutgers, The State University of New Jersey. This project was principally funded by the Prudential Foundation, the Ford Foundation, the Neighborhood Reinvestment Corporation, and the Farmers Home Administration, U.S. Department of Agriculture. We are happy to publicly thank Alex Plinio, Don Treloar, and Bill Brooks and the staff and Board of the Prudential Foundation; Nancy Andrews and the Board of the Ford Foundation; William Whiteside, George Knight, Steve Allen, and Ellen Hagey at the Neighborhood Reinvestment Corporation; and Ronnie Tharrington, Matt Felber, and their colleagues at the Farmers Home Administration for their indispensable support. We are also very grateful for the support of the University and in particular the encouragement given by Myron Aronoff, past Chairman of the Political Science Department, Barbara Callaway, Associate Provost, Paul Leath, Provost, T. Alexander Pond, acting President, and Frances Lawrence, President.

We also thank Marshall Wolfe, Executive Vice President at Midlantic Bank (New Jersey), for providing the project with both support from Midlantic Bank and his personal encouragement, and Jerry Greco, President of First Fidelity Community Development Corporation, for First Fidelity's financial support. Indeed, we are grateful to all of the corporate and foundation sponsors of the Institute's work. We also express our appreciation to Mark E. Brossman and the law firm of Chadbourne and Parke in New York City for contributing valuable legal advice to this project, while acknowledging that any misunderstanding of this advice is the fault of the authors. We thank our friend Michael Rappeport, principal,

v

RL Associates, for his advice, encouragement, and polling expertise that he brought to the project. We also acknowledge the valuable advice, financial support, and friendship offered by the leadership of the New Jersey Housing and Mortgage Finance Agency, including Jim Logue, Art Maurice, Kevin Quince, Stuart Bressler, and Ron Jampel.

In the earliest days of the project, many people associated with national housing organizations and publications provided encouragement and visibility for our work. John Simon (President of the National Housing Conference), John Atlas (President of the National Housing Institute), Paul Grogan (President of Local Initiatives Support Corporation), Mary Nenno (Associate Director for Policy Development at the National Association of Housing and Redevelopment Officials), Michael Carliner (National Association of Home Builders), Carl Riedy (then Executive Director of the National Council of State Housing Agencies), Linda Tarr-Whelan (Center for Policy Alternatives), and Johanna Shreve (National Association of Homebuilders) all offered invaluable support and advice.

Throughout the processes of research and writing, we have been sustained by the interest and help of wonderful people working on housing issues at state and local governments across America, and increasingly in the business and labor communities. Among these, we especially acknowledge Amy Anthony and Joseph Flatley (Massachusetts Executive Office of Community Development); Lynn Luallen (Louisville Housing Development Corporation); John Martinez (Kentucky Housing Corporation); Marvin Ziflinger (Massachusetts Housing Finance Agency); Tom Lawrence and Vicki Thomas (Tennessee Housing Development Authority); Neal Barber (Virginia Department of Housing); Bruce Blumenthal (New York State Department of Housing); Terry Duvernay (Michigan Housing Finance Authority); Jeanne Engel (Rhode Island Housing Finance Agency); Ted Koebel (Virginia Polytechnic University); Peter Dreier (Boston Redevelopment Authority); John Leath-Tetrault (the Enterprise Foundation); Bud Kanitz (National Neighborhood Coalition); Laurie Ryerson (Coastal Housing Partnership); Tom Cook (Bay Area Council); Rick Cohen (the Enterprise Foundation); Gaylord Burke (Merrimack Valley (Massachusetts) Planning Council); Bruce Coe and Don Scarry (New Jersey Business and Industry Association); Robert Levy (New Jersey Mortgage Bankers Association); Richard Gens (General Electric Mortgage Insurance Company); Rick Mandell (Co-Chairperson, Orange County, Fla.

Affordable Housing Task Force); Kent Colton (National Association of Home Builders); John Tucillo, Fred Flick, and Forest Pafenberg (National Association of Realtors); Stephanie Sampson (U.S. League of Savings Institutions); William Tierney (Federal National Mortgage Association—Chicago); Robert Detjen (Federal National Mortgage Association—Atlanta); Dan Flynn (California State Senate Office of Research); Janet Gordon (University of Pennsylvania); Dominic Bozzotto and Bruce Marks (Local 26 Hotel Employees/Restaurant Employees); Floyd Hyde, Marvin Gilman, and William Tutt (AFL-CIO Housing Investment Trust); and Senator Frank Lautenberg (and his legislative staff, especially Bruce King) for their support, encouragement, and assistance.

We are very grateful, too, to Judy Abromaitis for her secretarial, editorial, and organizational assistance in producing this book.

The most significant contributions of all were made by our wives and family. To Sandra and Meredith Schwartz, Susan Lawrence, and Hillary Horn, we offer profound gratitude and love for their gifts, which words cannot possibly acknowledge sufficiently.

Contents

Chapter 1

Employer-Assisted Housing: An Overview

In the 1980s, there was a significant increase in the number of American employers offering housing benefits to their non-management workers. In the late 1980s and into the early 1990s, this trend has received such visibility and encouragement that employer-assisted housing may well become one of the "hottest" personnel benefits of the next decade. This book explains why companies are offering housing benefits; describes what companies are doing to provide housing assistance; outlines the widespread, intense interest that the trend toward employer-assisted housing is beginning to receive; identifies reasons for this interest; and notes the significance of employer-assisted housing in the rapidly changing real estate markets and housing policy environments across America.

Unlike the "company towns" constructed by employers in the 19th and 20th centuries (which have been criticized from many perspectives), the housing activities of American employers in the 1980s have been generally seen to be supportive not only of corporate objectives but of workers' aspirations and community goals.

A wide variety of housing benefits were adopted by U.S. employers in the 1980s. Housing benefits are not yet standardized, so companies have to customize these benefits to meet: (1) their own cash/debt/risk preferences; (2) the corporate objectives that motivate or prompt the adoption of the benefit; (3) perceived worker housing needs; and (4) community needs and desired community responses. Companies adopting housing benefits have sought to act in a cost-effective, risk-minimizing, image-enhancing manner, and have generally succeeded in this goal.

Employers are adopting housing benefits for nonmanagement workers for a number of bottom-line reasons, including:

- housing benefits can be of significant value in the recruitment and retention of needed workers (especially in, but not limited to, high-cost housing areas)
- housing benefits can be of significant value in enhancing employee productivity by reducing employee drive times
- housing benefits can be structured so that companies make money on, and/or save money in, wage and benefit budgets
- housing benefits can be structured so that third parties (e.g., lenders, builders) share some of the costs and risks of offering these benefits
- housing benefits can be structured so as to stabilize or improve the communities surrounding corporate facilities (and, sometimes, enhance corporate real estate values or corporate security)
- housing benefits tend to be highly valued by workers (and, where relevant, by labor unions), thus enhancing labor relations, morale, and productivity
- housing benefits are perceived as contributing something of significant value to communities and regional economies

Employer-assisted housing is already national in scope and multi-industrial in spread. Employer-sponsored housing benefits are being adopted all across America: among large employers and by small companies; in privately held businesses, publicly traded firms, and by public employers. The trend is growing both in high-cost housing regions and in relatively inexpensive housing markets. It is also a trend that is taking place among a great diversity of employers, including firms in manufacturing, health care, finance, high technology, research and development, consumer products, homebuilding, and educational institutions. Employer-sponsored benefits are being offered by individual companies and by groups of companies, by unionized firms and nonunion shops.

The trend toward offering employer-assisted housing has aroused widespread, intense interest in the media; among federal, state, and local governments; in the banking and building industries; among labor unions; and on the part of community groups and private charitable foundations. Each of these groups is working to encourage still more companies, chambers of commerce, and trade associations to consider and adopt housing benefits. New federal laws, new state housing finance programs, new standardized benefit products, new labor demands and programs, new community requests—all of these activities are encouraging American companies to make employer-assisted housing an essential part of employee benefit planning in the 1990s.

The driving force behind employer-assisted housing is the reality that the nation has been suffering for more than a decade with a severe shortage of affordable housing for working families— a shortage that seems unlikely to be met by current market trends or governmental policies. Simply stated, employer-assisted housing has the potential to meet a significant portion of America's pressing need for affordable housing.

Later chapters in this book elaborate upon the themes and findings stated in this introductory chapter. Chapter 2 details the different types of housing benefits that some employers currently offer their nonmanagement workers; identifies some of the partnerships that employers have begun to forge with lenders, builders, and others to offer these benefits cost effectively; and provides useful case studies of the adoption of employer-assisted housing benefits. Chapter 3 reports on a national study of America's young and middle-aged nonhomeowning work force— indicating that a large majority of these workers (representing about 16 million households) want and need housing benefits and would make wage, benefit, and/or working condition trade-offs to receive such benefits from their employers.* Chapter 4 reports on a national survey of 461 top-level American business executives that reveals that, although modern concepts of employer-assisted housing are new and unfamiliar to most business leaders, 21 percent of interviewed executives have already decided that they want to consider or work toward a housing benefit for their workers.** Extrapolating from innovation diffusion studies, it is estimated that 33 percent to 50 percent of U.S. employers will consider or adopt housing benefits in the fore-

---

*Throughout this book, various statistics are cited regarding employee attitudes or interest in employer-assisted housing. All of this data, unless otherwise cited, stems from polling undertaken as part of the research of the American Affordable Housing Institute, Rutgers University. For additional methodological information, see Appendix 1.

**Throughout this book, various statistics are cited regarding employer interest in employer-assisted housing. All of this data, unless otherwise noted, derives from polling undertaken at the American Affordable Housing Institute, Rutgers University. For additional methodological information, see Appendix 2.

seeable future. Recent national studies by the International Foundation of Employee Benefit Plans and several state-level studies are estimating similar levels of employer interest in housing benefits. Chapter 5 describes the housing activities and orientations of America's labor unions today, activities and orientations that strongly support employer-assisted housing. Chapter 6 shows how modest changes in federal housing and tax policies could encourage employer-assisted housing. Finally, Chapter 7 summarizes the concept of employer-assisted housing and identifies additional trends in American society and business culture that are likely to encourage employer participation in national housing policies, including employer-assisted housing.

Defining "Employer-Assisted Housing"

As the term is used within this book, *employer-assisted housing* means the offering of one or more housing benefits to non-management workers. These housing benefit programs are being implemented in a wide variety of ways, but most housing benefit programs can be characterized as being in one of two broad categories. The first category of program enhances the affordability of existing housing, enabling employees to obtain housing that is already available on the market. Such programs, known as demand programs, do not add to the regional supply of affordable housing. The other category of program is supply-oriented; these programs bring additional housing units into regional markets.

Demand programs more closely resemble other types of personnel benefit programs in that employer involvement is usually indirect and all eligible employees may access the program at any given time. Supply programs, by definition, limit the number of participants to the number of homes being built or rehabilitated. Supply programs can develop fee simple ownership housing, rental units, or limited equity housing. Demand programs currently tend to provide only home ownership opportunities.

Employer-assisted housing is not the company town! Employer-assisted housing has its roots not in the company towns of the early 20th century, but in the more modern programs of employee compensation that expanded swiftly during and after World War II, and now contain such diverse offerings as flex-time, child care, and cafeteria-style benefits packages. The differences between employer-assisted housing benefits and the archetypical organization of the company town must be clear. For the most part, company towns grew up in isolated areas and provided a stable work force for extraction industries (principally mining, oil, and logging) and among textile mills in New England and the South. While such employers saw the provision of housing as a method for limiting employee turnover, similar to employer-assisted housing today, it was also used as an important means of social control. The tainted image of the paternalistic employer and owner of a company town derives from rental arrangements that allowed employers a high degree of control on a day-to-day basis over the housing tenure of the worker. Most leases required almost immediate eviction for anyone fired or leaving employment, acting as an effective deterrent to unionization and organized efforts to impact any management prerogative. In a powerful example of company control, the records of the United Mine Workers document that, "between 1922 and 1925 in West Virginia, employers evicted over 10,000 miners and their families, about 50,000 people."[1]

Modern employer-assisted housing breaks that link between control, ownership, and housing tenure. A paternalistic relationship is something that, today, neither the employer nor employee seeks. The emphasis of employer-assisted housing benefits is on cash or cash equivalent subsidies that help people—low-, moderate-, and middle-income workers—buy homes. The large variety of relocation and executive compensation packages that rely on comparable financial enhancements for home ownership certainly do not recall the company town legacy. Even where employer-assisted housing benefits are designed as rental arrangements for lower-income employees, protections from potentially uncomfortable relationships on the part of both the employer and the employee are built into the benefit package by creating partnerships and/or intermediary organizations that remove the employer from the management aspect of any rental units that they may help finance.

Unlike yesterday's company housing, today's employer-assisted housing benefits are eagerly sought by the members of the economy's diverse and changing work force. Human resource managers preparing for the new generation of workers are finding that "traditional approaches to employee pay and benefits, targeted to the traditional worker of the mid-20th century, may well become impractical. In their place, employers, either unilaterally or through the collective bargaining process, may try to design compensation packages that can be tailored to individual workers' needs, while continuing to seek ways to control labor costs."[2] The character of employee benefits has been evolving since the 1940s, when employers were encouraged to offer nonwage forms of compensation that were noninflationary. During the following decades, benefits spread as group discounts, and tax incentives lowered rates for various insurance programs exempting large portions of compensation packages from taxation. As examined in Chapter 5, changes in the character of the work force and changes in the family structure have made traditional benefits less attractive, and have spurred an increase in various new types of benefit packages. Employer-assisted housing is part of the trend toward new benefit plans, which include flexible benefits, reimbursement accounts, parental leave, and child care.

Employer-assisted housing, as the term is used here, does not include corporate purchases of low-income housing tax credits nor does it include corporate philanthropy directed to nonprofit housing organizations. Prior to the Tax Reform Act of 1986, a number of tax incentives, most particularly accelerated depreciation schedules and passive loss allowances, fueled the development of rental housing. The Tax Reform Act of 1986 eliminated these incentives, but Congress, concerned that little incentive for the production of low cost rental housing then existed, created a new, highly targeted incentive, the Low-Income Housing Tax Credit, to encourage for-profit corporations to invest in housing units that would be made available exclusively for the poor. Since the credit was established, more than $9 billion in credits (which routinely earn a 15 percent return or more) have been bought by major corporations, including BP America, Prudential, Amoco, Allstate, and Fannie Mae. While the role of businesses in funding affordable housing has grown as a result of the tax credit program, employer-assisted housing programs differ from tax credit investment in that tax credits do not make the explicit connection between the company and housing, since units built with tax credit assistance cannot be reserved for the investing company's employees. In Chapter 6, on federal incentives for employer-assisted housing, ways in which the tax credit program can be improved are explored, including provisions that will enable employers to invest in the credit for use by their low-income employees.

Just as business' social investment in housing is not employer-assisted housing, neither is the important role that business plays as a charitable contributor to a variety of housing organizations. Since 1980, when the federal government dramatically reduced its commitment to funding housing, a wide variety and growing number of nonprofit organizations that develop housing for low- and moderate-income people have come into existence. Recent studies show that this new group of housing providers produce up to 30,000 new or renovated affordable units annually. Organizations such as The Enterprise Foundation, the Local Initiatives Support Corporation, and the federally chartered Neighborhood Reinvestment Corporation, are bringing business and nonprofit community organizations together in hundreds of cities, creating public/private partnerships for housing. Business and corporate foundation philanthropic support has been, and will continue to be, vital to the success of these efforts. But these business–community partnerships fill only a small portion of the need, and business charitable programs do not have the capacity nor the responsibility to deal with the magnitude of the problem. Of the $17.1 billion donated by businesses and foundations to nonprofit causes in 1985, less than $500 million went to housing and community development efforts.[3] Business contributes, on average, 2 percent of profits to charity, and much of this goes to support other worthy projects including education, the arts, social welfare, and hospital programs.

Finally, employer-assisted housing does not include the real estate arrangements found in relocation plans. These forms of employer housing assistance, which are a direct personnel benefit expense, are part of a well-established industry, needing no new explanation or advocacy. Indeed, the relocation benefits business is now a $17 billion business annually, with most of the activity assisting middle and upper management and other professionals.[4] Similarly, housing-related executive compensation packages are also well established, with annual costs of $3 billion, and corporate leaders who receive these benefits do not require a volume such as this in order to articulate the need for such benefits.

Why Employer-Assisted Housing?

A shortage of affordable housing for workers is harming businesses and major regional economies all across the United States. In the American Affordable Housing Institute's 1990 survey of 461 top-level executives, representative of the nation's business leaders, a significant percentage of respondents reported difficulties in recruiting and/or retaining needed employees because of "the unavailability of nearby affordable housing." Many also remarked that the length of worker commutes were "a productivity issue" for their firm. As might be expected, about two-thirds of business executives who perceive that their firms experience housing-related business problems are interested in considering or working toward housing benefits for their employees. Exhibit 1.1 summarizes the problems that high housing costs are imposing on employers.

Exhibit 1.1   Problems Due to High-Cost Housing

Individual Businesses:

1. Difficulty and added expense in recruiting personnel.
2. Loss of key personnel to lower-cost housing regions (i.e., problems and costs associated with targeted labor retention efforts).
3. Wage rate distortions (e.g., demands for salaries and cost of living adjustments or "COLAS" tied not to productivity but to costs of housing).
4. Diminished productivity due to absenteeism, tardiness, and fatigue factors associated with long commutes (as workers move further away from developed work sites in search of affordable housing).
5. Resistance to, and costs of, relocating managers.
6. Problems and costs associated with moving corporate facilities or corporate functions to lower-cost housing regions.
7. Lost competitiveness when firms pay (unproductive) housing cost factors in wages.

Regional Economies:

1. When major firms move, the regional economy loses jobs, investments, and business activity.
2. Housing costs are passed along to other businesses and to the general consumer in the form of wages, premiums, and price increases—all factors that contribute to "regional inflation" and regional noncompetitiveness.

Communities:

1. Traffic congestion, lost "greenspace," lost farmland—as workers are forced to buy homes further away from developed work sites.

How Housing Costs Hurt Businesses

Boston

In October 1987, a study on the relationship between housing affordability and economic growth was completed by Ann Greiner of MIT's Urban Studies and Planning Department and published by the Boston Redevelopment Authority.[5] That study found Boston to have the nation's worst housing affordability index (a 7.3 to 1 ratio of home prices to annual wages) and that high housing costs were perceived by business leaders to be limiting economic growth, imposing high relocation costs on business, creating a labor shortage by inhibiting worker in-migration, while encouraging the loss of key personnel to lower housing cost areas, and forcing up wages.

The study confirmed previous press accounts of Boston's labor shortage, finding extreme shortages in many skill classifications. For example, 80 percent of firms hiring clerical workers, 50 percent of companies seeking high technology employees, and 90 percent of hospitals recruiting nurses reported labor shortages. Overall, 80 percent of small businesses reported having difficulty in finding qualified employees. The Greiner report also revealed Boston's labor force growth in the 1980s to be only one-third that of the nation's, caused largely by a very low in-migration rate. Experts at Harvard's Joint Center for Housing Studies, at the Federal Home Loan Bank of Boston, and at the Associated Industries of Massachusetts, all attributed these labor problems largely to skyrocketing housing prices.[6]

Personnel executives from many firms, representing a wide diversity of industries, all testified to housing cost as both a barrier to attracting needed workers and a key factor in driving up relocation costs (and as a brake on economic growth). Analysis showed Boston's increasing housing costs exerting "upward pressure on wages in every industry sector."[7] What does it mean for companies that are not in the most profitable position? They either cut back or move out. "We now only see this in the manufacturing industry (but we expect to) begin to see its impact on other industries," the chief economist of the Associated Industries of Massachusetts said recently.[8] He also concluded that "housing costs are choking the natural growth that could happen."[9] For example, two-thirds of business leaders responding to a 1987 New England Board of Higher Education survey thought housing costs were "an obstacle to future economic growth" in the region,[10] and half of those businesses responding to a New England Council survey called the cost of housing "a very important issue in terms of future growth and employment opportunities."[11]

The New York Metropolitan Area

Several recent analyses of the economy of the New York metropolitan area found high-cost housing to be a barrier, indeed a danger, to economic growth in the region—but business observers really do not need sophisticated studies to tell them that. The announced decisions of Grumman, Mobil Oil, International Paper, J.C. Penney, and Deloitte, Haskins and Sells (now Deloitte Touche) in the mid-1980s to move key corporate facilities out of the metropolitan area explicitly blaming *high housing prices* made the point very forcefully.

Grumman, Long Island's largest employer, was the first to go. With the opening of engineering centers in Florida and Texas, Grumman effectively relocated several thousand jobs out of the New York area. The company's announcement cited the lack of affordable housing as one of the prime reasons for moving. Grumman had experienced severe recruitment difficulties and high relocation expenses directly attributable to New York area housing costs. "The engineers we've interviewed," said a Grumman spokesperson, "simply said, 'No, we won't go to Long Island.' "[12] He added that a home costing $125,000 near Grumman's new Florida facility would cost over $200,000 on Long Island. Grumman's executives noted that the company has to offer housing bonuses and other premiums to lure engineers to Long Island—the housing bonus alone often being as high as 20 percent of salary. Grumman obviously found these added business expenses to be what one national expert recently termed "a non-productive use of capital (which) makes it increasingly difficult for (regional) employers to compete in a national marketplace."[13]

Grumman's decision, coming on top of announced plans to cut 1,500 jobs from its New York work force, was followed by Mobil's announcement that it would relocate its national headquarters and 1,700 jobs from New York City to Virginia; International Paper's planned move of jobs from Manhattan to Memphis; J.C. Penney's relocation of its national headquarters and 3,100 jobs from New York to Dallas; and the action of Deloitte, Haskins and Sells, one of the nation's largest accounting firms, to move its national headquarters out of Manhattan. In each case, the shortage of affordable housing was a critical factor in the decision to leave New York for another region of the country.

Long Island's planning board director estimated that Grumman's decision would cost the area about $50 million in lost investment, jobs, and tax revenues. Using his formulas, the actions of Mobil, International Paper, J.C. Penney's, and Deloitte imposed a loss of more that a quarter of a billion dollars on the metropolitan area.[14]

The New York/northern New Jersey area has one of the "worst" housing affordability gaps in the nation. This situation has caused the Regional Plan Association and the Port Authority of New York and New Jersey to see the regional economy as endangered by the shortage of affordable housing for workers.

Beginning in 1985, the Regional Plan Association warned that "without adequate housing provision and satisfaction of housing needs, the region may not sustain its projected strong growth in employment and output."[15]

In 1987, the Port Authority of New York and New Jersey's annual analysis of the region's economy made the point even more forcefully: "Companies just are not going to expand here when their employees can't afford homes."[16] The report noted a worsening shortage of affordable housing, high housing costs, the need to double present levels of home construction in each of the next three years to bring prices down, and the negative consequences to businesses when they experience difficulties in attracting out-of-area employees to the region.

In 1989, 43 percent of businesses surveyed by the New Jersey Business and Industry Association said that they had experienced difficulty in recruiting and/or retaining employees due to the high cost of housing. Among larger businesses the percentage was even more acute, with 56 percent of firms employing 100 to 499 persons reporting difficulty, and 75 percent of employers with 500 or more employees reporting difficulty.[17]

An hour outside of New York, in affluent Fairfield County, Connecticut, towns are experiencing a labor shortage and a housing affordability crisis that mirrors New York's. A much publicized report, "Fairfield County 2,000," prepared by a nonprofit research group, predicts that because of high housing costs, Fairfield County will have a hard time maintaining an adequate work force.[18] The report recommends that the area's municipalities work with developers to produce 60,000 housing units for workers who earn less than $45,000.[19]

California

The same kind of warning sounded by the Regional Plan Association and the Port Authority concerning the New York/New Jersey region has been voiced by economists and business executives in California. At the start of this decade, *The New York Times* reported that "many economists say the high price of housing in California is increasingly turning back would-be migrants . . . as well as potential employers, in a pattern they say is jeopardizing the state's economic health."[20] In 1981, the prestigious California Roundtable asserted that "the high cost of housing is having a feedback effect on the entire economy and is posing a serious threat to continued economic growth in California."[21] The impact in the early 1980s was felt in a number of urban areas, particularly San Diego, and in a number of industries.

The negative economic impact of high-cost housing grew into the late 1980s. According to the California Association of Realtors, the median family's income rose by 234 percent between 1970 and 1987, but during this same time period housing costs soared by 580 percent.[22] As a result, only 21 percent of California households could afford to purchase a median-priced home.[23]

There is now substantial recognition on the part of business leaders that housing unaffordability is imposing real problems and costs upon their firms and their regions. Seventy-one percent of California's manufacturers recently reported that the high cost and unavailability of housing is having a negative effect on business.[24] They are reporting that employees are moving farther away from work sites in search of affordable housing, leading to longer commutes and reduced productivity. Concern over commuter-generated auto pollution has caused the South Coast Air Quality Management District to consider denying permits for some new facilities.

Employers are finding it difficult to fill jobs, retain vital personnel, and expand their businesses. For example, Patagonia, an outdoor clothing manufacturer, recently moved its prosperous mail order division from Ventura, California, to Montana because, according to a company spokeswoman, "housing costs made it difficult to recruit entry-level workers."[25] Joel Singer, chief economist for the California Realtors, sums up the situation by saying that high housing costs "ultimately could make California a non-competitive economy."[26]

Advantages to Companies and Workers

The business problems associated with high-cost housing are not only increasingly recognized, but are also spreading rapidly across the nation. Some very large companies may run, but even they will not be able to hide, from these problems for very long. Ignoring these problems will not solve them, either. Accordingly, forward-looking executives have begun to very carefully examine their options for dealing with these problems, and a growing number are deciding that a housing benefit for nonmanagement workers ought to be a key component for solving housing-related business problems.

Generally, there are four ways that companies can cope with housing-related business problems. They can

1. advocate and support governmental policies to make housing more affordable;
2. contribute philanthropic funds to nonprofit community-based housing groups;
3. grant wage increases designed to match housing costs (and cost increases); and
4. adopt one or more housing benefits for nonmanagement workers.

Each of these activities can be useful to companies, workers, and communities. Business support for improved governmental housing policies would be very helpful in many localities and states and is long overdue at the national level; charitable funds can certainly be put to good purpose by nonprofit housing groups in almost every community. Yet these are highly indirect, limited, uncertain, and long-term strategies. Granting wage increases that track the costs of (and cost increases in) housing may also be part of an appropriate strategy for a given company. But as Exhibit 1.2 shows, there are five reasons why most firms will generally find it more advantageous to design and implement a housing benefit than to utilize a business strategy that relies (partly or exclusively) on wage increases.

Exhibit 1.2   Five Advantages of Housing Benefits

	HOUSING BENEFITS	WAGE INCREASE
1. Costs and risks can be shared with third parties (lenders, builders, insurers).	Yes	No
2. Costs and risks can be structured as an investment that can directly make money for firms.	Yes	No
3. Costs and risks can be structured to be tax free to workers.	Yes	No
4. Costs and risks can be amortized by savings in labor turnover.	Yes	No
5. Costs and risks can be structured to enhance corporate real estate values or corporate security.	Yes	No

It is important to expand on the areas described in Exhibit 1.2. First, the costs and risks (if any) of offering a housing benefit can be shared with third parties who will profit from the benefit's being offered. Lenders interested in the high volume of activity that an employer-sponsored mortgage program would provide may be encouraged to grant "discounts" to employees; lenders interested in reducing their collection costs and risks via payroll deduction can be (and have been) encouraged to make mortgage loans at rates that enhance housing affordability for workers; builders receiving purchase guarantees from employers can be (and have been) encouraged to offer significant home purchase price discounts to employees. Employers may structure housing benefit plans that share the costs and risks of the plan with third parties, whereas no such advantage is generally available for wage increases.

Second, housing benefit plans can be structured as an investment directly providing cash returns to the employer. If, for example, a company buys a mortgage revenue bond or mortgage-backed security at a discounted rate of interest (7 1/2 percent, for example) and allows the invested dollars to be lent to workers at below-market rates (8 percent or 8 1/2 percent, for example), the firm receives a return of principal and interest (which, in many cases, can be effectively guaranteed) while offering a benefit worth thousands of dollars to each participating worker over the life of the mortgage loan. Cash returns on wage increases are rarely as predictable for the employer, nor is the boon of most wage increases as great for most workers as is the opportunity to purchase a home.

Third, some employer-assisted housing benefits can be structured so as to be tax free to workers. Interested employers will want to consult their tax counsel, of course, but several of the forms of employer-assisted housing provide a real enhancement of housing affordability without incurring tax liabilities for workers. Wage increases, of course, are fully taxable to the worker.

Additionally, some employer-assisted housing programs can be amortized by savings in labor turnover. Consider an employer who knows that the labor turnover cost (recruitment, training, and productivity costs) for a given type of worker is $3,000 and who structures a downpayment loan of $10,000 forgiven at the rate of $2,000 per year for five years. By pegging the "forgiveness" at or below labor turnover costs, the benefit can be amortized.

Finally, those housing benefits that produce new or newly rehabilitated housing units near corporate facilities can stabilize or improve the community while enhancing corporate real estate values. Wage increases rarely achieve either of these objectives (at least in as direct a manner).

Although wage increases may have a role to play in helping companies cope with housing-related business problems, what an increasing number of business leaders are realizing, is that a housing benefit plan for nonmanagement workers can be a basic component of their firms' strategies of coping with the high cost of housing today, and with business problems that are caused by these housing costs.

Interest in Employer-Assisted Housing

In the late 1980s and into the 1990s employer-assisted housing came to be a subject of strong, widespread interest in the general and business media, in federal and state governments, in the mortgage banking and real estate industries, and among labor unions and community housing organizations. In fact, each of these sectors has acted in ways that will encourage still more companies, chambers of commerce, and trade associations to consider adopting housing benefits for nonmanagement workers. Accordingly, an employer who decides to offer housing benefits today is likely to find that lenders and builders are interested in sharing the costs and risks of offering the benefit; that nonprofit housing organizations and/or labor unions are interested in cooperating with the employer to publicize, administer, or otherwise advantage the benefit program; that federal and/or state government officials are interested in providing resources (which can reduce employer costs or enhance the impact of the employer's contribution); and that significant and generally very positive media attention will accompany the introduction of the program.

Media Attention

Not surprisingly, employer-assisted housing has caught the attention of writers and editors in many business publications. In the last three years, feature articles on this subject have appeared in the *Harvard Business Review, Fortune, Wall Street Journal, Journal of Commerce, Business and Society Review, Money Magazine, Employee Benefit News, Employment Relations Today, Employment Review, Dollar$ense, Employee Relations Weekly,*

Personnel Management, in addition to a variety of regional business journals. These articles have been highly supportive of the utility of employer-assisted housing—both for companies and workers.

While the interest of the business press might have been expected, the degree of editorial attention paid by the nation's daily newspapers to the subject of employer-assisted housing has been highly unusual. Opinion pieces favoring employer involvement in housing for their workers have appeared in the *Los Angeles Times,* the *Philadelphia Inquirer,* the *Hartford Courant,* the *Boston Herald,* the *Seattle Times* and elsewhere; news stories have run on page one of *USA Today* and prominently in the *New York Times,* the *Washington Post,* the *Christian Science Monitor,* the *Portland Oregonian,* the *Louisville Courier,* the *Newark Star Ledger,* and many others; and the concept has been featured in five separate nationally syndicated columns (appearing in hundreds of dailies across the country). In a related development, journals of social comment have begun report on employer-assisted housing—among them, the *National Journal* and *Social Policy.*

Major publications of the shelter industries have published one or more articles on employer-assisted housing, including the *Journal of Housing, Housing Economics, Builder* magazine, the *Journal of Real Estate Development, Realtor News,* the *Mortgage Banker, Shelterforce, Housing Affairs Newsletter, Affordable Housing Bulletin,* the *National Housing Conference Newsletter,* and many regional builder publications and community-based housing newsletters. Various labor-oriented publications, among them the *AFL-CIO News* and the *Midwest Labor Review,* have also written on the subject.

Who Is Talking About It?

Employer-assisted housing has been on the agenda of virtually every housing-related conference or workshop in the United States in the past few years. It has been the subject of high-level government briefings, industry-sponsored symposia, chambers of commerce meetings, and urban leadership breakfasts.

At the federal government level, employer-assisted housing has been discussed in committee meetings in both the U.S. Senate and House of Representatives; in the U.S. Departments of Labor, Agriculture (Farmers Home Administration), and Housing and Urban Development; in the White House; in the National Commission on Housing Affordability; at the National Housing Conference, the National Conference of State Housing Agencies, the National League of Cities, the National Conference of State Legislatures, and the National Association of Housing and Redevelopment Officials.

At the state and local government levels, special conferences, workshops, and symposia on employer-assisted housing have been held in recent years in Connecticut, Delaware, Kentucky, Massachusetts, New Hampshire, New Jersey, New Mexico, New York, North Carolina, Oregon, Tennessee, Vermont, and Virginia.

From 1988 through 1990, business workshops on employer-assisted housing were sponsored or cosponsored by Chambers of Commerce in Louisville, Hartford, Seattle, Burlington (Vt.), Lawrence (Mass.), and the State of New Jersey—sponsored by the National Association of Homebuilders, the National Association of Realtors, the American Apartment Owners Association, the New Jersey Mortgage Bankers Association, and the National Association of Personnel Benefit Managers.

Employer-assisted housing has also become interesting to nonprofit, community-based housing organizations, to philanthropic foundations, to labor unions, and to scholarly audiences. Nonprofit organizations have sponsored consideration of employer-assisted housing in Florida, Massachusetts, New Jersey and Pennsylvania; foundations in New Jersey and New York have discussed the subject; labor unions in Maryland, New Jersey, New York and Ohio (as well as national labor councils) have been talking about housing benefits for nonmanagement workers; and scholarly organizations in Kentucky, New Jersey, Washington, D.C. and even Paris, France, have had papers written or panels presented on the subject.

Support for Employer-Assisted Housing

Government

In April 1990, President George Bush signed into law a bill authorizing companies and labor unions to collectively bargain for one specific type of employer-assisted housing: a Taft-Hartley housing trust fund. This legislation, discussed here in several chapters, has already encouraged active interest in housing benefits on the part of many labor unions and business firms. In November 1990, Congress passed and President Bush signed the National Affordable Housing Act, which authorizes the provision of technical assistance on housing benefits to businesses and labor unions by the U.S.

Department of Housing and Urban Development (HUD), and permits employer-assisted housing programs to be part of local and state government affordable housing strategies and to receive federal funding as part of those strategies.

At the state level, North Carolina, New Jersey, and Pennsylvania, in their respective state housing agencies, have adopted programs to encourage firms to guarantee all or part of their workers' mortgages. Similar programs are under consideration in Connecticut, Kentucky, and Rhode Island. Many state housing agencies have announced their willingness to customize programs for employers.

Labor

In the winter of 1990 to 1991, a 14 million member organization of the American Federation of Labor and Congress of Industrial Organizations (AFL-CIO)—Union Privilege—adopted a group mortgage plan. The plan is designed to help union members attain home ownership (and/or to trade up) in a more affordable manner by utilizing their huge collective buying power. The plan has been designed to dovetail with various employer-provided benefits. Union leaders across America will receive information and training on bargaining for housing benefits. The plan, and the training, is likely to encourage a significant increase in employer-assisted housing by providing national and relatively standardized products and programs that employers can buy (and by stimulating organized labor's demand for housing benefits). The United Auto Workers voted to include employer-assisted housing on their 1990 bargaining agenda though they subsequently settled on a master contract without a housing benefit. Other national and international unions are expected to follow suit.

Lenders

In 1991, the Federal National Mortgage Association (Fannie Mae) announced a program to buy $1 billion in employer-assisted mortgage loans. National mortgage lenders and major secondary mortgage market players (in addition to Fannie Mae) are preparing to originate (and to buy and sell) employer-assisted mortgages. These actions are expected to spur hundreds of banks and mortgage companies to offer such mortgages (because they will now be able to sell them on the secondary market). Again, the existence of a national, standardized set of products and of a national set of players (lenders) interested in marketing these products is expected to spur many employers to offer housing benefits to their nonmanagement workers. Regional offices of Fannie Mae have already begun to work with employers on customized benefit plans. This type of activity is expected to increase corporate participation in employer-assisted housing programs.

Studies

The Enterprise Foundation and the Neighborhood Reinvestment Corporation are both currently exploring ways in which the community-based nonprofit housing organizations they serve can work with employers to provide housing benefits for workers, which will stabilize and/or upgrade neighborhoods. The Farmers Home Administration commissioned a study by the American Affordable Housing Institute on the potential utility that employer housing programs might have in rural America. As part of the National Affordable Housing Act of 1990, HUD has been authorized by Congress to undertake additional research on employer-assisted housing.

Sources of Interest

Enlightened self-interest motivates much of the interest in, and support for, employer-assisted housing. Lenders, builders, realtors, and personnel benefit consultants make money on housing benefit plans; labor unions leaders enhance their position with members when they can help to provide a new benefit; community-based nonprofit organizations see employer-assisted housing as a funding source for neighborhood improvement; government officials, facing budget constraints and popular tax resistance, reason that employer-sponsored housing benefits will help meet moderate income housing needs and allow government to target resources to the housing needs of those unable to work.

But all of the interest in employer-assisted housing (including media and foundation attention) also derives from two fundamental contextual facts: (1) there is a real, pressing, and growing housing need in this nation—a need that severely impacts workers and, therefore, businesses; (2) the federal government, once the most prominent entity addressing housing needs, has cut back on housing support to the point of virtual abandonment of responsibility for meeting these needs.

National Housing Needs Examined

In the 1980s, the United States experienced five broad housing trends, each of which evidenced a downturn in the living conditions of millions of American families—middle class, working class, and poor. First, there was a decline in homeownership, national in scope; following 35 years of steady increase, the percentage of Americans able to buy a home decreased every year from 1980 to 1987, a trend particularly marked among young families and first-time home buyers.[27] Second, a dramatic, explosive increase in homelessness took place. Third, the affordability, availability, and quality of the nation's rental housing stock decreased, to the point where a majority of America's tenants now live in dwelling units that the government considers to be inadequate, overcrowded, or cost-burdened.[28] Fourth, the shortage of housing affordable by the poor reached crisis proportions as more poor people, with less money, sought fewer available apartments, of declining quality, at sharply rising rents.[29] Finally, a pattern of stagnation and decline in the quality of the existing housing stock emerged, consigning 10 million families to inadequate or overcrowded dwelling units and 24 million families to units that the government classified as having "a housing problem."[30]

Employer-assisted housing has significant potential to help reverse the declining rate of home ownership and the mounting unaffordability of rents for working families. Accordingly, the following section examines these national housing trends in greater detail.

Declining Rates of Home Ownership

For most families, owning a home is a basic part of the "American dream"; a goal for which they save and sacrifice; a symbol of family security, stability, and success. The housing preferences of the American people have been surveyed repeatedly in the last 40 years and each survey confirms a fundamental and nearly universal aspiration to home ownership.[31] Despite great variability in the methods, the populations studied, and the era in which the studies were done, an overwhelming percentage of Americans (often 90 percent or higher) report themselves as wanting to own a home. A 1984 study by the Roper organization is illustrative: 9 out of 10 adult Americans under age 35 regarded home ownership as their highest personal priority.[32]

Between 1940 and 1980, the dream of home ownership came true for an ever larger percentage of Americans. In that period, American home ownership levels grew from 44 percent to 65 percent. In 1980, for the first time in 35 years, the percentage of citizens able to buy a home declined, and has declined every year since then. Exhibit 1.3 shows the overall drop in home ownership from 65.6 percent in 1980 to 63.9 percent in 1988 and the steep fall in home ownership among young families (which is discussed in detail later in this chapter). This overall drop in the home ownership rate means that more than 1.6 million American families who would have been able to own a home at the 1980 rate were denied that chance in the 1980–1988 period.[33]

Exhibit 1.3 Home Ownership Rates by Age of Household Head (Percent)

AGE	1973	1980	1983	1988
Under 25	23.4	21.3	19.3	15.5
25–29	43.6	43.3	38.2	36.2
30–34	60.2	61.1	55.7	52.6
35–39	68.5	70.8	65.8	63.2
40–44	72.9	74.2	74.2	71.4
45–54	76.1	77.7	77.1	76.0

Source: American Housing Survey, 1973–80; Current Population Survey, 1983–88.

The explanation for this decline in home ownership is clear.[34] In the 1980s, the costs of buying and maintaining a home skyrocketed, far outstripping the median family income and savings of the American worker. Home prices just about doubled in the decade of the 1980s (as did effective downpayment requirements); home prices and mortgage interest rates rose four to five times faster than incomes; downpayment requirements rose sharply and suddenly, while family savings rates first plummeted, then improved fractionally.

Today's young families confront barriers to home ownership that previous generations simply did not have to face. Figures from the Urban Institute and other national sources make this point graphically:

- In 1959, a typical 30-year-old had his or her real income increase 49 percent over the next 10 years, and paid 16 percent of income for the average home.
- In 1973, an average 30-year-old saw income decline slightly over the next 10 years and paid 21 percent of income for the average home.
- In 1983, a 30-year-old not only earned less than the typical 30-year-old in 1973 (in constant dollars), but paid 40 percent of income in mortgage payments.
- In 1990, a 30-year-old would be paying over 45 percent of income for that same first house.[35]

These unprecedented obstacles to home ownership among young families were put into context by Anthony Downs in a recent Brookings Institution publication: "The percentage of all potential first-time home buyers who can actually afford to purchase homes at today's interest rates and prices in much lower than it was in the 1950s, 1960s, and 1970s."[36]

Little wonder then that a 1986 report by the MIT-Harvard Joint Center for Housing Studies warned that "young households feel thwarted by the high cost of home ownership and alarmed about their prospects of ever being able to buy."[37] The MIT-Harvard study also found that an increasing percentage of discouraged young home buyers were limited by the downpayment requirement, not just by mortgage requirement totals.

Young families are thwarted, too, by the absence of new starter homes in many of America's regional housing economies. Mass production of small homes aimed at the first-time home buyer, once a staple of the home-building industry, is now largely a thing of the past. More than half of the country's active home builders are now aiming their product at the trade-up market rather than at the first-time home buyer market.

Employer-assisted housing has significant potential to reduce the declining rate of home ownership in America. The downpayment is the greatest single barrier to home ownership that young working families face today, and many of the forms of employer-assisted housing successfully address this barrier for the worker at little or no cost to the employer. Other forms of employer-assisted housing reduce interest rates on employee mortgages—another basic reason for the nation's declining rate of home ownership. Chapter 3 identifies the relatively modest level of employee housing benefit coverage that would be needed to meet virtually all of America's moderate-income home ownership needs.

Unaffordability of Rental Units

As home ownership has declined since 1980, the number and proportion of renter families has grown, reaching 36 percent of all American households in 1990. The Joint Center for Housing Studies attributes much of this growth in renting to high and expanding costs of home ownership and notes that the number of renters increased in all income classes and age groups from 1980 to 1988. And as the number and proportion of apartment dwellers grew, so did their housing problems.[38]

In 1985, 85 percent of poor renter householders paid at least 30 percent of income for housing, which means that, according to HUD standards, they live in cost-burdened units. The proportion of poor renter householders who spent 60 percent or more of their income for housing grew from 44 percent in 1978 to 55 percent in 1985, an increase of 1.4 million households.

Ten percent of all renters and 20 percent of poor renters in 1985 lived in substandard or overcrowded housing. As Exhibit 1.4 shows, in dollars adjusted for inflation, there were 600,000 fewer apartment units renting for no more than $250 a month in 1985 than in 1978, but 3.6 million more low-income renters in 1985 than 1978.[39]

The rapid rent increases in the Northeast and the West mirror the dwindling number of low-cost, privately owned, unsubsidized dwelling units. Between 1974 and 1985, the number of these units in the Northeast fell by nearly 40 percent, with particularly dramatic declines during the first half of the 1980s. Equally sharp declines occurred in the West, but percentage losses were somewhat more modest in the South and the Midwest. Indeed, the Midwest actually posted a small absolute increase in the total number of units renting for less that $300 per month—reflecting the addition of more than enough subsidized units to offset the decline of unsubsidized units."[40]

Exhibit 1.5 indicates that these problems grew worse throughout the 1980s with little easing of rent burdens in much of the nation even as the nation entered a recession in the late 1980s. Gross rents in the Northeast hit a record $447 in 1988 up from $366 at the beginning of the decade. In the West, gross rents rose from $406 in 1980 to $490 in 1990. In the somewhat overbuilt

Exhibit 1.4
Low-Income Renters and Low-Rent Units
1978 and 1985

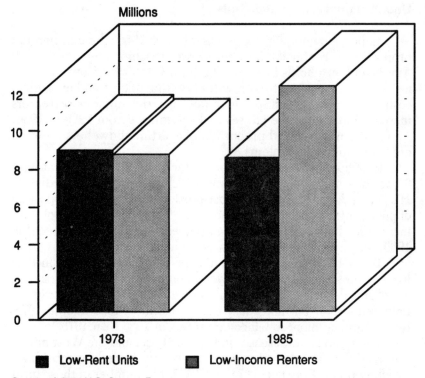

Millions

Source of data: U.S. Census Bureau.

South and slower growing Midwest rents peaked in the mid-1980s, but are still well above 1980 levels.[40a]

The important conclusion from these and related data has been provided by the National Low Income Housing Information Service: every state in the country has a shortage of rental units affordable to low- and moderate-income workers and every state has a worse shortage in 1990 than it had in 1980.[41]

A number of the forms of employer-assisted housing address the question of rental unit affordability for working families. While no adequate quantitative estimate yet exists as to the degree of national need that employer-assisted housing might meet in the rental housing area, it is clear that a significant portion of the need

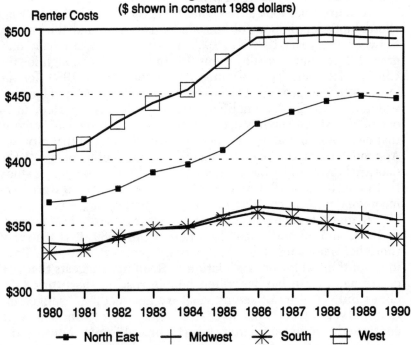

Exhibit 1.5
Increasing Rent Burdens
($ shown in constant 1989 dollars)

Source of data: *The State of the Nation's Housing: 1991* (Cambridge, Mass.: The Joint Center for Housing Studies of Harvard University, 1991) 25–26.

could be effectually addressed by the adoption of rental housing benefits for nonmanagement workers.

The Changing Real Estate Environment

As this book is being written, stories in the popular media are appearing regularly regarding the downturn in housing prices, particularly on the East and West coasts. Perhaps it is not surprising that the media finds any change other than skyrocketing housing costs to be newsworthy. But for employers unaccustomed to considering housing benefits, it is natural for the question to occur as to whether a housing benefit is necessary in what one may think is a period of falling housing prices.

A more sober look at the data, however, suggest that housing affordability for millions of households is not around the corner. Between the years 1982 and 1989, housing prices nationally only grew 4.3 percent annually,[42] but this increase was enough for the Chicago Title and Trust Company to report that in 1989, for the fourteenth year in a row, the gap between home prices and incomes widened.[43] As the National Housing Institute has reported, in 74 out of 80 cities a single wage earner earning the median wage in that city could not afford the median-priced home in that city (see Appendix 3 for a complete listing of cities and methodology).[44] The data are borne out by the Chicago Title and Trust Company's study that indicates that 79.3 percent of homebuyers in 1989 were two-income families in contrast to only 53.1 percent in 1976.[45]

In markets such as California, where prices rose 18.4 percent in 1988, and an additional 16.6 percent in 1989, it is true that there has been some fall-off in prices.[46] James P. Antt, Jr., President of the California Association of Realtors, suggests that real estate panics can happen when people read of sharp price declines but, "we're not seeing what we are reading," suggesting that market correction is all that is taking place.[47] Indeed, with continued strong population growth in California, housing demand will continue to remain strong, but home prices may well not rise 19 percent when wages rose only 2 percent as was the case in Santa Barbara, California.[48]

In New England, demand is down, as a function of both a slowing economy and as a result of overbuilding. During the mid-1980s, two units were added to the housing stock for every new person added to the population.[49] But even in this market, housing costs continue to be well beyond the means of most families. A similar situation exists in the Mid-Atlantic states. However, in the oilpatch states, after a decade of housing market declines, home price increases appear to be mirroring recent oil price increases.

In short, the declining rates of home ownership trend of the 1980s appears likely to continue during the 1990s, particularly among young workers. If employers are to successfully compete for employees, they may well want to take those actions that overcome the housing affordability problems encountered by their work forces, because it appears unlikely that, despite media attention, the market place is poised to come to the affordable housing rescue.

Federal Housing Cuts

It is clear that some of the interest in, and support for, employer-assisted housing derives from federal housing cuts. While it is not suggested that employers be asked to substitute for or replace federal housing funds, employer-assisted housing may play a part in this area.

The basic thrust of federal housing policy in the 1980s has been to diminish sharply the national government's involvement in virtually every aspect of the provision of shelter. The President and Congress have cut

- support for the construction of new housing in the private sector and governmental expenditures for the production and rehabilitation of public housing;
- funds granted to local governments to provide home ownership opportunities for low- and moderate-income families;
- the number of low- and moderate-income tenants that receive the reduced amounts of appropriated new aid;
- federal tax incentives to the private sector for the production of rental housing;
- federal loans to low- and moderate-income homeowners for the rehabilitation of substandard units; and
- housing assistance to elderly and handicapped persons, American Indians, and rural households.

Overall, expenditures on housing have been cut more deeply in the 1980s than have expenditures on any other federal activity. The HUD budget has declined from 7 percent of the federal budget in 1978 to about 1 percent today.

For the past three years, Congress has tried to reach a consensus regarding a new housing policy, one that might reverse these trends. During this time period a plethora of commissions, task forces, and studies have made their views known to Congress. In the Administration, HUD Secretary Jack Kemp has shown interest and energy in calling attention to national housing problems, but despite this activity little has happened. Between the Reagan HUD scandal, the cost of the savings and loan bailout, and continuing and worsening budget deficit problems, it appears that the funds necessary to reverse the housing trends of the 1980s will not be available in the foreseeable future. Thus, the federal government can not be relied upon by employers to solve the housing problems that they and their employees are confronted with today.

For an increasing number of employers, this means that they will have to take the lead in addressing those housing problems affecting their businesses and their workers. The balance of this book examines ways programs can be structured; the attitudes of workers, business leaders, and the shelter industries toward those solutions; and federal, state, and local policies that, if not providing large new sources of cash, will at least facilitate, and not complicate, the actions of those employers who do seek to address the housing problems they face.

Notes

1. S.D. Brandes, *American Welfare Capitalism 1880–1940* (Chicago: University of Chicago Press, 1976) 49.
2. G. Stelluto and D. Klein, "Compensation Trends into the 21 Century," *Monthly Labor Review*, February 1990, 42.
3. "Community-Based Development: Investing in Renewal," Report of the Task Force on Community-Based Development Council on Community Based Development, 1988, 53.
4. D.C. Schwartz, "Corporate Action on Affordable Housing," *Business and Society Review*, 65 1988; 4–8.
5. Ibid., 4.
6. Ibid., 5.
7. Ibid., 8.
8. Ibid.
9. Ibid.
10. *The Future of New England: 1987 Survey of Business, Government and Higher Education Leaders* (Boston: New England Board of Higher Education, 1987).
11. Ibid.
12. Schwartz, "Corporate Action on Affordable Housing," note 4, above.
13. Ibid.
14. Ibid.
15. Ibid.
16. Ibid.
17. *New Jersey Business and Industry Association 1988 Business Outlook Survey* (Trenton: N.J. Business and Industry Association, 1988, unpublished).
18. Schwartz, "Corporate Action on Affordable Housing," note 4, above.
19. Ibid.
20. Ibid.
21. Ibid.
22. D. Flynn and D. Hoffman, "A Boost for Homebuyers: Employers See Value in Subsidizing the Cost," *Los Angeles Times*, June 17, 1989, section 2, 8.
23. Ibid.
24. "State Choking on Growth," *The Sacramento Bee*, March 25, 1989, D5.
25. "Easing the Squeeze," *Los Angeles Times*, February 9, 1989, VC6.
26. Flynn and Hoffman, "A Boost for Homebuyers," note 22, above.

27. D.C. Schwartz, R.C. Ferlauto, and D.N. Hoffman, *A New Housing Policy for America: Recapturing the American Dream* (Philadelphia: Temple University Press, 1988), 3.
28. Ibid.
29. Ibid.
30. Ibid.
31. H.W. Christian et al., *Home Ownership: Celebrating the American Dream* (Chicago: Economics Department, U.S. League of Savings Associations, 1984) 146.
32. National Association of Home Builders (NAHB), National Association of Realtors, and Mortgage Bankers Association of America, *Toward a National Housing Policy* (Washington, D.C.: The Associations, 1987) 3.
33. Schwartz, Ferlauto, and Hoffman, "A New Housing Policy for America," note 27, above.
34. See D.C. Schwartz, R.C. Ferlauto, and D.N. Hoffman, *The State of the Nation's Housing: 1989* (Cambridge, Mass.: The Joint Center for Housing Studies, Harvard University, 1990); and M.E. Stone, *One-Third of a Nation* (Washington, D.C.: Economic Policy Institute, 1990).
35. *A Call for Action to Make Our Nation Safe for Children: A Briefing Book on the Status of American Children* (Washington, D.C.: Children's Defense Fund, 1988) 5.
36. "The Nation's Housing: An Affordability Crisis," *New York Times*, March 16, 1986, E-5.
37. J. Brown and J. Yinger, *Home Ownership and Housing Affordability in the United States, 1963–1985* (Cambridge, Mass.: The Joint Center for Housing Studies, 1986) 6ff.
38. *The State of the Nation's Housing: 1989* (Cambridge, Mass.: The Joint Center for Housing Studies, 1990) 16–19.
39. *A Place to Call Home*, (Washington, D.C.: Center for Budget and Policy Priorities, 1989) 15.
40. *The State of the Nation's Housing*, note 38, above.
40a. *The State of the Nation's Housing: 1991* (Cambridge, Mass.: The Joint Center for Housing Studies of Harvard University, 1991) 25–26.
41. C.N. Dolbeare, *Out of Reach—Why Everyday People Can't Find Affordable Housing* (Washington, D.C.: Low Income Housing Information Service, September 1989).
42. "After 80s Housing Boom, A Decade of Flat Prices?" *New York Times*, April 6, 1990, A1.
43. "Home Buyers Fall Behind," *New York Times*, February 6, 1990, D:5-1.
44. "Working Papers for Affordable Housing: Number 14, P. Dreier (Orange, N.J.: National Housing Institute, 1990).
45. "Buyers Finding a House is Not Always a Home," *Newark Star-Ledger*, March 26, 1990.
46. "Market for Resale Houses is Cooling Off," *New York Times*, September 9, 1990, Sec. 10, 5.
47. Ibid.
48. Ibid.
49. Ibid.

Chapter 2

Housing Benefits: Structuring Effective Employer-Assisted Programs

Housing benefit programs are entering labor/management relations on an ad hoc basis. The notion that employers should offer, or that employees should want, housing benefits has not been central to employee benefits planning or the collective bargaining process. Yet, increasingly, employers are offering and employees are seeking housing benefit programs in response to the housing problems affecting both employers and employees. Because housing benefits have been developed principally on an ad hoc and customized basis with little guidance from the shelter industries, government, or other employer or employee organizations, a variety of approaches have been adopted by employers and employees who have brought great creativity, but oftentimes limited housing knowledge, to the housing problems affecting them.

While an ad hoc approach does not encourage the rapid expansion of housing benefit coverage, it has allowed useful experimentation. This may ultimately serve to inform employers and employees as to the cost-effectiveness, administrative feasibility, and utility of various housing benefit approaches. This chapter reviews the various ways in which housing benefit programs have been implemented, and proposes additional models that employers may want to consider.

Selecting the type of housing benefit program to offer requires a more extensive set of considerations than are made when selecting other types of now familiar, standardized, employee benefits, such as health care or life insurance. Standardization of these products has facilitated the decision-making process and truncated the number of considerations that must be made in order to determine the desired type of product. Standardization of benefit products has routinized employer participation in the offering of the benefits. In the example of health insurance, employers typically provide some administrative support and, most importantly, participate by writing a check to a third-party provider so that the employer's employees can access the service. Standardization of product has made comparisons of various products feasible and that comparison can be made largely on the basis of cost for service.

In contrast, housing benefit programs are not yet standardized, which makes a range of activities possible. And, whereas cost for service may be the central consideration in comparing and choosing a health care benefit plan, other factors, such as corporate debt and cash flow capacities; the need or desirability of improved corporate real estate values; or the value of improved civic, community, and political relations, may be very influential considerations for the firm when determining the cost of a housing benefit. It is not that housing benefit decisions cannot be analyzed in terms of costs and benefits just like other benefit programs; rather, it is that the costs and benefits to the employer may be distributed throughout the firm instead of solely in the human resource department budget. As a result, the involvement of broad, top-level corporate judgment, rather than human resource leadership alone, is needed to determine the overall value of a housing benefit for a firm and which sector of the firm is best able to incur the costs.

Unlike health care coverage, where different policies may influence the quality of coverage but not the number of employees who can take advantage of a program, the structure of a housing benefit influences the number of program participants, as some benefit programs do not enhance affordability enough to enable all employees to enter the housing market. The solution to this problem may not be a more expensive program, but rather a program structured differently, requiring employers to know something about the housing market in which they operate and the kinds of housing affordability and availability problems that confront their employees.

Some employers have chosen to minimize costs and maximize benefits by restricting the number of communities or neighborhoods in which a program is offered. By placing geographic restrictions on a program, employers can achieve both cost savings and additional benefits. For example, by targeting assistance only to neighborhoods proximate to a facility, an employer can improve employee productivity and reduce absenteeism as employees are no longer faced with long commutes to and from communities where the housing is affordable. Similarly, by targeting neighborhoods adjacent to corporate facilities, employers may find corporate real estate values improving in response to a housing benefit that has stabilized or revitalized a community. Further, political, civic, or community relations can be improved by programs that are perceived as assisting in the revitalization of a neighborhood or city. Geographic restrictions may influence the number of participants in a program and hence cost since some employees will just not want to move into certain neighborhoods. All housing benefit programs can be offered on a geographically limited basis.

Aside from how a firm participates or where costs are incurred, housing benefits are different than other types of benefits because housing benefits result in employees obtaining a permanently valuable asset rather than temporary access to a service. Consequently, employees are willing to enter into a variety of nontraditional relationships with their employers. Employees responding to the 1989 American Affordable Housing Institute survey report a willingness to become financially indebted to employers or to have employer assistance subjected to recapture under certain circumstances. No employee is willing to repay last year's health insurance premium payment.

In addition to concessions that employees are willing to make in order to receive housing benefits, a variety of third parties are willing to discount the price of services in order to participate in employer-assisted housing programs. Employers can find mortgage lenders who will discount mortgage application fees, interest rates, and closing costs; real estate brokers who will reduce commissions; builders who will reduce sales prices; and state and local governments that will offer large subsidies to employers offering housing benefits to low- and moderate-income employees. As a result, employers can leverage their contributions to a housing benefit program with the contributions of others.

Housing benefits can be implemented in a variety of ways, but most housing programs fall into one of two categories. The first category enhances the affordability of existing housing, enabling employees to obtain housing currently available on the market. Such programs, known as demand programs, do not add to the regional supply of affordable housing. The second category can be described as supply-oriented; these programs add new or rehabi-

litated units to a regional affordable housing market. Demand programs more closely resemble traditional employee benefit programs
in that employer involvement is usually limited and all eligible employees can access the program at any given time (though utilization
rates will obviously be lower). Supply programs, by definition, limit
the number of participants to the number of homes being built or
rehabilitated. Supply programs develop fee simple ownership housing, rental units, or limited equity housing. Demand programs tend
to provide only home ownership opportunities.

Decisions regarding which category of program to offer are
strongly influenced by housing market factors in the area in which
the sponsoring firm operates, the level of employer involvement
desired, the number of employees who might be expected to participate (or the number of employees the employer wants to have
participate), and the immediacy with which the employer wants
the program to start. Although cost is always an important factor
in determining what benefits can be afforded by the employer,
cost is not necessarily a key issue in deciding whether to offer a
demand program or a supply program; supply programs are not
necessarily more costly than demand programs.

A description of 13 methods of offering employer-assisted
housing follows (see Exhibit 2.1). The first six methods are demand
programs, which enhance the affordability of existing housing. The
next five methods are supply programs. The final two methods are
special finance mechanisms that can either create new units or
enhance the affordability of existing housing.

Demand Programs

Group Mortgage Origination Programs

Group mortgage origination is the basic building block of demand-oriented employer-assisted housing programs. Group mortgage origination plans are essentially volume discount programs in
which a mortgage lender reduces interest rates, origination or discount points, and/or application fees in return for a bulk mortgage
lending commitment or some other expectation of a certain level
of mortgage lending activity.

There are four reasons why group mortgage origination is the
program that employers may want to first consider. The first two
reasons, ease of administration and cost, are traditional measures

Exhibit 2.1   Types of Employer-Assisted Housing Programs

TYPE OF BENEFIT	EMPLOYERS OR MARKETS FOR THIS TYPE OF BENEFIT	REMARKS
Demand Programs		
1. Group Mortgage Origination	Colgate Palmolive	Costs are shared with mortgage capital supplier.
2. Closing Cost Subsidy Programs	Wisconsin Electric, University of California	Can save workers from a few hundred to a few thousand dollars depending on cost of home and the magnitude of assistance.
3. Mortgage Guarantees	University of Pennsylvania; NJHMFA/ HOPE Program	Low-cost/low-risk for employers, lowers or eliminates downpayment requirements for workers.
4. Group Mortgage Insurance	Standardized products should be available shortly	Relieves firms of contingent liability incurred with guarantee programs.
5. Downpayment Assistance Programs		
5A. Third-party Second Mortgages	Allegheny General Hospital; Coastal Housing Partnership; Chicago "Walk Home" Program	Second mortgage loan arranged at below market rates in exchange for employer-administered payroll deduction, linked deposit arrangements, loan guarantees, and for program investments.
5B. Forgivable Downpayment Loans	First Federal Savings (N.C.); Church & Dwight (N.J.)	Costs are pegged at or below recruitment/ retention costs. Overcomes downpayment problem for workers.
6. Purchase of Securities	State and local housing agencies are seeking interested employers to purchase publicly issued bonds	Employer can make a modest profit from a personnel benefit. Employee receives lower rate mortgage or downpayment loan.

Exhibit 2.1 *Continued*

Supply Programs

7. Cash Contributions (direct grant or mortgage buydown)	St. Joseph's Hospital (Wisc.)	Except for financial institutions, requires upfront dollar commitments.
8. Construction Loan Financing	Builders who obtained construction financing at thrifts but now find loans unobtainable under new federal legislation regulating thrift lending for construction.	Enables developers to save on construction financing costs in single- and multi-family housing.
9. Purchase Guarantees	Coastal Housing Partnership (Calif.)	This benefit assures the developer of "take-out" financing on a date certain basis. This enables the developer to precisely know and limit construction financing expenses. In return for the "capping" of finance expenses, developers are able to discount home sale prices.
10. Donation of Development Sites (or subsidy via land lease)	P.C. Connection (N.H.); University of Calif.-Irvine; Hospital for Special Surgery (N.Y.); Peterson Industries	Attractive to "land rich" employers.
11. Master Leases		Enables owners of rental property to reduce or eliminate unit vacancies. By not having to include a vacancy factor in rent rates, owners can lower basic rent rates.

Specialized Benefit Programs

12. Employee Stock Ownership Plans/ Employee Home Ownership Plans	Employee Owned Firms (ESOPs)	Employee housing programs can be an alternative investment strategy for those funds held by the ESOP but not invested in company stock.
13. Taft-Hartley Trust Funds	Local 26-Hotel Employees/Restaurant Employees	Employer makes contribution of an amount per hour to a trust fund for housing programs that are jointly administered by labor and management.

for determining the feasibility of any employee benefit, while the other two reasons are unique to housing benefit programs.

First, employers offering group mortgage origination plans have the familiar administrative role of organizing the plan (in this case selecting a lender interested in providing mortgages on highly competitive terms) and informing employees of the availability of this benefit. Firms select only one lender in order to maximize the lender's volume; the greater the volume the larger the lender's concessions are likely to be. Group mortgage origination plans do not require an employer to be a mortgage lender or processor any more than group health care plans require an employer to be a doctor or medical technician.

Second, the cost to the employer for a group mortgage program can be as low as the cost of selecting a lender and informing employees of the availability of the service. Some lenders will provide some level of discount if the employer's outreach to employees is aggressive or if the pool of potential mortgage loan applicants is large (groups of employers working together can pool their work forces for this benefit and thereby enlarge the pool of potential mortgage applicants). In such instances, employers need not contribute any direct cash assistance to the employee in order to modestly enhance affordability. The lender subsidy will vary with the number of employees likely to participate in a program (a function of the size of the employer's work force, the demographics and income of those employees, and the cost of housing in the particular region), the lender's interest in increasing or maintaining market share or volume, the number of discount points typically being sought in the market, and the quality of the housing market in which the loans are being made. Still, a lender can be expected to reduce mortgage application fees, closing points (the sum of discount points and mortgage origination fees usually totaling not more than 4 percent of the mortgage), and mortgage interest rates (although usually by not more than 25 basis points). The value of these concessions are typically worth between $1,500 and $3,000 depending on the size of the mortgage, although an interest rate reduction can be worth somewhat more over the 30-year life of a mortgage.

In addition to actual cash savings, group mortgage programs provide employees with the comfort of knowing that with a minimal amount of shopping they have located a lender that has a good product line and that they have not made a serious mistake in the oftimes confusing process of choosing a mortgage lender.

Third, employers can provide additional subsidies in combination with lender-provided group mortgage origination programs. It is the ability of group mortgage origination to be combined with other forms of employer-assistance that makes it the building block of employer-assisted housing. By combining lender-provided assistance with employer efforts, employers are able to begin leveraging their contributions to a housing benefit program with subsidies provided by other sectors of the shelter industry. The ability to leverage value for employee benefit programs from providers is a trait unique to housing benefit programs.

Fourth, a group mortgage origination program establishes a relationship between the employer and a member of the shelter industry. By having a member of the shelter industry working with an employer, the employer can access housing sophistication beyond that which the employer alone has. By bringing to bear the experience and knowledge of those involved in the housing and construction finance industries, an employer can offer cost-effective housing benefit programs without having to learn substantially more about housing than an employer must learn about health care in order to offer health insurance. For employers not involved in housing or finance—and who have no desire to be—this is a distinct advantage.

Colgate-Palmolive

Colgate-Palmolive, a worldwide firm that has its corporate headquarters in New York City and production and research facilities in the New York metropolitan area, became increasingly concerned with the rapid escalation of housing prices in metropolitan New York in the mid-1980s. As a result, Colgate asked the mortgage bank that administered its relocation program for advice regarding the feasibility of structuring a housing assistance program for employees who were not relocating.

Tim Callahan, an account manager with Lomas Corporate Services, which established the program (Lomas was recently acquired by Fleet Mortgage Company, which continues to operate this program for Colgate), said Colgate "noticed the trend early-on that they were having problems recruiting and keeping employees in the tri-state (Connecticut, New Jersey, New York) area. They wanted a program that would help them keep a good work force. They didn't want a real expensive program, but they wanted to address the problem."[1]

In 1985, Colgate-Palmolive announced a group mortgage origination and closing cost subsidy program. The program was structured to provide employees with mortgages at highly competitive terms with no points or closing costs for mortgages eligible to be sold on the secondary mortgage market. For first-time homebuyers, the dream of home ownership had "become a very difficult dream," according to Terry Portale, Relocation Administrator for Colgate, so the program was structured to offer very real savings of $2,000 to $5,000 depending on the size of the mortgage.[2] While responding to a market in which interest rates were falling from 13 percent to around 10 percent, Colgate and Lomas also recognized the utility of offering the program to employees who owned a home and were interested in refinancing. Although Colgate was principally concerned with the issue of equity, that those who already owned a home should not be closed out of the program, Colgate understood that refinancing was important for those "who have a home with substantial equity but are now faced with college costs or have an elderly person in their home who has health care needs."[3]

Closing Cost Subsidy Programs

Closing cost subsidy programs help homebuyers meet some of the expenses associated with the purchase of a home. The inability to accrue a downpayment is the most significant barrier to home ownership today, and even those who have accrued a downpayment face thousands of dollars in additional expenses including closing points, legal fees, and title and mortgage insurance. Closing costs are typically between 5 percent to 7 percent of the purchase price of the home.[4] It is not unheard of for a customer to obtain a 5 percent downpayment mortgage, only to end up needing an additional 8 percent for various loan processing and closing costs.[5] A closing cost subsidy program, which can be readily combined with group mortgage origination plans, solves part of this problem.

Closing cost subsidies can be offered in several ways. One way is for an employer to pay closing points. Points are a fee expressed as a percentage of the mortgage (usually 1/2 percent to 3 1/2 percent) that are charged at the time of the closing. Points represent, in effect, an insurance premium charged by the lender to ensure that the loan will generate an expected rate of return. Lenders wanting to participate in a group mortgage program can offer some concession on closing points. An employer offering a closing cost subsidy program may be able to eliminate all or most of the remaining closing points, depending upon the extent of the employer's contribution. For example, an $80,000 mortgage carrying three points would require the employee to pay $2,400 for those points at the time of closing. This is a substantial sum if the borrower is struggling to save $8,000 for a downpayment. In this example, the lender might be expected to concede one point, or $800, and the employer might make a contribution of the remaining $1,600.

Legal assistance for homebuyers is another closing cost subsidy program that firms can offer. Legal expenses associated with purchasing a home frequently cost several hundred dollars. A limited, pre-paid legal insurance program for homebuyers is a benefit with which human resource directors are familiar and one that they can readily price. In a related vein, employers can subsidize other closing costs such as title insurance, title searches, and engineering studies.

Downpayment Barriers to Home Ownership

The American Affordable Housing Institute's survey of employed renter households indicated that 60 percent of those interested in purchasing a home thought that they might not be able to do so because they could not afford the downpayment. Another 14 percent of respondents said that the lack of a downpayment, in combination with other factors, had prohibited them from buying a home. When asked how much additional cash they would need to purchase their first home, 77 percent of respondents said that less than $10,000 was needed. This data, discussed in greater detail in Chapter 3, indicate that the inability of workers to fully fund a downpayment requirement is the principal barrier to home ownership for prospective homebuyers.

In considering how to overcome the downpayment barrier to home ownership, it is important to understand the lender's purpose in requiring a downpayment. Lenders require downpayments in order to reduce their risk in the advent of default. Downpayments reduce lender risk because the loaned amount is less than the value of the property that secures the loan. Should default and foreclosure occur, the home can presumably be sold for an amount at least equal to the loan. Further, there is substantial evidence that the larger the downpayment in terms of a percentage of the home's value, the less likely the borrower is to default (keeping in mind that more than 98 percent of all owner-occupied housing mortgage loans do not default).[6]

Aside from downpayments, the principal way of reducing lender risk for the past half century has been by insuring mortgages. Initially, the Federal Housing Administration (FHA) was the sole mortgage insurer, guarding lenders against losses of up to 90 percent of the mortgage amount on lower-priced homes. More recently, private mortgage insurers have been insuring lenders for smaller portions of mortgage lending risk, typically about 15 percent to 30 percent.

Employers can take additional actions to reduce lender risk, which in turn can reduce downpayment requirements or expand loan underwriting standards, permitting employees that might not otherwise qualify for a mortgage to do so. Three ways that employers can provide downpayment assistance are (1) mortgage guarantees, (2) mortgage insurance, and (3) direct downpayment assistance programs, each of which is discussed below.

Mortgage Guarantee Programs

Mortgage guarantee programs are a cost-effective way of reducing lender risk and thereby reducing borrower downpayment requirements. Mortgage guarantees reduce lender risk because security for the mortgage is no longer just the property or the borrower's other financial resources, but also the financial resources of the employer making the guarantee. Obviously, many corporations will have vastly greater resources than any employee and thus greater loan security is provided.

Mortgage guarantee programs advantage employers in three principal ways. The first advantage is cost—mortgage guarantee programs require no direct cash expenditures, although mortgage guarantees may be recorded as "contingent liabilities" on a firm's balance sheet because it is possible that should a default occur, the employer will incur a liability. About 2 percent of all home mortgages default and usually the value of the property is sufficient to secure the loan. Therefore, though *contingent* liability can be large, the actual *expected* liability that a firm would incur would be expected to be substantially smaller.

Second, mortgage guarantee programs can be used by employers to reduce employee turnover rates, thereby lowering recruitment, training, and other costs associated with undesired turnover. This occurs because mortgage guarantee programs can be structured to provide an incentive for an employee to remain with the employer by having the employer's guarantee offered only as long as an employee remains with the employer. When the guarantee is ended, the lender may require the loan to be refinanced because the ending of the guarantee has now increased the lender's risk. The cost of refinancing, including the potential of having to provide the lender with a substantial sum for a downpayment, can be a powerful incentive for the employee to remain with the employer.

Third, mortgage guarantees are easily linked with group mortgage origination programs, so that in addition to a reduced downpayment the borrower also receives a mortgage having reduced fees and a highly competitive interest rate. Employers with the capacity to carry contingent liability can negotiate with a potential lender regarding how much of a guarantee is required in order to lower downpayment requirements for employee borrowers and obtain other group mortgage benefits.

When choosing to offer a mortgage guarantee program, employers have to consider the impact of carrying significant sums as contingent debt on the corporate ledger, even though the likelihood of a mortgage default is small, and in the unlikely event that a default occurs, the employer's secured interest in the property should cover the outstanding mortgage debt. Another potential cost is that less well-capitalized firms may be required by the lender to establish a loan loss reserve fund to further insure the lender against mortgage default. Establishing such an account would be a direct cost, but this fund would be handled as an investment of the employer paying a market rate yield and all principal and interest not required to pay the costs of mortgage defaults would be returned to the employer.

Lenders who sell mortgages on the secondary market are required by secondary market purchasers not to lend at more than a 95 percent loan-to-value ratio. Some states and private mortgage insurers have similar requirements for lenders, even if the mortgage is to be held in portfolio. In these instances, 100 percent mortgages with an employer guarantee are not possible. But an employer guarantee can facilitate 5 percent downpayment loans without the borrower having to pay for private or federal mortgage insurance, both of which are not always available as a result of insurance company sales preferences and purchase price ceilings on federally insured mortgages. Mortgage guarantee programs can also increase loan underwriting flexibility by permitting gifts, second mortgages, and other financial assistance to count toward the 5 percent downpayment requirement. Employers may want to compare the guarantee required by lenders who sell mortgages on the secondary market and those who hold mortgages in their own portfolios as well as public sector housing entities, such as state housing finance agencies, as portfolio lenders and public agencies may have more flexible lending policies or require smaller guarantees.

The University of Pennsylvania and the New Jersey Housing and Mortgage Finance Agency

Perhaps the oldest, arms-length employer-assisted housing program is the one offered by the University of Pennsylvania. Unlike many college and university housing assistance programs that are offered only to senior faculty, the University of Pennsylvania program is open to all permanent university employees. The program, created in the late 1960s, offers a 100 percent mortgage guarantee. The value of a 100 percent guarantee is that it completely insures the lender against all loss of loan principal in the advent of a mortgage default. As a result of this 100 percent guarantee, the administering lender is able to waive all downpayment requirements. As the lack of a downpayment is the principal barrier to homeownership, this program completely overcomes the barrier, without the University making any cash expenditure.

Though open to any permanent university employee, the program does have certain restrictions, most notably, only homes in the west Philadelphia neighborhood adjacent to the campus are eligible to participate. The reason for this restriction lies in one of the original motivations for offering this program—wanting employees to participate in the revitalization of the area around the school. Peter Iacovoni of Meritor Mortgage Corporation, which administers the program for the University, reports that, "buyers tend to fix up homes with the dollars not spent on the downpayment. This creates immediate home appreciation and equity."[7] And the neighborhood certainly was not the "Gold Coast when the program was established in 1968," according to Janet Gordon, Associate Treasurer for the University, who coordinates the administration of the program with the lender.[8] Today, the neighborhood boasts many homes selling for $90,000 to $120,000, and some for much more.[9]

About 60 percent of the purchasers have been university staff, with the balance being faculty. About 1,200 employees have participated in the program,[10] but the current number of guaranteed loans is about 200.[11] The University has noticed that many purchasers are first-time homebuyers, who later trade up and leave the neighborhood, but leave an improved home behind.

The consequence of this program to the University is that the University carries a contingent liability of about $13 million in mortgage guarantees. A "footnote" is how Gordon describes this contingent debt on the University's ledgers, saying that it has no impact on the school's AA credit rating.[12]

If the nearly quarter-century old University of Pennsylvania mortgage guarantee program is among the oldest modern housing benefit programs, the mortgage guarantee program initiated by the N.J. Housing and Mortgage Finance Agency (HMFA) for private employers and their employees is among the most recent programs. Initiated in September 1989, the HMFA program—the first state-supported, employer-assisted housing program in the nation—is known as the Homeownership for Performing Employees (HOPE) program. HMFA raised $23 million via the sale of tax-exempt housing revenue bonds for a pilot program of about 250 loans made in partnership with state businesses. Art Maurice, then Executive Director of HMFA, said that in beginning this program he "felt that the agency's resources, expertise in mortgage financing, and legislatively mandated powers could be better employed in partnership with the private sector."[13] The HOPE program allows employers to offer a low-cost benefit to their workers that helps them afford the high cost of housing in New Jersey. Working through the HMFA, an employer guarantees 20 percent of its employee's mortgage loan for five years whether or not the employee stays with the employer for the total term. In return for the guarantee, the employee is eligible to receive a no-downpayment loan for the total cost of the home. In effect, the employer is guaranteeing the traditional downpayment portion of the loan. To be a qualified employer, the company must also submit to financial review that appraises the quality of the employer's guarantee. The program gives companies maximum flexibility to design their own eligibility requirements and operating procedures.

The program is open to employees with family incomes of up to $62,000. The program can be structured as a graduated payment mortgage so that monthly payments increase on the schedule of anticipated salary increases. Based on standard underwriting, HOPE expands borrowing capacity by 20 percent for participating employees. The 1989 bond allocation offers 30-year fixed rate mortgages at 8.7 percent, about 200 basis points below the then-prevailing market rate. More than 300 companies expressed interest in participating in the program when the program was announced.

One participating firm is Melrose Displays, Inc., based in Passaic. The firm employs 200 people who make display advertising for stores. Melvin Cohen, chief executive of the corporation, believes that the employer-assisted housing program "creates good will because employees see that the company is willing to go on the line for them."[14] His motivation for participating in the program is directed by his need to have a stable and trained work force. He says that, "some of the people around here cannot afford to get into a home. If I want to keep them, we've got to get them into a house."[15]

Cohen sees that he is at a competitive disadvantage with lower-cost regions and the New Jersey housing benefit will allow him to compete. "Down south, where a lot of our competitors keep their plants on the Mexican border or over the border, living expenses are much less and wages are much less. We're paying top wages; if I paid any more, I'd be out of business. But people around here can't afford to get into a house, even with the wages we are paying."[16] Cohen also emphasizes that the community at-large benefits when employers help make housing more affordable. For him, business altruism and social responsibility are important factors. "Not only does this help stabilize employees who want to have a future here, we help stabilize communities."[17]

Since 1983, AT&T, the largest private employer in New Jersey, has offered its own employee group mortgage program. The program saves employees 25 basis points on origination fees and up to $300 on home appraisal fees. However, AT&T also agreed to participate in the HMFA program. Lynn Newman, public relations manager at AT&T, believes that the program, "will help workers address the cost of housing in a high cost state and keep them close to the work place which translates into high productivity."[18]

George Zolnowski, the controller at Kay Elemetrics Corp., a high-tech electronic manufacturing firm with 65 employees, sees housing assistance as a key to attracting and keeping employees. "Most of our company's employees live at least 30 miles away. Any time you have a 60- or 70-mile commute, you know that (their commitment to the job is) a short-term proposition. Our downfall is we're located in North Jersey. For an engineer to buy a home close to the plant seems nearly impossible. Our main thrust is to attract and keep the people we want. That's getting tougher and tougher. A lot of people have a lot of trouble getting the start-up costs. The HOPE program helps you in that area."[19]

Group Mortgage Insurance Programs

An alternative to a mortgage guarantee program is a group mortgage insurance, or co-insurance, program. The principal advantage of group mortgage insurance is that the contingent liability incurred in a guarantee program is transferred from the employer to a private mortgage insurance company. Like existing mortgage guarantee programs, employer-paid mortgage insurance programs expand access to mortgage credit beyond that which conventional private mortgage insurance policies can provide.

Conventional private mortgage insurance costs about 50 to 100 basis points, depending on the extent of the coverage and whether the premium payment is made at the time the home is purchased or on an installment basis as part of the monthly payment. Coverage that the lender can obtain usually varies from 15 percent to 30 percent of the mortgage amount. With mortgage insurance, buyers can purchase homes with as little as a 5 percent downpayment.

Insurers are not able to insure mortgages with a loan-to-value ratio of greater than 95 percent. The reason for this is partly legal and partly economic. Legally, a California statute prohibits mortgage insurers doing business in the state to make loans more highly leveraged than 95 percent. This law also prohibits California mortgages from being traded in pools containing more highly leveraged loans, even if those more highly leveraged loans are permitted by other states. Because California mortgages are such a large portion of the national mortgage insurance industry, the effect of this law is to nationally ban the insuring of more highly leveraged loans. Economically, more highly leveraged loans are also more risky. Even if California law did not place a roadblock in the path of higher loan-to-value ratio loans, it is doubtful that insurers or lenders would be eager to make such loans and surely the premium costs for such coverage would be significantly higher than current mortgage insurance premiums. An additional roadblock to mortgages in excess of 95 percent of loan-to-value is that the Federal National Mortgage Association's (Fannie Mae's) federal charter (Fannie Mae is the largest purchaser of mortgages) prohibits it from purchasing more highly leveraged mortgages.

Mortgage insurers, lenders, and secondary market mortgage purchasers, however, have recently begun to take a more liberal view of how homebuyers can accumulate the required 5 percent downpayment. Mortgage insurers are beginning to insure, and secondary mortgage market purchasers are beginning to buy, mortgages in which homebuyers have received up to two-fifths of the 5 percent downpayment from other sources, including family and public agencies.

These new mortgage programs were initially targeted to meet needs of lower income borrowers who could afford the carrying costs associated with financing lower cost housing, but could not manage to accrue the required downpayment. These programs are often tied to special pre- and post-mortgage counseling programs that provide financial management information and training for new borrowers. These reduced downpayment programs also permit more flexible loan underwriting guidelines, permitting lenders to be more flexible in assessing the household income-to-loan ratios (typically mortgage payments cannot exceed 28 percent of income and total monthly debt costs cannot exceed 36 percent of income), and be more willing to waive requirements regarding mortgage payment reserve accounts, in addition to third-party assistance in making the 5 percent downpayment requirement.

Based upon the success of this flexible approach toward the sources of downpayment funding for a 5 percent downpayment, Fannie Mae announced in April 1991 that it will purchase $1 billion of mortgages in which employers provide two-fifths of the 5 percent downpayment. Employers can provide this assistance in several ways, including a grant, loan, or forgivable loan.

Group mortgage insurance programs have not yet been offered to employers on a regular basis by mortgage insurance companies. Model mortgage insurance programs are available, however. A number of state housing agencies have funded co-insurance programs in association with private mortgage insurers. In these programs, the public sector creates a co-insurance fund, which is a sum of money placed at risk to cover a predictable level of mortgage defaults. The size of the fund needed is proportionate to the risk as anticipated by the underwriting guidelines chosen. However, programs can be structured so as to permit co-insurers to select a level of risk (and cost) with which the co-insurer is comfortable. Based upon these public sector models, it seems likely that co-insurance programs will only be offered by mortgage insurers to employers or groups of employers capable of generating at least

100 mortgages annually, so as to facilitate mortgage pool risk assessment and mortgage packaging and resale.

Employers could participate in co-insurance programs in one of two ways. The first is for employers to be co-insurers by capitalizing the co-insurance account. Employers who participate as the co-insurer will be required to invest in a co-insurance trust fund. The cost of capitalizing the fund is estimated to be about $3,000 per participating employee, depending upon the size of the mortgage, the housing market in which the house is located, and the specific underwriting criteria used. Funds used to capitalize this account are at risk, and should defaults occur at a rate above that for which the lead mortgage insurer is responsible, the fund will incur losses. Funds not needed to pay defaults are invested by a trustee in liquid securities (so that funds can be readily drawn upon to pay defaults) for a period of three to seven years. The employer earns a market rate return on these securities during this period and any principal or interest not used to pay for defaults are returned to the employer at the end of the seven-year period. After seven years, mortgages no longer require private insuring.

The second way employers could participate in a group mortgage insurance program is with public agencies and/or private intermediaries and investors who are interested in capitalizing the co-insurance fund and who will charge employers a premium, enabling employers to access the co-insurance fund. Sources of third-party investment include local or national trade associations to which employers belong, pension funds, and public capital (including state government pension funds, state housing finance agency reserves, and local taxable bonds). Private lenders seeking investments necessary to meet Community Reinvestment Act[20] lending goals, and charitable investors (including church and foundation funds), may also be interested in capitalizing a trust, especially if the employee population receiving the benefit is of low or moderate income or the area in which the loans are generated is part of a local revitalization effort. By paying a premium to the third party that is capitalizing the co-insurance trust, employers would participate in group mortgage insurance programs in much the same way as they participate in other types of insurance benefits—by paying a premium. Unlike health insurance, the premium for mortgage insurance would be a one-time fee of about $600 to $1,800. The Neighborhood Housing Services (NHS) programs in Pittsburgh and Chicago are establishing this type of program, which these nonprofit housing corporations will offer to local employers in association with other NHS first-time homebuyer programs.

While the costs associated with each method of participation in a group mortgage insurance program are very different, some employers may have reasons to consider, and invest, in the more expensive participation form. Paying co-insurance premiums requires direct employer expenditures; however, some employers may find it feasible and attractive to invest funds, especially pension funds, to capitalize the co-insurance trust. By using pension funds (for the trust can be structured to pay a market rate return), employers will be able to pay for a benefit that assists employees from funds that are not part of the corporate operating budget. Funding an employee benefit through the use of pension funds, without violating the Employment Retirement Income Security Act (ERISA) provisions, should enable employers lacking otherwise available cash to invest in group mortgage insurance programs, and thus provide an important new employee benefit without their increasing wage and benefit costs.

Downpayment Assistance Programs

Corporate recruiters and relocation program administrators have long recognized the utility of direct downpayment assistance programs. While such programs are a mainstay of corporate housing programs, they have been viewed as too expensive to offer beyond the select group of employees who have traditionally received this assistance. This view is changing; some employers have structured new, more cost-effective methods of offering downpayment assistance and have begun accounting for the cost of these programs in ways that show the benefits of even very substantial direct assistance.

Third-Party Second Mortgage Programs

One way employers are providing downpayment assistance is by entering into new relationships with lenders that yield second mortgage downpayment loans. Employers offer to provide a payroll deduction program for payment of first or second mortgages, linked deposit and other corporate banking agreements, and loan guarantees for the second mortgage. Some employers make second mortgage loan origination a condition for selection as the group mortgage originator. As a result of these agreements, lenders offer second mortgage loans at or near first mortgage rates. Employers have been able to obtain 95 percent and more highly leveraged loans for employees without the employees incurring any expense for mortgage insurance. This can be done because an 80 percent loan to home value first mortgage is readily marketable without mortgage insurance. Financing for the balance of the home purchase is accomplished with a second mortgage, which is secured by both the property being financed and by the various agreements employers have made with lenders. In Santa Barbara, California; Hartford, Connecticut; and Chicago, employer consortia have been formed and these groups are working with single lenders to increase volume for the selected lender, enabling a more standardized program to be established.

As with group mortgage origination programs, all lending terms for employer-secured second mortgages are negotiable, including origination fees, application fees, closing costs, loan terms, and interest rates, particularly if the employer is reducing lender risk through loan guarantees, payroll deduction programs, and linked banking agreements.

An employer organizing a downpayment assistance program is able to do so without actually funding the downpayment and incurring that substantial expense. The benefit may in fact be cost-less, as the lender is responsible for the administering of the program and the banking relationships with the lender may be ones that the employer wants to have for other business reasons. In addition to the lack of cost, an employer also benefits from this program by incurring little or no risk, as not all lenders require a guarantee of the second mortgage, and if they do, the risk is limited to not more than 20 percent of the home's value. The employer retains a secured interest in the home.

Allegheny General Hospital and St. Joseph's Hospital. Community partnership is a key ingredient in Allegheny General Hospital's (Pittsburgh, Pennsylvania) housing benefit program. The hospital, the largest employer on Pittsburgh's northside (employing about 4,700 people), established a group mortgage origination and downpayment loan program for all hospital employees in 1989.

The hospital began the program as a way to "promote the community in conjunction with community groups," according to Mike Gayso, Manager of Allegheny Health Services Federal Credit Union, a partner in the program. Union National Bank, a local savings bank, and neighborhood groups who help make prospective participants aware of homes on the market and of public and non-profit housing assistance programs that are available, are also partners in the program.[21]

The program combines a 1/2 percent discount on mortgage interest rates on loans made by Union National Bank with a credit union loan of up to 2.5 percent of a home's sale price for downpayment and closing costs. The hospital guarantees the loan made to the employee by the credit union. Union National Bank is provided additional security for its loan through a direct deposit payroll deduction program. The program is offered in a three zip code area of north Pittsburgh where home prices range from $30,000 to $80,000. A mortgage committee meets on at least a quarterly basis to both approve loans and meet with the neighborhood groups who participate in the program.

For employees interested in owning a home within the 20-block neighborhood surrounding Milwaukee's St. Joseph's Hospital, two home ownership housing benefit programs are available. One program gives workers a grant of 3 percent of the purchase price of a home for downpayment and/or closing cost expenses, or $1,000, whichever is greater. Alternatively, employees can opt for a second program in which the hospital lends the employee up to 15 percent of the cost of the home in the form of a second mortgage. The second mortgage loan is made to the employee at an interest rate equal to the hospital's cost of funds and is for a three- to five-year term. By amortizing the second mortgage over a relatively short term and at a lower interest rate than the homebuyer would otherwise be able to obtain, the homebuyer is able to build equity in the property faster than more traditional methods of financing. During the period when both the first and second mortgage rates are being repaid, the effective cost of what is, in effect, a blended rate mortgage, is below the cost of a 95 percent loan-to-value conventional mortgage with private mortgage insurance. The first mortgage being at 80 percent of loan-to-value needs no mortgage insurance.

William Tierney, Midwest director of low- and moderate-income programs for Fannie Mae, who helped design the project, comments, "One of the most important benefits to the employer is that, if successful, this project should help stabilize the local real estate market and protect the hospital's significant real estate investment in the community."[22] Fannie Mae purchases the first mortgages from the local lender.

As in the case of Allegheny General Hospital, St. Joseph's chose to organize its housing benefit so as to stabilize a neighborhood in which it has a substantial investment but that is in need of general revitalization. Each hospital also recognized that by targeting the program to the community surrounding the hospital, employees will be able to walk to work, which will save money and improve worker productivity by reducing commuting times.

Employer Consortia: The Coastal Housing Partnership and Chicago Walk Home Programs. Santa Barbara, California, is among the most expensive communities in the nation. With median home prices in excess of $300,000, affordable housing has come to mean housing available to couples earning $70,000 to $80,000 annually who, although vital to the local economy, have been priced out of the local housing market. In response to this problem a dozen employers have joined together to form their own nonprofit corporation, the Coastal Housing Partnership, which is charged with developing housing benefit programs for all of the participating employers. The Partnership, the first all-employer housing partnership in the nation, grew out of a shared recognition within the business community that the high cost of housing hurt the ability of business, government, educational, and health care institutions to attract and keep the personnel they wanted. Participating employers pay annual dues to the corporation ranging from $500 to $3,000 annually, plus a one-time "access" fee of $1,000 for each program in which they choose to participate.

The Partnership has established three programs during its four-year existence. One program assists renters who lack the $1,000 or more that can be needed as a rent security deposit for an apartment in the community. The Partnership has established a revolving loan fund to provide money for security deposits. Low-interest loans are then repaid to the fund over a 24-month period.

A second program is a second mortgage downpayment loan program for homebuyers. This program enables homebuyers to obtain 80 percent financing, which saves the buyer approximately 1 percent at the time of closing since no mortgage insurance coverage is required. The homebuyer is responsible for a minimum 5 percent downpayment and the balance of the home financing is provided by the second mortgage program. The second mortgage is provided by a local lender who agreed to offer the program in part because of the involvement of multiple local employers. Employers participate by either guaranteeing the loan, having other corporate banking agreements with the lender, or by assisting the lender in loan collection by servicing the loan through a direct payroll deduction program. In return for the employer's relationship to the loan, which provides the lender with additional security, the lender has agreed to make these loans at a rate roughly equal to the cost of a first mortgage, although second mortgage loans are typically somewhat more costly.

A third program offered by the Partnership is a purchase guarantee program. The Partnership acquired options on 16 condominium units from a developer for purchase by employees. By acquiring the option on all 16 units at once, the Partnership was able to obtain a substantial price discount. The units carry deed restrictions regarding resale so that the units will be available as a future source of affordable housing to the members of the Partnership.

Laurie Ryerson, Director of the Coastal Housing Partnership, says that the consortium approach provides "strength in numbers," adding that the "CHP represents a far greater number of potential homebuyers than any single member and thus enjoys a real negotiating advantage," with lenders and builders.[23] The Partnership concept also provides employers with needed information regarding what housing benefits are and how they can help employees. "Participating employers have ready access to information and assistance that they would have to otherwise develop independently," Ryerson explains.[24]

In northwest Chicago, a very different type of neighborhood from Santa Barbara, another employer partnership offers a somewhat different program. There, an employer consortium has been formed to address workers' needs for affordable housing and the business community's need for a stable neighborhood and a reliable work force. The Chicago Walk Home Program is offered by a consortium of seven companies, which in aggregate employ approximately 2,000 workers in a 50-square block area in northwest Chicago. The program is offered in coordination with the nonprofit Neighborhood Housing Services (NHS), a neighborhood-based organization that promotes neighborhood stabilization and renovates affordable housing. Like the Coastal Housing Partnership, the NHS provides a source of information regarding employer-assisted housing programs so that individual employers need not re-invent a benefit program, but rather can simply access an existing program.

The benefit program offered through the Chicago Walk Home Program is a revolving loan fund, in which the employers-investors earn a modest return, on low-interest downpayment loans that are made available to employees seeking to buy homes in the area.

The loan pool is administered by the NHS, which is also responsible for program promotion, application intake, and approval of borrowers. Employers make a sliding scale investment in the fund based on their number of employees for a term of three years, and earn a return of 5 percent per year, payable at the end of the term. Qualified employees of the companies are eligible to borrow up to $8,000 at 6 percent interest for up to seven years. The average loan is for 10 percent of the $60,000 purchase price of neighborhood homes. The program is designed to help workers build equity at a quicker rate and to supplement employee savings so that workers can put 20 percent of the cost of the house toward a downpayment, which lowers monthly payments. By making a 20 percent downpayment, borrowers also avoid the costs of private mortgage insurance, which also lowers closing costs and monthly costs. Participating employers, which range in size from 20 workers to 800 workers, include Pride Container Corp., Helene Curtis, Inc., Pioneer Bank and Trust Co., Continental White Cap, Finzer Roller Co., Universal Allied/Imaging Co., and Bayer Black Smith.

Richard Sharfstein, President of Pride Container Corp. with 130 employees, comments about his company's involvement in the Walk Home program: "I know the importance of the relationship between area businesses and the surrounding residential area because we operate literally across the street and next door to three-flats and bungalows. I have a receptionist who has worked for us for eight years and lives two blocks from the plant. I'd like to see more employees become homeowners in the area."[25]

From the employee's perspective, a second mortgage downpayment loan is helpful because such a program significantly reduces downpayment costs and eliminates mortgage insurance costs. Lender-financed second mortgage programs require borrowers to begin the repayment of the second mortgage immediately following closing, unlike some employer or public sector deferred loans. As a result, although downpayment costs are reduced, they are reduced at the expense of higher monthly carrying costs. This problem also arises in mortgage insurance and guarantee programs in that these programs provide downpayment assistance, at least in part, by transferring downpayment costs to higher monthly carrying costs. In this era of unstable incomes, many homebuyers cannot afford a program that further increases their monthly housing expenses. For these prospective homebuyers, second mortgage programs, group mortgage insurance programs, and mortgage guarantee programs do not solve the housing affordability problems they face; thus, these programs do not solve an employer's housing-caused work force problems. In these instances, employers may want to consider directly funding a forgivable downpayment loan program.

Forgivable Downpayment Loan Programs

The 1990 American Affordable Housing Institute Survey of employer interest in employer-assisted housing asked employers about the cost of recruiting and training entry-level employees. Twenty-nine percent of the responding employers indicated costs of $1,000 to $3,000 to recruit employees and 38 percent indicated that a similar amount was needed to train them. The 1988 *National Cost Per Hire* survey of The Employment Management Association indicated that the average cost per hire for all employees was $6,078.[26] The cost of employee turnover in the United States exceeds $11 billion annually and the average cost to refill a position is between 10 to 20 times the weekly wage.[27] The average turnover in some industries is 80 percent and, according to the Department of Labor, 50 percent of new hires do not remain with the employer more than nine months.[28] In short, it is expensive to hire people; it is expensive to train people; and it is even more expensive to have to regularly repeat the process as a result of continual employee turnover.

While not all turnover is undesirable, most is. Of course, turnover is not always the result of a housing problem. However, home ownership remains a major economic aspiration of 65 million nonhomeowning households, millions of which will never own a home without assistance external to their regular household income because their incomes are insufficient to accrue a downpayment. Thus, an employer who assists these families in fulfilling their aspirations would seem to be at a competitive advantage in recruiting and retaining employees.

Employers are beginning to understand the link between an employee's housing aspirations and the problem of employee turnover. In response, some employers are offering cost-effective downpayment loan programs that enable employees to meet their housing aspirations while reducing the rate, and thus the cost, of employee turnover. By offering downpayment loans that are forgiven at a rate that is less than the annual cost of recruiting and training employees multiplied by the turnover rate, employers have created programs that reduce turnover costs while helping meet employee housing objectives. For example, if it costs an employer $3,000 to recruit and train an employee and the position turns over every other year, at the end of five years the employer will have spent $9,000 to keep that position filled. If, on the other hand, an employer loans an employee $7,500 and forgives the loan at an annual rate of $1,500 per year, at the end of five years the loan will be completely forgiven, but the employer will have saved $1,500 as compared with the expected costs of recruitment and training. Employers can structure forgivable loans to be recapturable should the employee leave before the forgiveness period is over, with a portion, or all, of the loan becoming callable. The inability to conveniently repay the loan will encourage some employees to remain with the employer, but even in those instances where the employee chooses to leave and repay the employer, the recapture feature ensures that the employer emerges from the incident financially whole. Because forgivable loans require no monthly servicing, these programs are administratively simple to operate.

First Federal Savings and Loan and the Church and Dwight Company. "We were tired of acting like a technical institute providing job skills only to have trained employees leave for other jobs," says Alice Wilson, Vice President for Mortgage Banking at First Federal Savings and Loan in Raleigh, North Carolina.[29] In response to this situation, First Federal established a program tailored to the housing needs of its young, entry-level work force. The program offers a $6,000 downpayment loan to an employee purchasing a condominium (typical new condominiums cost $75,000 to $80,000 in the Raleigh market), but in return the employee must agree to remain an employee of First Federal for five years. During the five-year period, the downpayment loan made by First Federal is forgiven on a pro rata basis, so that at the end of five years First Federal has completely forgiven the $6,000 loan. First Federal has calculated that the cost of recruiting and training entry-level employees, combined with a high turnover rate for this personnel, is such that it is less expensive to forgive a $6,000 loan than it is to repeatedly recruit and train new employees. By amortizing the cost of the loan against the cost of recruitment, training, and lost productivity due to job vacancies, First Federal believes that this program is saving the thrift money, not raising personnel costs. About 350 employees are eligible to participate in the program.

In addition to reducing employee turnover, the program also benefits the lender by increasing mortgage lending activity (First

Federal writes the first mortgage) and by stimulating a sluggish condominium market. Wilson reports that some employees who believed that they could only purchase a home with employer assistance were encouraged by the program to get into the market, only to subsequently learn that they had the resources without the employer assistance. As a result, the program was sometimes not used to finance a home, but Wilson believes that the program still played an important catalyzing role in motivating employees to discover that they could afford home ownership. The thrift also benefited in these cases because the lender wrote the first mortgages for these homebuyers, too.

For Church and Dwight, offering a housing benefit does not have the collateral advantages of increasing business as it does for First Federal's mortgage lending business; but, "It makes sense to have more employees living in the same town the company headquarters are located," says John Langsdorf, Public Affairs manager for Church and Dwight, which has offered a housing benefit program for its employees since 1988.[30] When Church and Dwight, best known as the maker of Arm and Hammer products, moved its corporate headquarters from New York City to Princeton, New Jersey, few of its 300 employees lived in the area. According to Langsdorf, "We have employees who live in Pennsylvania and commute 40 or 50 miles."[31] The company, seeking to establish good community and employee relations, began the program to induce its workers to locate in Princeton.

Church and Dwight teamed up with Griggs Farm Development in Princeton Township, a project created by a nonprofit housing development organization, to market units in the development to their employees. Employees are eligible to receive a loan up to $23,000 or 15 percent of the cost of the house, which ever is less, for a downpayment on a home in the development. The company forgives the loan on an amortized basis over five years. If the employee leaves the firm involuntarily before the period, a prorata portion of the loan plus interest is due the company. A voluntary move before five years requires the employee to repay the loan in full with an accumulated interest rate of 10 percent. Langsdorf believes that the program could be an important part of their employee benefit package in the future so that they can "remain competitive" in the market for qualified employees.[32]

Poll data reveal that about two-thirds of all employees would willingly agree to work for their employer for an additional five years in return for downpayment assistance. For employers that have the cash flow capacity to fund downpayment loans and that have significant recruitment and retention problems, a forgivable downpayment loan program may prove to be surprisingly cost-effective.

Purchase of Security Programs

Employers can purchase publicly and privately issued mortgage bonds issued at negotiated (below market) rates. Proceeds from the sale of these bonds can be lent to employees for mortgage loans or second mortgage downpayment loans at rates that reflect the below market interest rate being paid on the bonds that are capitalizing the loan fund. For example, an employer could purchase a bond bearing an interest rate of 8 percent. The proceeds from the bond could then be lent at a slightly higher rate, say 8.5 percent, to allow for administrative costs. Although an 8 percent return is relatively low, this rate in combination with savings gained by facilitating recruitment and lowering the turnover rate (leaving the employer could trigger mandatory refinancing) may make the rate of return acceptable to many employers. Certainly, an 8 percent return is better than the nonexistent return earned by most other employee benefits. Additionally, because this security is being purchased not as an investment, but rather as a way of offering an employee benefit, the difference between the market rate return and the negotiated rate may be subject to favorable tax treatment.

Using the proceeds of the bond sale, employers can offer employees first mortgages at reduced interest rates and do so with more flexible underwriting criteria. Employers could agree to reduce or waive mortgage insurance requirements and reduce downpayment requirements. Employers could also leverage this fund against conventional mortgage lending programs (including group mortgage origination programs). For example, a conventional group mortgage originator could write a standard 80 percent loan to value mortgage, with reduced origination and application fees. The employer using the bond proceeds could then provide a second mortgage for up to all of the remaining 20 percent of the purchase price of the home, overcoming the downpayment barrier for prospective homeowners.

While it is feasible for large employers, working with a public or private bond issuer, to sponsor this type of housing benefit, this method may be more suitable for groups of employers working together on a local or regional basis, with organizations such as chambers of commerce, trade associations, and local housing partnerships taking on the role of organizing these programs, as could local governments and state housing agencies. The public agencies could also serve as the issuers of the taxable, and in some instances, tax-exempt securities.

A purchase of security program should also be of interest to lenders who can participate as employers, program administrators (as traditional mortgage loan processors and servicers), bond issuers, and bond agents for the redemption of bonds. Lenders, however, should also be interested as investors with a responsibility for meeting Community Reinvestment Act obligations. Purchase of these bonds, which could carry an employer guarantee or credit enhancement, could be an excellent way of meeting community reinvestment lending needs.

Other Programs

There are, of course, other ways of offering affordability enhancing (demand) housing benefit programs. Two programs, mortgage buydowns and shared appreciation mortgages, are familiar to many employers engaged in relocation activity and deserve special mention in that, although familiar to employers, these methods may not be appropriate for large-scale employee benefit programs.

Mortgage buydowns reduce home mortgage interest rates on either a permanent or temporary basis. A permanent buydown is obtained by paying a fee, referred to as "points" (1 point equals 1 percent of the mortgage amount), to the lender at the time of closing in return for a mortgage interest rate reduction. The lender accepts this payment in return for making a permanent interest rate concession.

Many lenders offer temporary buydowns as well. Temporary buydowns enable a borrower to qualify for a larger mortgage by increasing the borrower's income-to-monthly housing expense ratio, a ratio used to qualify borrowers for a mortgage. The cost of a temporary buydown is the difference between the amount of interest a loan would generate at market rate and the interest generated by the subsidized rate. A typical temporary buydown program might have an employer providing a 300 basis point buydown in year one, a 200 basis point buydown in year two, and a 100 basis point buydown in year three with no subsidy being provided thereafter. A $100,000 loan carrying a 30-year term and a 10 percent interest rate would require a monthly payment of $878. The same mortgage at 7 percent requires a $665 monthly payment. Thus, the first year subsidy required to implement this program is $2,556. Program costs in years two and three are less than this amount, but the total three-year cost for this program is a hefty $5,160.

Employers considering permanent or temporary buydown programs may want to review this decision in light of information suggesting that these programs do not address the major problem facing most people trying to enter the housing market—the need for help with the downpayment rather than help in managing monthly costs—which is what buydown programs provide.

Temporary buydowns can create financial problems for borrowers whose incomes do not keep up with rising housing expenses. Receiving temporary assistance may be a useful subsidy for upper management, which can count on rising incomes, but there is less reason to expect nonmanagement incomes to keep up with rising housing expenses. Employers should avoid programs that result in employees incurring housing expenses that may not be manageable in the future. Another reason to question the feasibility of large-scale buydown programs is that they are expensive, particularly in that they can be less explicitly linked with efforts to slow employee turnover than some of the other programs previously discussed. In the case of temporary buydown programs, one might require an employee to repay the buydown while the program is providing assistance, but it would be difficult to require repayment after the brief, but expensive, assistance period ends.

Permanent buydowns avoid the problem of employees buying more house than ultimately affordable, but like temporary buydowns, they are difficult to link to retention strategies. As with a temporary buydown, the employer is required by the lender to pay the full cost of the buydown at closing. Should an employee subsequently leave the employer, there is nothing about the mortgage instrument or the mortgagee's relationship with the lender that would necessitate refinancing, as is the case with an employer who ends a mortgage guarantee or calls a downpayment loan. It may be possible to require the repayment of the points paid to the lender, but, in that the employee never actually saw that payment, it may be difficult to communicate what the employee owes to the employer and why.

Employer participation in shared appreciation mortgages is another method of providing housing assistance. This phenomenon has been particularly noticeable in very high-cost markets, where homes rapidly appreciate. Shared appreciation mortgages (or shared equity mortgages as they are sometimes called) address the borrower problem of an insufficient downpayment. A shared equity relationship requires the investor (the employer) to co-invest in the purchasing of a home with the homebuyer (the employee). The homebuyer and the co-investor each make mortgage payments on the home based upon their respective percentage interests in the home. Each party shares in the tax advantages and costs of owning a portion of a home. However, the homebuyer is also responsible for paying a fair market rent to the co-investor for the right to exclusively use the property. At some contractually specified future date, the home must be refinanced and the investor receives a share of the appreciation of the property with the homebuyer receiving whole interest in the property. The theory of shared equity is that even after paying off the investor, the homebuyer has sufficient equity from appreciation to provide a downpayment for the refinanced home.

Aside from the fact that there is no guarantee that there will be sufficient appreciation to provide for the downpayment, there can be other problems with shared appreciation mortgages in which the employer is the investor. First, shared appreciation participation can be expensive for an employer. In some California examples, co-investors (employers) have paid more than $100,000 per home, an amount too great for even the largest employers to incur on a regular basis.[33] Second, shared appreciation mortgages are the antithesis of an arms-length relationship, as the employee is now, in part, a tenant of the employer. Third, shared appreciation can be complicated. Shared appreciation programs usually require the homebuyer to rent the co-investor's portion of the home, and the co-investor usually needs a property management agent to represent the co-investor's interest in the property and receive monthly rental payments. Fourth, most employers and employees do not want such an intimate financial relationship. Survey data indicate that only between 17 percent to 27 percent of renters would want to purchase a home under such an arrangement if they were not entitled to all of the appreciation. Renters believe that it is difficult to purchase a home, but they know that when they do buy, they want to own all of the home. For all of these reasons, employers should carefully weigh all the available options before considering shared appreciation housing benefit programs.

To summarize, six demand-oriented employer-assisted housing programs are clearly appropriate for employers to consider by reason of their cost, utility to the employee, ease of administration, ability to solve important business recruitment and retention problems, and the nature of employer–employee relationships. These programs—group mortgage origination, closing cost subsidies, mortgage guarantees, group mortgage insurance, downpayment loan (third-party and forgivable), and the purchase of securities—can all be implemented on a geographically targeted basis to address other business problems such as reduced employee productivity and absenteeism as a result of long commutes between work sites and affordable housing, and the need for a stabilized neighborhood offering reasonable security to corporate facilities or personnel.

Demand-oriented programs enhance affordability by reducing downpayment and carrying costs for homebuyers. In some markets, demand programs, however, do not meet the affordable housing needs of employers or employees. In some instances, supply programs are better suited to employer goals and employee housing needs. Supply programs are particularly appropriate in blighted areas in need of redevelopment or stabilization, in markets of housing scarcity, or in areas so expensive that demand programs alone do not offer enough assistance to solve the existing housing problems.

Supply Programs

Supply programs, in contrast to demand programs, do not provide direct assistance to the homebuyer (or to the renter, as supply programs frequently work best in developing rental housing), but rather they provide indirect assistance by reducing financing or development costs; the savings on which are then passed on to the purchasing or renting employee.

Employers can choose to expand employee access to affordable housing by facilitating new construction, by encouraging the substantial rehabilitation of substandard or abandoned housing units, or by facilitating the conversion of nonresidential property to housing. In making this choice, employers must consider how they want to relate to the development process. They can participate as a supplier of equity (on an investor or grant basis), as a supplier of debt, or as a guarantor of debt. In selecting one or more of these options employers will want to consider the risk, cash, cash flow, and role preferences of the firm, as well as the term during which the employer is willing to participate in a housing venture. Even more than with demand programs, supply programs have the potential of placing the employer in the development process, which may or may not be desirable. These considerations are also central in deciding whether to encourage the development of rental or for-sale housing.

Cash

Unlike the programs previously discussed, in which some minimal level of participation must be achieved in order to provide an implementable benefit, cash participation in a project can be offered at widely varying levels and terms.

At the most expansive level, employers can participate in the construction of rental housing as an equity investor holding a limited partnership in a project. Because corporations remain exempt from passive loss tax limitations (to which individual taxpayers are subject), equity investment in a project can make sound investment sense. Yet a firm, by limiting its return generated from the payment of rent by employees/tenants (as opposed to returns generated by tax advantages), can provide a very useful housing benefit. Equity investment requires a substantial contribution from the employer, but as a limited partner (as opposed to directly being a general partner/developer) the firm can have the limited legal exposure and none of the management responsibilities of a landlord. Developers of rental housing in today's credit market frequently find themselves in need of equity investment. Employers, as a new source of equity, would be welcomed into the rental housing development industry. In return for equity participation, employers would negotiate for a commitment of priority access to some percentage of the building and rent rate concessions for the firm's employees.

In a less-involved option, many corporations, particularly those in financial industries, have made substantial equity contributions toward the development of rental housing, usually in association with nonprofit developers.[34] These contributions have been charitable and, as a result, the newly constructed units could not be rented on a priority basis to the employer's employees, as to do so would be a violation of Internal Revenue Service regulations regarding charitable contributions. Employers, however, could make corporate (noncharitable) donations without the long-term return relationship of an investor. In return, developers would agree to reserve units and reduce the rent for employees of the participating firm.

A third option is for an employer to lend money to a project rather than to invest in it. Employers who make loans at below market rates or on a delayed, or otherwise flexible, payback basis can provide a valuable resource to developers.

While larger levels of employer cash support will clearly lead to the creation of affordable housing, some employers, particularly smaller employers, will not have the capacity to make substantial investments or contributions. These employers, however, may have an interest in making smaller contributions in association with other employers. Some developers, particularly nonprofit developers, will be able to aggregate these contributions in ways that produce affordable units. Participation in this type of program may be of great interest to employers when the units being developed are proximate to the employment site and the development is seen as facilitating neighborhood revitalization or as enhancing the security of the area. Employers who draw on the local neighborhood to provide a work force should be similarly motivated. In return for smaller contributions, nonprofit developers may be willing to offer some units to the employees of contributing firms through a lottery process, with winners receiving units at concessionary rent rates.

Whether the appropriate role for an employer is as investor, lender, or grantor of funds, employers as a source of capital can be an important part of the development process—one in which both employer and employee can reap substantial reward for participation.

Construction Loan Financing

A short-term form of cash participation is the provision of construction financing. The Financial Institutions Recovery, Reform, and Enforcement Act of 1989 (FIRREA) has made construction financing increasingly difficult for developers to obtain. FIRREA requires that lenders limit their lending for any project to 15 percent of assets, rather than the previous standard of 100 percent. As a result, developers of large projects now have to piece together construction financing from multiple sources, raising transaction costs associated with already expensive construction loan financing. Although developers are having a more difficult time raising short-term financing, large corporations continue to borrow at, or near, prime rates. An important, short-term, way in which employers could facilitate the development of housing is by borrowing at favorable rates on behalf of developers needing short-term construction loan financing or by guaranteeing all or a portion of a construction loan, thereby providing a credit enhancement that enables the developer to borrow at a more favorable rate. At the conclusion of the development process, the project gains permanent financing and the employer is repaid or the employer's guarantee is ended. At this point the employer's involvement with the project ends, except that its employees continue to receive priority access and sales price or rent rate concessions on units built.

This type of participation does have risks. Some projects are never developed or are built only after great difficulty. On the other hand, if the development goes smoothly this form of assistance has no direct cost or impact on corporate cash flow. Multi-family projects (condominium or rental) typically benefit the most by this form of assistance since developer capital requirements are generally greater than when building single-family homes.

In addition to sales price and rent rate concessions, nonprofit developers may also be interested in trading construction financing assistance for shares in cooperative or mutual housing projects. Employers hold these shares so that if an individual employee moves, the employer retains control of the unit and can continue to offer it to other employees.

Purchase Guarantee Programs

Instead of providing front-end affordability enhancements for new construction or rehabilitation as construction loan financing assistance does, some employers may want to consider a back-end risk reduction program. For example, by agreeing to purchase some number of units if those units are not otherwise purchased by an agreed upon date, an employer may be able to extract substantial sales price discounts for purchasing employees. This is because lenders and developers view the employer's guarantee as a way of transferring their risk that units built will not be sold. In return for this risk reduction, lenders and developers are willing and able to make price concessions. From the lender's perspective, the risk being reduced is that construction financing loans will not be repaid in a timely way, while from the developer's perspective, the risk of carrying the property for an indefinite period (while paying construction loan finance charges, taxes, and other costs) is eliminated by an employer purchase guarantee.

An employer need not guarantee all of the units being built in a development, but rather just that number of units that reduces the risk of the overall project to a point where the lender and developer are comfortable that the remaining project is readily marketable. For example, in a market experiencing slow but steady sales, an employer might guarantee the purchase of the number of units that might be expected to remain unsold after 90 or 120 days, or an employer might guarantee 20 percent of a project. In this way, a partial project guarantee reduces the risk of unsold inventory at the margin while still requiring that the project be generally marketable. Alternatively, an employer could choose to guarantee 100 percent of a project, enabling lenders and builders to build "risk free," even in a severely depressed market. Barring some special conditions that require an employer to have housing available at a particular site, however, no right thinking employer would want to offer a guarantee that masked the general marketability of a project. A project built solely in response to an employer purchase guarantee might prove to be housing in which neither employees, nor the general public, would want to live.

In return for a purchase guarantee, a developer would be expected to offer substantial sales price concessions on the number of units guaranteed by the employer if purchased by the employer's workers. Sales price discounts will vary by region and market conditions, but price reductions of 20 percent, and more, are achievable.

For those projects that "sell out" prior to the time when the developer would call upon the guarantee, this benefit has no programmatic cost. In those instances when the employer's guarantee is called upon, however, the cost to the employer is not the cost of purchasing the units, but rather the cost of carrying the units until they can be sold, including any price concessions necessary to facilitate a sale. To further reduce the risk of cost, employers should carefully analyze the incomes and housing needs of their employees to ensure that the units being built are affordable and meet employee housing goals. Poll data suggest that employees have a good idea of the type of housing to which their social-economic status should "entitle" them; the evidence also suggests that housing not up to this standard will not be accepted by workers, regardless of affordability. The data also suggest that the home-buying aspirations of employees are not significantly above what their incomes would realistically permit.

From the employee's perspective, a 20 percent sales price discount is a significant affordability enhancement. On a $90,000 home, a 20 percent discount amounts to a savings of $18,000 on the sales price, $3,600 on the downpayment (assuming a conventional mortgage requiring a 20 percent downpayment), and $126.44 a month in carrying costs (assuming a 10 percent, 30-year mortgage).

Development Sites

Although employer cash can be used to acquire land or structures capable of being rehabilitated or converted to housing uses, some firms already own surplus land or obsolete buildings that could be developed for employee housing. Firms need not be the actual developer of housing. The site could be sold at a discount, leased, or donated to a developer in return for employees obtaining occupancy priority and sales price or rent rate concessions. Both for-profit and nonprofit developers would be interested in working with employers on this basis, as may public development entities and prospective condominium associations formed by employees interested in living in the project. Developing corporate property in association with community land trusts or mutual housing associations—both limited equity forms of ownership—provides the employer with a continuing ability to control the property so that housing is recycled to current employees rather than being lost to the general market as employees leave the employer.

Employers also can prevent the loss of for-sale housing to the open market, with the employee acquiring all of the employer's subsidy as well as the developer's concessions, by retaining a right of first refusal to buy the property or by placing a lien on the property for the difference between the discounted price at which the employee acquired the unit and its true market value. This lien need not be repaid if the unit was resold at a discounted price to another employee of the firm. In addition, the employer could forgive the lien over time as the value of the subsidy could be amortized against savings on employee turnover. If an employee left an employer shortly after obtaining a home, the full lien could immediately be called.

Developing new housing opportunities for workers while also getting rid of obsolete or blighted properties can be an affordable and attractive solution for many employers. Employers may also find that the removal of substandard property improves neighborhood and civic relations and engenders public financial support for the desired housing project, which can further reduce employer housing program costs.

PC Connection and Peterson Industries

PC Connection, one of the largest computer mail order firms in the country, located in the town of Marlow in rural New Hampshire, is building homes for its employees. As the company grew from 2 employees in 1982 to more than 250 in 1990, the absence of affordable housing in the area was putting a break on the firm's growth that, according to *Inc.* magazine, was the second fastest growing privately held firm in 1987.[35]

"People started coming to us saying they couldn't find a place to live. We compete with companies in Boston and Connecticut. If people can't find housing here, they'll go to companies where they can," explains Patricia Gallup, President of PC Connection. The average age of the PC Connection work force is 29 years old. "We've had 14 marriages and 15 pregnancies in the past year; we had to do something."[36]

"What we are planning to do is build a home and charge the employee basically what it costs us, so it's not really costing us anything to do the project, and it's a cost saving to them," states Gallup. PC Connection spent about $1.2 million to build a 90-acre subdivision of 10 three-bedroom homes. The company anticipates that it will completely recover its costs upon sale of the units to its employees.

As an affordability enhancement to its employees, PC Connection sells the subdivision units to employees at cost for $120,000 to $160,000. The firm holds a second mortgage on the property for the difference between the built cost and the market cost of the unit—usually $30,000 to $40,000. Over a five-year period the company "bonuses out" the second mortgage, essentially forgiving it at an amortized rate.

Ron Karvosky, Comptroller for the firm, explains, "Should the employee leave the company or should they decide to move out of the area, and buy another house somewhere else, the second mortgage would be payable upon the sale."[37]

The company owns another 110 acres of land that they plan to subdivide once this project has been completed.

PC Connection would not appear to have much in common with Peterson Industries in Decatur, Arkansas, and, in many ways, these two firms do have little in common. However, each is the largest employer in a small community and each concluded that by offering a new, construction-oriented housing benefit program they could alleviate some of the problems they faced resulting from a lack of readily available affordable housing proximate to the work site.

For PC Connection, the solution was to develop housing on land it owned, but for Peterson Industries, the solution was a downpayment grant program specifically tied to the construction of new housing. According to Curtis Bond, Director of Human Resources at Peterson Industries, "we wanted to make this (the housing benefit) a community benefit, not just a company benefit."[38] As a result of this philosophy, the downpayment program is only offered on new units built within the Decatur School District boundaries. By restricting the program to this area, the company was able to encourage employees to "live local instead of driving 40 or 45 miles to work," as many employees do.[39] Bond says that, "it is too early to tell," but he has "a sense that it is helping reduce turnover."[40] The community benefits from the program by new growth, which is leading to an increase in school enrollments, an improved local tax base, and increased local commerce.

Specifically, the Petersen Industries' program offers employees a $1,000 downpayment grant for homes built by a company-selected developer. Two basic home designs are offered, one costing about $30,000 and the other costing about $50,000. Buyers have the ability to add or choose various customizing features, but the company believes that by negotiating an exclusive agreement with one builder it has been able to obtain the best possible home at the best possible price.

While in many markets a $1,000 grant would not be seen as very helpful, in this lower cost area of northwest Arkansas a $1,000 grant can be as much as two-thirds of the amount needed for a downpayment on a lower cost home purchased with a 5 percent downpayment, or as little as 10 percent of the amount needed to purchase the more expensive unit with a 20 percent downpayment. Regardless of which home is purchased or how much of a downpayment is made, the employer contribution of $1,000 in this market is significant. Perhaps the most convincing proof of the significance of the program is that about 30 workers moved to the community from other locations during the first 18 months of the program's existence.

In citing these examples of how employers offer housing benefits, one sees that employer-assisted housing programs are indeed a national phenomenon, occurring in virtually every region of the nation, including regions typically thought of as not having a housing affordability problem. While the type of employer varies, the reasons employers offer housing benefits do not. All employers cite concerns about the ability to recruit and retain key personnel, the impact of long commutes on worker productivity and reliability, and the need to operate corporate facilities in a neighborhood or community that is viable and secure.

Master Leases

Changes in the federal tax code, investor preferences for not owning property on a long-term basis, and difficulties in obtaining financing have resulted in a shortage of rental housing in many markets. In some urban areas the rental housing that exists proximate to employment opportunities is badly substandard. As a result, employers have opportunities to play a role that is neither excessively risky nor costly. As master leaseholders, employers can provide housing assistance for moderate- and low-income employees while addressing important business recruitment, retention, and neighborhood security issues.

A master lease is the rental unit equivalent of a purchase guarantee program. A master lease ensures the property owner that a contracted number of units within a rental project will be rented by the entity that is the master lessee. The concept of a master lease is well known to employers who regularly rotate or relocate employees, as these employers frequently enter into master lease agreements on behalf of the relocating employees. Master lease agreements can be made with a prospective apartment house developer or with an owner of existing units. Both for-profit and nonprofit developers, and owners of existing housing, find master lease agreements desirable. Master leases do not require the master lessee to be involved with the ownership or management of the property, but rather simply require the master lessee to pay rent on a unit if it is not being paid for by a sublessee (the employee).

For a prospective developer, a master lease is something that can be shown to a loan underwriter as evidence of the financial feasibility of a project. Indeed, given the FIRREA loan underwriting standards and the poor economic state of many housing markets, having a master lease may be one of the few ways in which project financing can be secured from lenders skittish that an apartment, once built, would remain unrented. For a master lease that secures project financing, developers are willing to offer rent rate concessions to the master lessee (the employer)—concessions that can be passed on to employees.

Owners of already built units may also have reasons for entering into master lease agreements. Owners of property with a significant vacancy rate or owners who want to rehabilitate or refinance property may find that a master lease improves cash flow, marketability, and lender security so that refinancing is obtainable.

A master lease program can be structured to encourage reduced rates of employee turnover. Employees can be required to leave a unit within a specified period of time or have the rent rate increased to the prevailing market rate if the employee leaves the employer. Poll data suggest that approximately one-quarter of surveyed employees are interested in receiving a rental benefit even if it means living proximate to the work site and requires the employee to vacate the unit within six months of leaving the employer. The problem of the employee having to leave the unit could be further mitigated by having the former employee's rent increased to a market rate, with the next available market rate unit in the building reverting to the control of the employer's master lease, assuming that the employer does not have a master lease on the entire building.

Specialized Benefit Programs

The various methods of offering a housing benefit previously discussed each result in one specific form of housing benefit being offered to employees. In addition, each of the 11 programs reviewed heretofore can be offered by most employers either alone or in association with other employers.

The last two programs to be examined, Employee Stock Ownership Plans (ESOPs) and Taft-Hartley Housing Trust Funds, differ from those previously discussed in that these programs do not directly establish a specific benefit, but rather result in a pool of money being assembled that in turn can fund a variety of employer-assisted housing benefit programs.

ESOPs and Taft-Hartley trusts also differ from previously discussed programs in that only specialized types of employers can implement them. An ESOP-financed housing benefit program quite obviously requires a firm to be structured as an employee-owned firm under the terms of the Internal Revenue Code of 1986, Section 4975(e)(7),[41] while Taft-Hartley trusts are only available to unionized firms. Although most employers are in neither of these categories, it is appropriate to discuss both concepts because they represent large numbers of employees (more than 10 million employees work for corporations having ESOPs,[42] while more than 14 million employees are affiliated with unions).[43,44]

Employee Stock Ownership Plans (ESOPs)

ESOPs are a method of corporate finance that enable firms to sell all, or a portion, of a firm to employees on a tax-advantaged basis. In creating an ESOP, the original owners of the firm receive cash for their interest in the firm while the employees receive stock in the firm, which is held in trust by what is essentially a pension plan for the individual employee.

In a typical leveraged ESOP, the trust that is to hold the purchased stock borrows money to purchase the stock.[45] The stock collateralizes the loan.[46] Each year the employer contributes cash or pays the trust dividends sufficient to repay the loan. As the loan is repaid, the trust distributes shares into individual employee accounts.

Most ESOP trusts consist primarily of stock from the firm participating in the ESOP, but trusts routinely hold other financial instruments as well.[47] Although ESOPs have not held financial instruments linked to the housing of employees participating in the ESOP, it is feasible for the trust to do so without violating ERISA fiduciary standards regarding the safety of such investments. By making investments in employee-occupied housing, ESOP trusts could greatly facilitate home ownership and rental housing affordability for plan participants.

One way in which an ESOP could assist homebuyers is by permitting a portion of an individual's plan holdings, or the trust's holdings, to be invested in a first or second mortgage downpayment loan made to that plan participant. The mortgage could bear a below market rate based upon the reduced cost of obtaining funds, reduced transaction costs (the loan need not be resold on the secondary market), individualized knowledge of the borrower, and the borrower's income and long-term job prospects. Individuals borrowing from their own ESOP account might also consider a shared appreciation mortgage. A shared appreciation mortgage might require the home to be refinanced at some agreed upon date in the future, but all appreciation would go directly back to the borrower's own account. The trust could also make shared appreciation mortgages, but since repayment would be to the trust and not the borrower's own ESOP account, an investment of this type would be somewhat less attractive to the individual borrower.

ESOPs could also act as lenders to, or equity investors in, newly constructed or existing multi-family properties; these properties could be rented in whole, or in part, to employees at preferential rates. At some future date the building could be sold to a private owner or to the residents as a cooperative or condominium, enabling the trust to make a return on the building's appreciation.

A less project-specific role for the ESOP would be for the trust to invest in a group mortgage insurance co-insurance fund, enabling employees to receive the benefits of lower downpayments, reduced mortgage insurance costs, and more flexible underwriting criteria. In each of these instances an employer could, in effect, fund a housing benefit using the assets of another, already existing benefit. In this regard again, housing benefits are different than most other benefits that employers regularly offer.

Taft-Hartley Trust Funds

In April 1990, Congress amended the National Labor Relations Act of 1949, the so-called Taft-Hartley Act,[48] permitting, for the first time in 17 years, an expansion in trust fund benefit programs. The adopted amendment permits employers to contribute to a tax-exempt housing trust managed jointly by a board representing labor and management. Employer contributions are made on the basis of a sum per hour/worker. Many other benefit programs for unionized workers, including health and pension plans, are frequently offered to unionized workers through trust funds capitalized similarly.

Taft-Hartley housing trusts are significant because they can fund a variety of housing benefit programs enabling diverse housing needs to be met. "My dream was to find a decent, safe place to raise my family—and the union made it possible," says Joseph Benoit, a Haitian immigrant who lived in slum housing in the Dorchester area of Boston. His union, Local 26 of the Hotel Employees/Restaurant Employees, has been a leading force in the country for work place housing benefits and an advocate for union-sponsored housing to help the working poor. Local 26 was the first union in the nation to collectively bargain for a housing benefit. The union now offers several programs, including downpayment assistance, grants and low interest loans to leverage new construction activities, and no interest loans and grants to employees who are unable to obtain better rental housing because they lack the money for a security deposit—a significant issue for a low-income union membership in one of the nation's most expensive housing markets. The incentive to offer a variety of programs is facilitated by the fact that Taft-Hartley trusts are exempt from ERISA standards requiring funds to be invested at a rate of return commensurate with the risk taken. Although unions have always been able to negotiate for specific benefit programs, such as mortgage guarantees or downpayment assistance, this new form of benefit funding should enable some unions having economically diverse memberships to better service this diversity.

In an era when labor–management relationships have become increasingly strained, placing a housing benefit on the negotiating table—a benefit that may be more valuable to labor and less expensive for management—may provide a way for labor and management to meet worker needs in an era where large wage increases are not likely.

Motivation of Partners

Throughout this chapter, ways in which employers can leverage their participation in employee housing benefit programs with the contributions of lenders, nonprofit organizations, builders, the public sector, and even the employees themselves have been reviewed. In this concluding section, reasons why the shelter industries are motivated to be participants in housing benefit programs are discussed in greater detail.

Mortgage Lenders

The residential mortgage lending industry principally consists of three types of loan originators: (1) mortgage banks, (2) commercial banks, and (3) thrifts.[49] Each lending sector has an interest in expanding their lending activities, but each sector also has some different capacities and legal responsibilities that influence the receptivity of these lenders to employer overtures.

The most obvious common motivation for such participation is expansion of business activity in order to generate more corporate income. The behavior of the nation's housing markets in the late 1980s and early 1990s, specifically, declining homeownership rates,[50] declining numbers of new units constructed,[51] and declining numbers of home purchases,[52] have made the expansion of market share more difficult; and it is likely that these conditions will continue. As a result, many lenders are now facing an overcapacity crisis and they therefore need to maintain an aggressive lending posture in order to maintain or increase local, regional, or national market share.[53] The ability to interface with thousands of potential mortgage loan applicants via an employer or employer consortia is attractive to lenders in this time of heightened competition.

When selecting a lender for a group mortgage origination program or a downpayment loan program, employers will want to keep in mind their work force size and location relative to the lender's market. Large, national employers will often be best served by national mortgage lenders. Smaller employers are more likely to find local or regional lenders more responsive to the volume that smaller employers (or groups of employers) provide (although given the soft lending market, local or regional employers should not dismiss the possibility of working with a national lender).

Unlike mortgage banks, which are not depository institutions (mortgage banks obtain funds primarily from institutional investors), commercial banks and thrifts are subject to the federal Community Reinvestment Act (CRA), which requires lenders to make affirmative efforts to meet the credit needs, including mortgage credit needs, of low- and moderate-income communities within their service area. Many lenders have had difficulty in meeting this obligation because they have been unable to effectively reach out to low- and moderate-income families, even though they are under increasing pressure to do so. Since July 1, 1990, federal regulators have publicly evaluated the effectiveness of lenders in meeting CRA obligations (previously, these ratings were confidential). Lenders, eager to avoid the appearance of discriminatory lending practices, are looking for new ways of reaching low- and moderate-income people who can qualify for loans. Working with employers who have low- and moderate-income employees can be an effective way for commercial banks and thrifts to market their services to two-paycheck families, many of whom earn $18,000 to $35,000 annually but are unable to afford to purchase a home through conventional mortgage programs. The pressure on thrifts to market to this population is even more intense because FIRREA regulations require many thrifts to expand their mortgage lending operations in order to continue having access to the Federal Home Loan Bank System's cash advance program. In order to remain eligible, thrifts must have an asset base in mortgages or mortgage securities of at least 70 percent. Many thrifts are having difficulty meeting this requirement. These changes in the banking and thrift industries are motivating lenders to partcipate in employer-sponsored affordable housing efforts.

Thrifts, in addition to being pressured by FIRREA to increase mortgage lending, also have been given some new financing tools as a result of FIRREA. Working through the Federal Home Loan Bank (FHLB) system, thrifts have three special programs that can be used in association with employer-provided housing benefit programs. The Community Investment Program makes funds available to lenders at the FHLB cost of funds plus 5 basis points. This results in an interest rate about 20 basis points lower than what is normally available. Mortgage loans from this fund are restricted to families having household incomes of less than 115 percent of the area's median income.

The Affordable Housing Program is another source of targeted, below market financing. The FHLB makes Affordable Housing Program funds available on a grant basis to serve the mortgage needs of those earning 80 percent of median income or less and for rental projects with 20 percent of the units reserved for low-income tenants. The amount of money available is limited to about 5 percent of the FHLB's preceding year's net income. Because funding is limited, each bank is looking to significantly leverage its funds with a variety of sources, including employers.

The loans made through the Community Investment Program and the Affordable Housing Program do not conform to the standard underwriting needs of secondary mortgage market purchasers, as interest rates on the mortgages are lower and loan underwriting is somewhat more flexible than standard mortgages. As a result, these mortgages are frequently held in portfolio by the originating thrift, a practice that helps many thrifts meet FIRREA requirements to increase their holdings in mortgages and mortgage securities. By holding these mortgages in portfolio, lenders also have increased underwriting flexibility in how they can relate to employer programs. For example, the secondary market has difficulty accepting corporate guarantees from all but the largest publicly traded firms. This is because the market needs to track the reliability of the guarantee. But a local lender may not feel so restricted, particularly if the lender already has a business relationship with the local employer. Similarly, second mortgage downpayment loans can be of concern to secondary market mortgage purchasers, but may not to a local lender who finds security in the employer's relationship to the second mortgage.

The third program available through the FHLB system is the Community Development Program, which does not have strict income eligibility requirements. This program makes funds available to thrifts at the FHLB cost of funds plus 10 basis points. Lenders participating in this program must restrict loans to lender-selected, under-served neighborhoods. For employers interested in a housing benefit program that yields neighborhood stabilization, or for those employers wanting to improve productivity by encouraging shorter commutes to and from work, this program can be an excellent way to leverage an employer contribution.

With each of these three programs, employers should find lenders eager to use these newly available resources and eager to leverage these resources with the types of programs that employers are interested in offering.

Nonprofit Housing Developers

As with the mortgage lending industry, the latter half of the 1980s witnessed great changes for nonprofit developers. Prior to 1980, nonprofit developers produced units through mechanisms largely derivative of federal housing subsidy programs. With the end of these programs, nonprofits had to learn how to finance housing by combining a multitude of funding programs, including federal low-income housing tax credits and state, local, and philanthropic sources. Using these multiple sources of financing required more expertise and time to assemble projects, but the total dollars available from all of these sources fell far short of replacing the diminished federal resources as the HUD budget fell from $36 billion in 1980 to $15.3 billion in 1990.[54]

Meanwhile, the need for nonprofit developers to produce more housing has increased despite diminished project financing. As a result, nonprofit developers are under pressure to find additional partners who can provide financial assistance and, at times, political credibility (important when seeking scarce local and state public funding) in return for providing housing finance and development skills and access to public funds that can be leveraged against private contributions, including employer participation.

The idea of employers and nonprofit developers working together has been gaining acceptability since the Low-Income Hous-

ing Tax Credit program was authorized in the Tax Reform Act of
1986. Since 1986, $9 billion in Low-Income Housing Tax Credits
have been purchased, mostly by corporations interested in earning
the 15 percent to 18 percent return on investment that tax credit–
assisted projects regularly pay. Corporations, rather than individuals, have been more interested in investing in tax credit–assisted
rental housing because corporations continue to be eligible to deduct unlimited passive losses from taxable income. Due to federal
regulations regarding the selection of tenants in tax credit–assisted
housing, however, employers purchasing tax credits cannot do so
in return for leasing preferences for the purchasing firm's employees. Employer-assisted housing programs (principally supply programs) and relationships with nonprofit developers, particularly
neighborhood-based nonprofits, enable community-based developers to shift their focus from limited tax credit–driven programs
and corporate philanthropy to a business relationship with area
employers in which the nonprofit is responsible for producing, or
rehabilitating, housing for the participating firm's low- and moderate-income employees.

Other Partners

Like lenders and nonprofit developers, builders and state and
local governments were severely impacted by changing economic
conditions and federal fiscal policies during the 1980s. As the 1990s
unfold, builders and state and local governments are in need of
new partners if they are to continue to build (low- and moderate-
income) housing.

With the collapse of the housing market in many areas of the
country in the 1980s, builders have faced major difficulties in financing, building, and selling recently developed units. FIRREA,
the national response to the savings and loan scandal, has affected
responsible builders who find that lenders are requiring stricter
loan underwriting and making development loans that are substantially smaller. FIRREA prohibits construction loans to one borrower in excess of 15 percent of the lender's asset base; prior to
FIRREA restrictions, a lender could provide a construction loan
for up to 100 percent of asset base. Because financing construction
and selling housing in some areas of the nation is a problem, builders in many areas are in need of new partners. This need of developers means that employers capable of guaranteeing the purchase
of units, guaranteeing construction financing, or entering into a

master lease that provides additional security for a mortgage loan will not be viewed by builders simply as providing a novel financing convenience, but rather as an essential participant in a project. And employers, because of this leverage, will be able to obtain appropriate reward for their participation.

The public sector has also been squeezed by federal policies. State and local housing policy prior to 1980 was largely derivative of, and financed by, federal policies. This is no longer the case. In response to federal housing program cuts many state and local governments have moved to fill some of the gap, but a funding void still exists. State and local governments need new partners, including employers. Just as employers seek to leverage their resources with those provided by others, the public sector is also looking for leverage. As a result, state housing revenue bond programs have begun in which the employer provides downpayment assistance or partial loan guarantees. Interest also exists in having the public sector capitalize a group mortgage co-insurance fund into which private employers could pay participation premiums.

State and local governments are likely to receive significant new federal funds for housing from the National Affordable Housing Act of 1990 (NAHA). This law permits state and local governments to provide technical assistance and funding for employer-assisted housing programs serving the needs of low- and moderate-income families. Planning for NAHA is now taking place, so it is an opportune time for employers to begin discussions with local and state officials and to build relationships that lead to housing policies helpful to their communities, employees, and themselves.

The 1980s witnessed a dramatic change in national housing policies that resulted in unprecedented declines in home ownership rates for families, particularly young families. The decade also witnessed new burdens being placed on lenders, nonprofit builders, for-profit builders, and state and local governments as each sector tried to cope with changes in the housing market caused by federal policy changes, national economic changes, and national demographic changes. As a result, each of these sectors has a new need for new partners that can provide assistance in addressing the housing problems that are threatening industries. As employers continue through the 1990s, trying to cope with housing-related business difficulties, it is important for them to know that they can turn to highly skilled and motivated partners for assistance. In Chapter 3, nonhomeowning employees responding to the national survey indicate that despite declining home ownership rates, they continue to have hope that they, too, can participate in the "American dream" of home ownership. These employees also reveal that if the opportunity to become a partner in employer-assisted housing with their employer was available, they would be willing to make a variety of concessions in order to obtain the types of housing benefits that have been considered in this chapter.

Notes

1. T. Callahan, "Business and the Housing Crisis," (Unpublished transcript, AAHI Conference, Princeton, N.J., December 6, 1988) 24.
2. Janelle Biddinger, "Companies Finding It Pays to Help Their Employees Buy Homes," *Realtor News*, May 8, 1989, 14.
3. Ibid.
4. Shawn G. Kennedy, "The Rising Cost of Closing on a Home," *The New York Times*, May 20, 1990, Section 10, 1.
5. Interview with Candace Ludwig, Vice President, Project Financing Division, Lumbermens Mortgage Corp., at the N.J. National Association of Industrial and Office Park Employer-Assisted Housing Workshop, Woodbridge, N.J., May 4, 1990.
6. G.T. Barmore, "Housing the Rank and File," *Mortgage Banking* (Washington, D.C.: Mortgage Bankers Association of America, August 1989) 26–30.
7. Interview with Peter F. Iacovoni, Divisional Vice President, Meritor Mortgage Corporation, East, Philadelphia, March 14, 1989.
8. J. Gordon, "Business and the Housing Crisis," (Unpublished transcript, AAHI Conference, Princeton, N.J., December 6, 1988) 55.
9. Iacovoni.
10. J. Gordon, "Business and the Housing Crisis," note 8, above, 17.
11. Ibid.
12. J. Gordon, "Business and the Housing Crisis," note 8, above, 53.
13. A.J. Maurice, "New HOPE for Employers and Employees Alike," *Shelterforce*, January/February 1990, 18.
14. Rachelle Gabarine, "Companies Help Workers Buy Homes in New Jersey," *New York Times*, August 3, 1990, A18.
15. Richard Remington, "Firms Sign Up with State Programs to Offer Home Loans for Employees," *Newark Star-Ledger*, January 21, 1990, 42.
16. Ibid.
17. Ibid.
18. "Companies Help Workers Buy Homes in New Jersey," *New York Times*, note 14, above.
19. "Firms Sign Up With State Programs to Offer Home Loans for Employees," *Newark Star-Ledger*, note 15, above.
20. The Community Reinvestment Act was enacted as Title VIII of the Housing and Community Development Act of 1977, P.L. 95-128.
21. Interview with Mike Gayso, Manager, Allegheny Health Services Federal Credit Union, Pittsburgh, Pa., September 5, 1990.
22. W. Tierney, "Fannie Mae Supports Employer-Assisted Demonstration Project," *Shelterforce*, January/February 1990, 19.

23. Interview with Laurie Ryerson, Executive Director, Coastal Housing Partnership, Santa Barbara, California, September 12, 1990.
24. Ibid.
25. "Walk Home Aims to Revitalize Neighborhood," *Chicago Tribune*, May 16, 1989, Section 3, 3.
26. *The Employee Management Association Report of National Cost per Hire Data for 1988* (Raleigh, N.C.: The Employee Management Association, 1989) 2.
27. "Employee Turnover: Measurement and Control," *Small Business Report* (Monterey, Calif.: Business Research and Communications, February 1987) 1.
28. Ibid.
29. Interview with Alice Wilson, Vice President for Mortgage Banking, First Federal Savings and Loan, Raleigh, N.C., September 5, 1990.
30. Douglas A. Sachs, "Employer-Assisted Housing: A Benefit for the '90s," *The Princeton Packet*, October 31, 1989, 1B.
31. Mindy Fetterman, "More Firms Help Workers Buy Homes," *USA Today*, February 7, 1990, 2B.
32. Douglas A. Sachs, "Employer-Assisted Housing: A Benefit for the 90s," *The Princeton Packet*, note 30, above.
33. Employee/Employer Equity Sharing (Redwood City, Calif.: The Equity Sharing Benefits Consulting Group, 1990).
34. There are more than 20 cities or counties throughout the United States that have active housing partnership programs or equity funds. Cities in which these programs exist include Boston, New York, Philadelphia, Cleveland, Chicago, Minneapolis, and Seattle. In each instance among the forces behind these partnerships have been the major corporate firms and foundations headquartered or associated with these cities. For example, John Hancock in Boston, BP America in Cleveland, Harris Bank and Trust and Amoco Oil in Chicago, and 3M in Minneapolis-St. Paul.
35. "More Firms Help Workers Buy Homes," *USA Today*, note 31, above.
36. Ibid.
37. Ibid.
38. Interview with Curtis Bond, Director of Human Resources, Peterson Industries, Decatur, Arkansas, September 10, 1990.
39. Ibid.
40. Ibid.
41. J. Kaplan, "Is ESOP a Fable? Fabulous Uses and Benefits or Phenomenal Pitfalls?," *Taxes—The Tax Magazine*, December 1987, 788.
42. "Rostenkowski Seeking ESOP-Loan Benefit Cut," *New York Times*, June 8, 1989, D7.
43. John Zaluski, Director of the Office of Wage and Industrial Relations, AFL-CIO, reports 14.1 million workers are affiliated with the AFL-CIO. There are, however, non-affiliated bargaining organizations the largest of which is the state affiliates of the National Education Association, which adds to the 14.1 million worker figure. Interview with John Zaluski, Director of the Office of Wage and Industrial Relations, AFL-CIO, Washington, D.C., June 29, 1990.
44. There is an overlap in the count between workers employed by firms having an ESOP program and unionized workers. The extent of the overlap is not

precisely known. About 27 percent of ESOPs are unionized according to the ESOP Association. Ten percent of all ESOPs have more than 1,000 employees and 30 percent of these firms have unions. *See* "1989 ESOP Association Survey Results," *ESOP Report*, (Washington, D.C.: The Employee Stock Association, January 1990) 3.

45. According to the 1988 ESOP Association membership survey, most employee purchases of stock are purchased with borrowed money rather than self-financed by the employer.

46. John Case, "Owner's Manual: Are ESOPs Dead or Alive?," *Inc.*, June 1988, 95.

47. "1989 ESOP Association Survey Results," *ESOP Report* (Washington, D.C.: The Employee Stock Ownership Association, January 1990) 3.

48. The National Labor Relations Act, or the Taft-Hartley Act, P.L. 101, 80th Congress. The amendment authorizing housing trust funds is P.L. 273, 101st Congress.

49. Between 1985 and 1989, 97.41 percent to 98.49 percent of all single-family mortgage lending was made by these three classes of lenders. Thrifts made about half of this volume with commercial banks and mortgage banks dividing the balance fairly evenly. Interview with Stephanie Sampson, U.S. League of Savings Institutions, Washington, D.C., August 2, 1990.

50. *The State of the Nation's Housing* (Cambridge, Mass.: The Joint Center for Housing Studies at Harvard University, 1989) 12.

51. Interview with Tina Trent, Economics Department, National Association of Home Builders, Washington, D.C., July 30, 1990.

52. Interview with Trisha Morris, Office of Public Affairs, National Association of Realtors, Washington, D.C., July 30, 1990.

53. *See* M.F. Cooper, "Overcapacity," *Mortgage Banking*, October 1988, 139–145; and M.F. Cooper, "Market Share Slavery," *Mortgage Banking*, November 1989, 37–40. *Also see* "Chevy Chase S&L Cuts 100 Jobs," *The Washington Post*, July 24, 1990, D1.

54. D.C. Schwartz, R.C. Ferlauto, D.N. Hoffman, *A New Housing Policy for America: Recapturing the American Dream* (Philadelphia: Temple University Press, 1988) 47.

Chapter 3

Worker Attitudes Toward Employer-Assisted Housing[1]

In the fall of 1989, the American Affordable Housing Institute completed a major national survey of the housing conditions, problems, and plans of the United States' young and middle-aged work force. In this study, 1,200 telephone interviews were completed on a national probability sample of American adults between the ages of 18 and 44 who were working full time (and/or whose spouse was so employed). See Appendix 1 for additional survey methodology.

The survey revealed a pattern of worker attitudes that are highly supportive of employer-assisted housing: millions of American workers want and need employer-sponsored housing benefits and would be willing to trade significant wage growth, job mobility, payroll/banking flexibility, and various other benefits in order to receive employer-provided housing benefits. The conclusions of our study, stated generally and then explained in detail in this chapter, are as follows:

1. The vast majority of young and middle-aged workers want to own and expect to own their own homes and to save the money needed to purchase that home on their own.
2. Nonetheless, about half of these workers are uncertain that they can achieve their goal of home ownership in the next five years, and almost 30 percent are uncertain and/or doubtful that they will ever attain that goal.
3. For 60 percent of the labor force studied, downpayments (and not monthly carrying costs) were perceived as the chief obstacle to achieving home ownership for their family.
4. The housing benefits these workers need are limited in cost because the homes that they want to purchase are modest

in price and because the average gap between current savings and anticipated downpayment needs is rather small.

5. A majority of the workers interviewed expressed interest
in one or more specific employer-assisted housing benefits.

6. A majority of employees interested in receiving housing
benefits from their employer reported a willingness to trade
anticipated wage increases, job mobility, and payroll/bank-
ing flexibility in order to receive these benefits. A sizeable
minority of these workers (projecting to 3 million to 8 million employee households) reported themselves as willing
to trade some portion of their health care benefits and/or
to move close to their work sites in order to receive housing
benefits from their employers. Forty-eight percent of the
respondents also expressed interest in rental benefits.

These findings suggest that employers who adopt cost-effective
housing benefits for their nonmanagement workers will be able to
achieve significant improvements in the recruitment, retention,
morale, and productivity of their work force.

Home Ownership for Young and Middle-Aged American Workers

The "American dream" of home ownership still burns brightly
in the hearts of America's workers. Exhibit 3.1 shows that for 75
percent of the working families interviewed, home ownership is
either their top financial priority or a "very important" priority that
they hope to achieve in the next half-decade. It is not surprising
that home ownership was significantly more important to families
in their prime first-homebuying years (ages 26 to 34), for married
workers, and for workers with higher earning power (who are more
likely to achieve their goal). Employers will be especially interested
in the fact that home ownership aspirations are about equally important to employees in all job classifications and skill levels; across
all lines of business; of both sexes; and in most regions and county
sizes across the nation. Exhibit 3.1 documents that home ownership
is especially important to urban-located workers and those employed in the northeastern United States, areas that track higher
housing costs.

Although the vast majority of the working household members
interviewed want to become homeowners in the next five years,

Exhibit 3.1 Homeownership for Young and Middle-Aged American Workers: Percentage Rating Home Ownership as Their "Top Financial Priority" or "Very Important Priority" for the Next Five Years

TOTAL	MALE	FEMALE	AGE 18–25*	AGE 26–34*	AGE 35+*	MARRIED*	SINGLE*	SINGLE PARENT
75	72	77	71	79	71	83	67	72

Annual Household Income

$15,000	$15,000–$25,000	$25,000+
67	74	78

County Size (1 = Largest, 4 = Smallest)

URBAN*	RURAL*	1	2	3	4
78	72	77	78	72	71

Region*

NORTH-EAST	MID-WEST	SOUTH	FAR WEST
82	73	77	68

Industry Employed In

UNION MEMBER	MFG/INDUSTRIAL	RETAIL/WHOLESALE	FINANCIAL
81	78	74	75

Occupational Classification of Worker

GOVERNMENT PROFESSIONAL	PRIVATE SECTOR PROFESSIONAL	CLERICAL/SALES	SKILLED LABOR	UNSKILLED
72	75	75	76	72

Source: All exhibits in this chapter are taken from the 1989 American Affordable Housing Institute Survey.
*Note: Percentage differences within starred categories achieve statistical significance at the .05 level or greater.

only about half of the respondents are very confident that they will achieve their goal during that time frame (see Exhibit 3.2). Indeed, the study indicates that almost 30 percent of the nation's young and middle-aged workers are uncertain or doubtful that they will ever be able to own a home (Exhibit 3.3).

When asked about their expectations for the next five years, upper-income workers, professionals, married workers, and employees of prime homebuying age are somewhat more confident that they will attain home ownership in the next half-decade, but a significant degree of doubt and uncertainty, over that time frame, extends across workers in every line of business, in urban and rural areas alike, and among both men and women. Single-parent heads of household (overwhelmingly female workers) are especially uncertain of their ability to become homeowners in the years immediately ahead (see Exhibit 3.2).

A similar, but not identical, pattern occurs among the nearly 30 percent of respondents who are uncertain or doubtful that they will ever achieve home ownership. Younger, married, upper income, and male workers are significantly more confident that they will be able to buy a house at some point in their lifetime, but a similar and sizable degree of doubt extends across workers in every line of business studied, in urban and rural areas alike, and among union and nonunion families. A majority of single-parent heads of households doubt their ability ever to purchase a home of their own (see Exhibit 3.3).

Exhibit 3.4 presents data showing why so many American workers are doubtful or unsure of their ability to become homeowners. The data document that it is downpayments, rather than monthly carrying costs or other factors, that are overwhelmingly perceived to be the primary obstacles to purchasing a home. Fully 60 percent of respondents see downpayment costs as the key barrier to home ownership—a percentage that varies only insignificantly across workers in every line of business, every region of the nation, every age category, and in both urban and rural areas. Female, upper-income, and married workers tended to regard downpayments as a barrier significantly more often than did other workers, while less skilled employees more frequently perceived monthly payments and other factors (other than downpayments) to be prohibitive of home ownership (see Exhibit 3.4).

The workers and spouses interviewed are correct in perceiving downpayment requirements as something of a problem for them: home prices have outstripped real wages and family incomes in

Exhibit 3.2 Near Term Home Ownership Expectations of Young and Middle-Aged American Workers and Their Families (Percentage)

	TOTAL	MALE	FEMALE	AGE 18–25*	AGE 26–34*	AGE 35+*	MARRIED*	SINGLE*	SINGLE PARENT*
Rating home ownership as almost certain or very likely	52	54	50	50	57	42	58	45	40
Rating home ownership as somewhat likely or not very likely	48	45	50	50	43	59	42	54	5

	Annual Household Income*			County Size (1 = Largest, 4 = Smallest)					
	$15,000	$15–25K	$25,000+	URBAN	RURAL	1	2	3	4
Almost certain/very likely	34	49	61	53	50	53	54	50	51
Somewhat likely/not very likely	65	50	38	46	49	47	47	49	48

Exhibit 3.2 *Continued*

Region*

	NORTH-EAST	MID-WEST	SOUTH	FAR WEST
Almost certain/very likely	47	55	55	45
Somewhat likely/not very likely	52	44	44	54

Industry Employed In

	UNION MEMBER	MFG/INDUSTRIAL	RETAIL/WHOLESALE	FINANCIAL
Almost certain/very likely	59	57	53	47
Somewhat likely/not very likely	41	42	47	52

Occupational Classification of Worker

	GOVERNMENT PROFESSIONAL	PRIVATE SECTOR PROFESSIONAL	CLERICAL/SALES	SKILLED	UNSKILLED
Almost certain/very likely	50	57	51	53	47
Somewhat likely/not very likely	50	43	49	46	53

*Note: Differences from 100 percent due to rounding or "don't know"; starred categories contain percentage differences that achieve statistical significance at .05 level or greater.

Exhibit 3.3 Lifetime Home Ownership Expectations of Young and Middle-Aged American Workers and Their Families (Percentage)

	TOTAL	MALE*	FEMALE*	AGE 18–25*	AGE 26–34*	AGE 35+*	MARRIED*	SINGLE*	SINGLE PARENT*
Fully expect to own	56	73	60	78	69	43	69	63	41
Doubtful or unsure	29	23	36	19	29	47	27	32	56
Other	4	4	4	2	3	10	6	5	4

	Annual Household Income*			County Size* (1 = Largest, 4 = Smallest)					
	$15,000	$15–25K	$25,000+	URBAN	RURAL	1	2	3	4
Fully expect to own	54	64	74	64	68	60	67	69	65
Doubtful or unsure	43	31	23	32	29	33	29	28	37
Other	3	5	3	5	3	6	4	2	7

Exhibit 3.3　*Continued*

Region* ／ Industry Employed In

	NORTH-EAST	MID-WEST	SOUTH	FAR WEST	UNION MEMBER	MFG/INDUSTRIAL	RETAIL/WHOLESALE	FINANCIAL
Fully expect to own	57	69	66	66	63	70	65	63
Doubtful or unsure	39	25	27	31	31	27	29	34
Other	4	5	3	4	6	3	5	3

Occupational Classification of Worker

	GOVERNMENT PROFESSIONAL	PRIVATE SECTOR PROFESSIONAL	CLERICAL/SALES	SKILLED	UNSKILLED
Fully expect to own	65	72	65	67	61
Doubtful or unsure	30	23	31	28	35
Other	5	5	5	6	4

*Note: Differences from 100 percent due to rounding; starred categories contain percentage differences that achieve statistical significance at .05 level or greater.

Exhibit 3.4 Perceived Barriers to Achieving Home Ownership Among Young and Middle-Aged American Workers and Their Families (Percentage)

	TOTAL	MALE*	FEMALE*	AGE 18–25	AGE 26–34	AGE 35+	MARRIED*	SINGLE*	SINGLE PARENT*
Unable to make needed downpayment but able to afford monthly carrying costs	60	54	65	58	60	62	65	55	60
Able to make downpayment but unable to meet monthly carrying costs	16	18	13	18	14	15	15	56	14
Unable to afford either downpayment or carrying costs	14	13	14	13	12	16	11	16	19
Other	10	14	8	11	13	8	10	14	6

	Annual Household Income*					County Size* (1 = Largest, 4 = Smallest)			
	$15,000	$15–25K	$25,000+	URBAN	RURAL	1	2	3	4
Unable to make needed downpayment but able to afford monthly carrying costs	53	59	65	62	59	63	61	57	62
Able to make downpayment but unable to meet monthly costs	22	15	13	15	16	14	16	17	13
Unable to afford either cost	18	16	10	12	14	13	12	15	14
Other	5	9	12	10	10	10	13	11	12

Exhibit 3.4 *Continued*

Region*

	NORTH-EAST	MID-WEST	SOUTH	FAR WEST	UNION MEMBER	MFG/ INDUSTRIAL	RETAIL/ WHOLESALE	FINANCIAL
						Industry Employed In		
Unable to make needed downpayment but able to afford monthly costs	62	65	55	60	66	59	62	58
Able to make downpayment but unable to meet monthly costs	14	16	16	16	15	17	17	21
Unable to afford either cost	14	11	15	14	10	11	12	13
Other	10	8	15	10	10	13	9	8

Occupational Classification of Worker

	GOVERNMENT PROFESSIONAL	PRIVATE SECTOR PROFESSIONAL	CLERICAL/SALES	SKILLED	UNSKILLED
Unable to make needed downpayment but able to afford monthly costs	58	65	60	59	56
Able to make downpayment but unable to afford monthly costs	13	10	14	20	23
Unable to afford either costs	14	10	16	10	13
Other	15	16	10	10	9

*Note: Differences from 100 percent due to rounding; starred categories include percentage differences that achieve statistical significance at .05 level or greater.

the 1980s and downpayment requirements have risen faster than family savings rates in that period.[2] Nonetheless, it must be noted that the downpayment assistance that America's young and middle-aged workers need is quite modest. This is true because (1) the homes that these workers aspire to purchase are inexpensive (generally at or below regional median prices); (2) the perceived dollar gap between what the workers have already saved and the downpayment they think they need is small; and (3) the majority of workers expect to save all of the downpayment themselves, meaning that only a minority of the nonhomeowning labor force are likely to be "takers" of an employer-assisted housing benefit.

Exhibit 3.5 indicates that 60 percent of the workers interviewed hope to purchase homes at or below $75,000 in price, and that 80 percent of respondents aspire to buy houses selling for under $100,000 (i.e., at or below median sales prices of existing homes in their region). The data in Exhibit 3.5 indicate that not only are American workers seeking modest homes, but that they are quite sensitive to and/or reasonable about regional and family housing economics. Thus, lower-income workers, rural-located workers, and single-parent heads of households aspire to especially modest priced homes whereas workers in the Northeast (and in larger counties generally), where home prices are higher, aspire (as they must) to buy more expensive houses. It is interesting to note that the home-price aspirations of American workers do not vary significantly by gender, age, marital status, or union membership.

If the homes that America's workers want to buy are relatively inexpensive, then, of course, the downpayments these workers need (which are computed as constant fractions of the home price) must be relatively modest, too. Exhibit 3.6 shows the size of the dollar gap between what the workers interviewed have already saved and the downpayment that they think is needed. It will be noted that 77 percent of the employees perceive a gap that is less than $10,000, and that fully 25 percent perceive a gap that is less than $5,000. It also appears that employee downpayment needs may be somewhat overstated as measured by comparing the cost of the home sought versus the size of the downpayment required. Perhaps this is due to unfamiliarity with privately insured lower downpayment mortgages.

A number of the findings warranted by the data in Exhibit 3.6 indicate, again, that the workers interviewed were sensitive to and/or reasonable about housing economics. It "makes sense"

Exhibit 3.5   The Approximate Cost of Homes Desired by Young and Middle-Aged American Workers (Percentage)

	TOTAL	MALE*	FEMALE*	AGE 18–25	AGE 26–34	AGE 35+	MARRIED*	SINGLE*	SINGLE PARENT*
Under $25,000	4	4	3	5	4	2	3	4	5
$25,000 to $50,000	33	30	35	37	30	33	33	32	48
$50,001 to $75,000	22	24	21	24	23	19	22	23	20
$75,001 to $100,000	21	22	20	18	21	24	20	22	14
$100,001 to $175,000	11	11	10	8	12	12	12	9	8
Over $175,000	10	9	10	8	10	11	10	9	6
Average in Thousands	$79	$79	$79	$73	$82	$82	$80	$78	$66

	Annual Household Income*					County Size* (1 = Largest, 4 = Smallest)			
	$15,000	$15–25K	$25,000 +	URBAN	RURAL	1	2	3	4
Under $25,000	6	3	2	3	4	3	3	4	5
$25,000 to $50,000	52	39	19	17	44	11	24	40	57
$50,001 to $75,000	14	31	21	19	25	13	25	27	18
$75,001 to $100,000	16	15	27	23	19	18	27	20	17
$100,001 to $175,000	6	7	16	20	4	27	12	5	2
Over $175,000	5	4	16	18	3	28	8	4	1
Average in Thousands	$62	$66	$96	$100	$64	$117	$83	$67	$55

Exhibit 3.5 *Continued*

Region* / Industry Employed In

	NORTH-EAST	MID-WEST	SOUTH	FAR WEST	UNION MEMBER	MFG/INDUSTRIAL	RETAIL/WHOLESALE	FINANCIAL
Under $25,000	4	4	5	2	3	5	3	4
$25,000 to $50,000	16	48	39	18	33	41	38	20
$50,001 to $75,000	8	25	26	24	22	20	23	24
$75,000 to $100,000	22	18	18	27	20	19	22	16
$100,000 to $175,000	25	4	7	14	13	7	5	29
Over $175,000	25	1	5	15	9	7	9	8
Average in Thousands	$112	$59	$67	$94	$80	$70	$74	$92

Occupational Classification of Worker

	GOVERNMENT PROFESSIONAL	PRIVATE SECTOR PROFESSIONAL	CLERICAL/SALES	SKILLED	UNSKILLED
Under $25,000	2	1	2	5	7
$25,000 to $50,000	25	20	29	43	43
$50,001 to $75,000	27	24	26	20	21
$75,001 to 100,000	22	28	21	19	15
$100,001 to $175,000	13	14	13	7	9
Over $175,000	11	13	10	6	6
Average in Thousands	$85	$92	$83	$68	$68

*Note: Differences from 100 percent due to rounding; starred categories include percentage differences that achieve statistical significance at .05 level or greater.

Exhibit 3.6   Perceived Downpayment Gap (Amount Needed Over Savings to Achieve Home Ownership) Among Young and Middle-Aged American Workers and Their Families (Percentage)

	TOTAL	MALE*	FEMALE*	AGE 18–25	AGE 26–34	AGE 35+	MARRIED*	SINGLE*	SINGLE PARENT*
Less than $5,000	25	23	27	27	25	23	26	24	51
$5,000 to $10,000	52	54	51	55	53	48	53	52	33
$10,001 to $15,000	7	7	6	5	5	11	7	6	8
$15,001 to $20,000	9	12	8	8	10	10	9	10	3
Over $20,000	7	5	8	4	7	9	6	8	5

	Annual Household Income*					County Size* (1 = Largest, 4 = Smallest)			
	$15,000	$15–25K	$25,000+	URBAN	RURAL	1	2	3	4
Less than $5,000	36	32	18	18	31	11	24	29	36
$5,000 to $10,000	52	55	51	47	56	43	51	58	51
$10,001 to $15,000	4	5	8	9	4	10	8	5	3
$15,001 to $20,000	6	4	13	14	6	17	10	5	9
Over $20,000	2	4	9	12	2	17	6	3	1

Exhibit 3.6 *Continued*

Region* — Industry Employed In

	NORTH-EAST	MID-WEST	SOUTH	FAR WEST	UNION MEMBER	MFG/INDUSTRIAL	RETAIL/WHOLESALE	FINANCIAL
Less than $5,000	12	28	39	14	27	28	31	24
$5,000 to $10,000	41	62	49	53	52	55	54	39
$10,001 to $15,000	7	5	8	9	3	4	5	6
$15,001 to $20,000	24	5	3	12	11	10	5	9
Over $20,000	15	1	3	12	6	3	4	21

Occupational Classification of Worker

	GOVERNMENT PROFESSIONAL	PRIVATE SECTOR PROFESSIONAL	CLERICAL/SALES	SKILLED	UNSKILLED
Less than $5,000	19	13	22	30	41
$5,000 to $10,000	56	51	56	52	45
$10,001 to $15,000	6	8	7	7	3
$15,001 to 20,000	12	19	8	6	7
Over $20,000	7	8	8	5	4

*Note: Differences from 100 percent due to rounding; starred categories include percentage differences that achieve statistical significance at .05 level or greater.

that lower-paid workers, rural workers, and single-parent heads of households would tend to need smaller levels of downpayment assistance (since they aspire to less expensive homes) and that employees in the Northeastern United States would need more help significantly more often. It is worth noting that neither gender nor marital status impact significantly on the savings/downpayment dollar gap, but that older workers and employees of financial institutions perceive themselves as needing a higher dollar amount to bridge that gap.

Whatever an individual's need for downpayment assistance, and whatever the average employee's savings/downpayment dollar gap, *most American workers expect to save all of the downpayment needed to buy their first home themselves.* Exhibit 3.7 indicates that fully 56 percent of the workers (and/or their spouses) interviewed expect to save the entirety of their downpayment themselves. This expectation is remarkably constant across the American work force: a similar percentage of workers in all regions, all income categories, all job classifications, and all marital statuses expect to be wholly self-reliant in this matter. On the other hand, female workers and younger workers (key components of the work force of the future) report themselves as needing outside help significantly more often than do others in the study.

The data arrayed in Exhibits 3.1 through 3.7, taken together, suggest that millions of young and middle-aged workers perceive themselves to need some help in achieving home ownership, but that only a minority of workers express that need; the help they need is one-time in nature (i.e., downpayment assistance) rather than continuing in character (i.e., monthly rent or mortgage assistance); and the amount of the help they need is modest.

Worker Preferences and Tradeoffs

We asked America's young and middle-aged workers to select only two benefits from a list including health care plans, child care, pension programs, college tuition reimbursement, and an employer-assisted housing program. The housing benefit was the third most popular benefit—rating significantly above child care and college reimbursement programs and below health care and pension plans. Exhibit 3.8 shows that this preference ranking is remarkably stable across the American labor force. There are no significant differences by age, sex, marital status,

Exhibit 3.7 Expected Source of Downpayment Savings Among Young and Middle-Aged American Workers and Their Families (Percentage)

	TOTAL	MALE*	FEMALE*	AGE 18–25	AGE 26–34	AGE 35+	MARRIED*	SINGLE*	SINGLE PARENT*
Expecting to save all the downpayment themselves (without gifts or borrowing)	56	60	52	50	58	59	58	54	58

Annual Household Income*

County Size* (1 = Largest, 4 = Smallest)

	$15,000	$15–25K	$25,000+	URBAN	RURAL	1	2	3	4
Expecting to save all the downpayment themselves (without gifts or borrowing)	54	57	57	56	56	55	56	55	57

Exhibit 3.7 *Continued*

Region*

	NORTH-EAST	MID-WEST	SOUTH	FAR WEST	UNION MEMBER	MFG/INDUSTRIAL	RETAIL/WHOLESALE	FINANCIAL
						Industry Employed In		
Expecting to save all the downpayment themselves (without gifts or borrowing)	52	59	56	55	60	62	57	42

Occupational Classification of Worker

	GOVERNMENT PROFESSIONAL	PRIVATE SECTOR PROFESSIONAL	CLERICAL/SALES	SKILLED	UNSKILLED
Expecting to save all the downpayment themselves (without gifts or borrowing)	54	60	51	59	59

*Note: Differences from 100 percent due to rounding; starred categories include percentage differences that achieve statistical significance at .05 level or greater.

Exhibit 3.8   Employee Benefit Preferences Among Young and Middle-Aged American Workers and Their Families (Percentage)

BENEFIT	TOTAL	MALE*	FEMALE*	AGE 18–25	AGE 26–34	AGE 35+	MARRIED*	SINGLE*	SINGLE PARENT*
Comprehensive health and hospitalization plan	71	74	68	65	75	71	70	72	64
Retirement pension plan	45	51	40	44	45	48	39	52	54
Employee housing assistance plan	31	28	32	29	30	34	30	31	32
College education reimbursement program	23	22	23	29	20	21	24	22	17
Child care/nursery school program	20	12	27	25	20	12	26	14	20

BENEFIT	Annual Household Income*			URBAN	RURAL	County Size* (1 = Largest, 4 = Smallest)			
	$15,000	$15–25K	$25,000+			1	2	3	4
Comprehensive health and hospitalization plan	68	70	71	72	70	70	74	70	69
Retirement pension plan	44	46	44	43	47	42	45	45	50
Employee housing assistance plan	33	29	31	33	29	41	25	29	29
College education reimbursement program	22	25	21	21	24	19	22	25	22
Child care/nursery school program	21	18	22	21	19	20	22	20	17

Exhibit 3.8   *Continued*

Region* / Industry Employed In

BENEFIT	NORTH-EAST	MID-WEST	SOUTH	FAR WEST	UNION MEMBER	MFG/INDUSTRIAL	RETAIL/WHOLESALE	FINANCIAL
Comprehensive health and hospitalization plan	72	75	67	70	66	69	78	66
Retirement plan	42	51	44	43	41	52	48	39
Employee housing assistance plan	34	25	31	34	30	28	28	33
College education reimbursement program	23	20	25	21	25	21	21	19
Child care/nursery school program	18	19	21	21	25	21	14	30

Occupational Classification of Worker

BENEFIT	GOVERNMENT PROFESSIONAL	PRIVATE SECTOR PROFESSIONAL	CLERICAL/SALES	SKILLED	UNSKILLED
Comprehensive health and hospitalization plan	68	74	72	67	67
Retirement pension plan	40	43	44	53	47
Employee housing assistance plan	35	32	31	27	35
College education reimbursement program	27	21	23	24	22
Child care/nursery school program	22	19	22	12	20

*Note: Differences from 100 percent due to rounding; starred categories include percentage differences that achieve statistical significance at .05 level or greater.

Exhibit 3.9 The Appeal of Different Housing Benefits to Young and Middle-Aged American Workers and Their Families

		PERCENTAGE OF RESPONDENTS INTERESTED IN BENEFIT
1.	Downpayment loan that is interest-free for five years	60
2.	Five-year forgivable downpayment loan (20 percent forgivable for each year of employment tenure)	67
3.	Employer-guaranteed mortgage loan	41*
3a.	Workers interested in guaranteed loan also willing to trade off one year's wage increase to obtain benefit	63**
3b.	Workers interested in guaranteed loan also willing to trade part of health care coverage to obtain benefit	29**
4.	Group mortgage discount on closing costs	48
5.	Group mortgage discount on mortgage rate	56
5a.	Group mortgage discount with loan serviced via payroll deduction	66***
6.	Low-rate mortgage but appreciation on house shared with employer	27
7.	Participate in employer-sponsored "build your own home" program	62
8.	Prefers employer-sponsored downpayment grant lottery to $4 per week wage increase	50

---

*Based upon anecdotal analysis of poll responses, it appears that surveyed workers may not have fully understood how a mortgage guarantee would be helpful to them; as a result, perhaps a lower level of interest was recorded than might actually be the case.

**This percentage is of those expressing interest in an employer-guaranteed loan.

***This percentage is of those expressing interest in group mortgage programs in 5 above.

income, job classification, line of business, urban versus rural location, union membership, or single-parent head of household status. Employees in the Northeastern United States and in large counties generally have a significantly higher degree of interest in housing benefits.

What kind of housing benefits would be most attractive to America's young and middle-aged workers and their families? The data arrayed in Exhibit 3.9 show that downpayment loans with employer-sponsored affordability features would be of greatest interest to respondents:[3] 61 percent of those interviewed would be interested in a loan that was interest-free in the early years and later converted to a market rate of interest; and 68 percent expressed some interest in staying with their employer for five years (foregoing job mobility) in order to receive a forgivable downpayment loan. An employer-guaranteed loan was of interest to 41

percent of respondents. In addition, a majority of interested employees expressed willingness to trade one year's anticipated wage
increase in order to receive an employer-guaranteed loan, while a
sizeable minority of workers interested in a guaranteed loan would
trade part of their health care benefits.

Exhibit 3.9 also indicates that about half of the working
families in the study reported themselves as interested in a program under which their employer negotiated with a lender for
a group mortgage discount on closing costs and/or mortgage interest rate (programs that typically cost the employer nothing
except the time of negotiation and the administrative costs, if
any, of program monitoring); two-thirds of the workers interested
in a group mortgage discount would be willing to have the monthly
mortgage costs handled via payroll deduction. Sixty-two percent
of respondents expressed some interest in an employer-facilitated "build your own home" program, and 50 percent would
prefer participation in an employer-sponsored downpayment lottery to a modest wage increase.

Each of the housing benefits described in Chapter 2 are attractive to millions of American working families. But different
benefits appeal to different groups or types of workers (and are,
therefore, likely to be differentially appealing to different types of
employers). Accordingly, it is important to review, in detail, the
appeal of each housing benefit to different sectors of the American
work force.

Exhibit 3.10 shows the high degree and broad nature of the
appeal of downpayment loan programs to the workers and their
spouses interviewed. These loan programs have an appeal to a
clear majority of American working families across all regions,
in both urban and rural locations, and appeal about equally to
male and female workers. Not surprisingly, they are especially
appealing to upper-income workers and to those in higher status
job classifications.

Employer-guaranteed mortgage loan programs appeal to about
two-fifths of respondents—a percentage that does not vary significantly by sex, job classification, line of business, region, union
membership, single-parent status, income, urban versus rural location, or county size (see Exhibit 3.11).

Exhibit 3.12 presents data on the trades that workers would
be willing to make in order to receive a guaranteed mortgage loan
from their employer. As reported above, a majority of workers
would be interested in giving up one year's wage increase to receive

Exhibit 3.10   The Appeal of Employer-Sponsored Downpayment Loan Programs to Different Types of Young and Middle-Aged American Workers and Their Families

The Percentage of Workers Interested In:

	TOTAL	MALE*	FEMALE*	AGE 18–25	AGE 26–34	AGE 35+	MARRIED*	SINGLE*	SINGLE PARENT*
5-year interest-free loan, converting thereafter to market rate	60	59	60	57	63	57	59	60	61
5-year forgivable loan (20% forgiven for each year of employment tenure)	67	66	69	61	70	72	71*	64*	67

	Annual Household Income*					County Size* (1 = Largest, 4 = Smallest)			
	$15,000	$15–25K	$25,000+	URBAN	RURAL	1	2	3	4
5-year interest-free loan, converting thereafter to market rate	54	54	65	58	60	60	57	60	60
5-year forgivable loan (20% forgiven for each year of employment tenure)	58	66	73	67	68	65	70	68	65

Exhibit 3.10 *Continued*

	Region				Industry Employed In			
	NORTH-EAST	MID-WEST	SOUTH	FAR WEST	UNION MEMBER	MFG/ INDUSTRIAL	RETAIL/ WHOLESALE	FINANCIAL
5-year interest-free loan, converting thereafter to market rate	58	56	60	61	59	60	55	72
5-year forgivable loan (20% forgiven for each year of employment tenure)	67	67	69	66	65	67	67	72

Occupational Classification of Worker*

	GOVERNMENT PROFESSIONAL	PRIVATE SECTOR PROFESSIONAL	CLERICAL/SALES	SKILLED	UNSKILLED
5-year interest-free loan, converting thereafter to market rate	66	67	63	54	54
5-year forgivable loan (20% forgiven for each year of employment tenure)	72	76	69	65	64

*Note: Starred categories include percentage differences that achieve statistical significance at .05 level or greater.

Exhibit 3.11 The Appeal of Employer Guaranteed Mortgage Loans to Different Types of Employees Among Young and Middle-Aged American Workers and Their Families (Percentage)

	TOTAL	MALE*	FEMALE*	AGE 18–25	AGE 26–34	AGE 35+	MARRIED*	SINGLE*	SINGLE PARENT*
Definitely or contingently interested in employer-guaranteed loan	41	43	39	37	42	43	41	39	44

	Annual Household Income*					County Size* (1 = Largest, 4 = Smallest)			
	$15,000	$15–25K	$25,000+	URBAN	RURAL	1	2	3	4
Interested in employer-guaranteed loan	36	37	44	42	39	45	40	39	37

Exhibit 3.11 *Continued*

Region

	NORTH-EAST	MID-WEST	SOUTH	FAR WEST	UNION MEMBER	MFG/INDUSTRIAL	RETAIL/WHOLESALE	FINANCIAL
Interested in employer-guaranteed loan	42	40	39	40	44	40	42	45

Industry Employed In

Occupational Classification of Worker

	GOVERNMENT PROFESSIONAL	PRIVATE SECTOR PROFESSIONAL	CLERICAL/SALES	SKILLED	UNSKILLED
Interested in employer-guaranteed loan	41	42	46	36	36

*Note: Starred categories contain percentage differences that achieve statistical significance at .05 level or greater.

Exhibit 3.12   Wage and Benefit Trades That Young and Middle-Aged Workers and Their Families Would Be Willing To Make

Percentage Interested in Employer-Guaranteed Loans:

	TOTAL	MALE	FEMALE	AGE 18–25*	AGE 26–34*	AGE 35 + *	MARRIED*	SINGLE*	SINGLE PARENT*
Willing to trade one year's wage increase	63	65	61	45	67	73	68	59	66
Willing to trade part of health coverage	29	26	32	23	29	36	29	28	28

	Annual Household Income*			County Size* (1 = Largest, 4 = Smallest)					
	$15,000	$15–25K	$25,000 +	URBAN	RURAL	1	2	3	4
Willing to trade one year's wage increase	44	42	43	46	39	46	45	42	26
Willing to trade part of health coverage	26	26	38	29	29	24	33	30	27

Exhibit 3.12 *Continued*

Region* / Industry Employed In*

	NORTH-EAST	MID-WEST	SOUTH	FAR WEST	UNION MEMBER*	MFG/INDUSTRIAL	RETAIL/WHOLESALE	FINANCIAL
Willing to trade one year's wage increase	62	61	59	60	72	60	57	75
Willing to trade part of health coverage	19	28	31	33	28	29	19	55

Occupational Classification of Worker

	GOVERNMENT PROFESSIONAL	PRIVATE SECTOR PROFESSIONAL	CLERICAL/SALES	SKILLED	UNSKILLED
Willing to trade one year's wage increase	66	64	59	56	42
Willing to trade part of health coverage	29	30	26	23	44

*Note: Starred categories contain percentage differences that achieve statistical significance at .05 level or greater.

such a loan. Exhibit 3.12 shows that older, married, higher-status, and unionized workers would make this trade significantly more often than other employees.

Exhibit 3.12 also depicts those workers who would trade some portion of their health care benefits to participate in an employer-guaranteed mortgage loan program. An unusual combination of upper-income workers, employees of financial institutions, and workers in low-status jobs are significantly more interested in this trade; Northeastern employees are significantly less often interested; but, overall, about 28 percent of those interested in a guaranteed mortgage loan would trade some health care coverage for this housing benefit (whatever their gender, age, and/or urban or rural location).

Employer-arranged group mortgage discounts appeal to about half of the respondents—irrespective of their gender, marital status, urban versus rural location, or line of business. For most types of discounts, region and job classifications also make no difference upon the percentage of workers interested (see Exhibit 3.13). Exhibit 3.13 also identifies those types of employees who report themselves as willing to participate in linked payroll deduction loan servicing in order to participate in an employer-arranged group mortgage discount plan. Two-thirds of those interested in such a discount would agree to a payroll deduction—a percentage not significantly affected by an employee's line of business, gender, income, urban versus rural location, or union status. Older and married workers tend to be significantly more accepting of linked payroll deduction programs whereas unskilled workers and Midwesterners tend to be significantly less interested.

Exhibit 3.14 reveals the types of workers interested in employer-facilitated "build your own home" programs. The data indicate that "build your own" programs are of greatest interest to skilled workers, in smaller counties of the South and Far West, and to lower-income workers.

It was concluded from this data that millions of American workers want and need employer-sponsored housing benefits to achieve home ownership, and that they would make business-advantageous tradeoffs to receive them. Also, different forms of housing assistance are of differing degrees of interest to different types of workers. These conclusions suggest, further, that employers can customize and combine different housing benefit programs to meet their unique mix of worker types and business objectives.

Exhibit 3.13   The Appeal of Group Mortgage Discount Programs and Tradeoffs Concerning Such Programs to Different Types of Young and Middle-Aged Workers and Their Families

Percentage Interested:

	TOTAL	MALE	FEMALE	AGE 18–25*	AGE 26–34*	AGE 35+*	MARRIED*	SINGLE*	SINGLE PARENT*
Interested in group mortgage closing point programs	48	47	49	41	54	47	48	48	59
Interested in group mortgage interest rate programs	56	58	61	50	59	55	55	47	62
Interested in B, willing to have mortgage payments deducted from payroll	66	65	67	63	67	71	67	66	72

	Annual Household Income*					County Size* (1 = Largest, 4 = Smallest)			
	$15,000	$15–25K	$25,000+	URBAN	RURAL	1	2	3	4
Interested in group mortgage closing point programs	44	43	43	50	46	55	46	50	33
Interested in group mortgage interest rate programs	56	59	53	56	55	55	58	58	47
Interested in B, willing to have mortgage payments deducted from payroll	63	64	68	67	67	67	67	69	62

Exhibit 3.13 *Continued*

	Region*				Industry Employed In*			
	NORTH-EAST	MID-WEST	SOUTH	FAR WEST	UNION MEMBER*	MFG/INDUSTRIAL	RETAIL/WHOLESALE	FINANCIAL
Interested in group mortgage closing point programs	55	44	46	50	38	52	46	46
Interested in group mortgage interest rate programs	53	53	58	58	54	55	51	67
Interested in B, willing to have mortgage payments deducted from payroll	63	60	66	72	69	71	62	63

Occupational Classification of Worker*

	GOVERNMENT PROFESSIONAL	PRIVATE SECTOR PROFESSIONAL	CLERICAL/SALES	SKILLED	UNSKILLED
Interested in group mortgage closing point programs	45	51	51	41	48
Interested in group mortgage interest rate programs	53	56	56	51	55
Interested in B, willing to have mortgage payments deducted from payroll	67	67	69	69	55

*Note: Starred categories contain percentage differences that achieve statistical significance at .05 level or greater.

Exhibit 3.14   The Appeal of Employer-Sponsored "Build Your Own Home" Programs to Different Types of Employees Among Young and Middle-Aged American Workers and Their Families

Percentage Interested in Program:

	TOTAL	MALE	FEMALE	AGE 18–25*	AGE 26–34*	AGE 35+*	MARRIED*	SINGLE*	SINGLE PARENT
Definitely want to	28	28	28	26	33	23	30	26	38
Might want to	34*	35*	33*	36*	32*	37*	34*	34*	26

	Annual Household Income*			County Size* (1 = Largest, 4 = Smallest)					
	$15,000	$15–25K	$25,000 +	URBAN*	RURAL*	1	2	3	4
Definitely want to	28	36	25	29	28	29	28	28	30
Might want to	38*	31*	33*	32*	36*	27*	37*	37*	34*

Exhibit 3.14 *Continued*

	Region*				Industry Employed In*			
	NORTH-EAST	MID-WEST	SOUTH	FAR WEST	UNION MEMBER*	MFG/ INDUSTRIAL	RETAIL/ WHOLESALE	FINANCIAL
Definitely want to	28	23	30	32	28	29	31	32
Might want to	27*	35*	35*	36*	32*	33*	41*	22*

Occupational Classification of Worker*

	GOVERNMENT PROFESSIONAL	PRIVATE SECTOR PROFESSIONAL	CLERICAL/SALES	SKILLED	UNSKILLED
Definitely want to	25	30	26	33	31
Might want to	34*	28*	36*	36*	27*

*Note: Starred categories contain percentage differences that achieve statistical significance at the .05 level or greater.

Worker Perspectives on Employer-Sponsored Rental Housing Benefits

Exhibit 3.15 indicates that:

1. about one-half of respondents would be interested in achieving modest savings on their monthly rent payments by living in an employer-assisted multi-family apartment complex;
2. significant majorities of those interested in such an arrangement would still be interested if all of the occupants were co-workers and if they would be required to move within six months of terminating employment;
3. living in a company-sponsored apartment complex would be of significantly greater interest in rural America, in the South generally, and among middle-income workers than among other types of workers.

Exhibit 3.15   The Appeal of Specific Rental Benefits to Young and Middle-Aged American Workers and Their Families

Percentage of Respondents Interested in:

Saving $50 per month by living in company-owned multi-family housing	48
If housing is near work	41
If all neighbors are co-workers (as a percentage of those previously interested)	61
Even if employee would have to move out within six months after employment termination (as a percentage of those previously interested)	63

A Concluding Consideration

Beyond their own interests and needs, workers obviously have important views on the appropriateness and desirability of employers involving themselves in the housing of their workers generally. Exhibit 3.16 shows that a clear majority of young and middle-aged American workers favor employer-assisted housing, but that they make useful distinctions among the types of involvements they favor. In general, workers prefer arms-length financial arrangements that do not create privacy and social control problems for the employee. Interestingly, programs having these characteristics also pose fewer cost and management burdens for the employer.

Exhibit 3.16   Attitudes Toward Employer-Assisted Housing, Generally, Among Young and Middle-Aged American Workers

Percentage of Respondents Believing:

Employers should help with financing . . . but they should not be directly involved in building or renovating housing for employees	56
Large employers or groups of smaller employers should be involved in building or renovating housing for their employees	15
Employers should never get involved in helping employees with their housing	24
Employer-assisted housing raises concerns about privacy and control of workers' lives	40

The data presented in Exhibit 3.16 suggest that workers want precisely the kind of housing benefits that their employers should want to provide. But what do their employers think? To answer that question, a second national survey was conducted, this time of top-level American business managers. The findings of that survey are presented in Chapter 4.

Notes

1. An earlier version of this chapter was published in the January/February 1990 issue of *Shelterforce* magazine. (*See* D.C. Schwartz, "Worker Attitudes Toward Employer-Assisted Housing," 16–17.) The authors gratefully acknowledge the assistance of *Shelterforce's* editorial staff and the permission of the National Housing Institute (*Shelterforce's* publisher) for permission to reprint portions of that article.
2. *See* D.C. Schwartz, D. Hoffman, and R. Ferlauto, *A New Housing Policy for America: Recapturing the American Dream* (Philadelphia: Temple University Press, 1988) 6–17 and *passim*.
3. The authors believe that the percentage of workers interested in employer-guaranteed loans (while substantial at 41 percent) may have been inhibited in the survey by the relative unfamiliarity of respondents with the nature and power of third-party mortgage guarantees.

Chapter 4

Employer Interest in Providing Housing Benefits

In Chapter 3, evidence was presented indicating that millions of America's workers want and need employer-assisted housing benefits; that these workers would be willing to make significant tradeoffs on wages, working conditions, and other benefits to receive employer-assisted housing; and that, therefore, businesses offering housing benefits might thereby achieve important savings regarding the recruitment and retention costs and productivity of their labor force. In this chapter, data on the attitudes and the interests of employers in providing housing benefits will be reviewed. More specifically, summarized here are the results of a national survey wherein 461 top-level business executives—broadly representative of the nation's human resource, personnel benefits, and chief executive officer leadership—were interviewed by telephone as to their interests in, and attitudes about, housing benefits for their nonmanagement workers. This survey, conducted between December 1989 and March 1990, yields six major findings, listed here, and documented and discussed below:

1. Modern concepts of employer-assisted housing are very new and unfamiliar to most business executives: 90 percent of respondents reported that their firms had never considered such a benefit, and 93 percent reported that their firms were not offering any housing-related benefits to non-relocating workers.
2. Despite the new and unfamiliar nature of these benefits, 21 percent of the managers and executives interviewed were already convinced (a) that their firms should consider

offering housing benefits to nonmanagement workers (15 percent) or (b) that they should work with their firm's credit union to provide a housing benefit for their employees (6 percent). Extrapolating from studies on the diffusion of innovation, this finding indicates that an estimated 35 percent to 50 percent of U.S. employers will consider or adopt housing benefits in the forseeable future.[1] Recent studies by the International Foundation of Employee Benefit Plans, the Virginia Housing Research Center, the New Jersey Business and Industry Association, and others are in conformity with this estimate of employer interest in housing benefits in the 1990s.

3. Executives who want to consider or work toward housing benefits are located in firms that are broadly representative of the American business system (e.g., in terms of geographical location, perceived business problems, and percent unionized).

4. Executives who want to consider or work toward housing benefits tend to be significantly more concerned about recruitment and retention issues and to be more cost-conscious about these functions than are managers not yet interested in such benefits. Executives favoring employer-assisted housing tend to be located in firms that offer more benefits and that spend more on recruitment and training of workers.

5. Executives favorably disposed toward offering housing benefits are overwhelmingly motivated by their perception that such benefits will aid in the recruitment and retention of their work force, and tend to perceive housing benefits as an important factor in improving productivity, community relations, labor relations, and in upgrading the communities surrounding their corporate facilities.

6. All of the different housing benefits described in Chapter 2 have some appeal to some of the executives surveyed. Deferred downpayment loans and mortgage guarantee programs are attractive to approximately one-third of those managers who are interested in considering direct housing benefits. Deferred downpayment loans would appeal to about 40 percent of these executives, provided the loan program can be funded by redirecting anticipated growth in wage and benefit budget. Child care programs and forgivable loans to employees to help employees build their

own homes proved less appealing to executives wanting to consider direct housing benefits (attracting about 19 percent and 25 percent, respectively).

These findings suggest that employer-assisted housing can be an important factor in resolving America's housing problems in the 1990s. First, it is widely agreed that the nation will need new efforts to enhance the affordability of home ownership for about 3.3 million young families (first-time homebuyers) who would otherwise be priced out of the market in this decade. If only one-fifth of all firms actually adopted an effective housing benefit program (and 21 percent of executives surveyed are already expressing interest), all of this need would be met. Second, both the data and contextual information strongly suggest that management's interest in employer-assisted housing will grow in the 1990s—as the concept becomes more familiar and as predicted labor shortages and demographic changes in the work force prompt increased concern for, and sophistication about, worker recruitment and retention. Executives who want to consider offering housing benefits to nonmanagement workers are operating in the same regional economies as those not yet interested in such benefits; they are concerned about many of the same problems and have business pressures and constraints similar to their counterparts; but they tend to be more concerned and more sophisticated about worker recruitment and retention and more willing to do something about it. It is believed that America's business managers in the 1990s are likely to become more concerned, and more sophisticated, about recruitment and retention issues (and therefore about the advantages of employer-assisted housing). In addition, it is believed that new and standardized benefit packages facilitating employer-assisted housing will be brought to market shortly—that will greatly facilitate employer interest in considering housing benefits for nonmanagement workers.

Survey of Employers

As indicated above, the American Affordable Housing Institute sponsored a national telephone survey of top-level human resource professionals and CEOs. Using a sampling methodology designed to yield results broadly projectable to (i.e., representative of) the total population of such executives (see Appendix 2 for methodology), RL Associates of Princeton, New Jersey, interviewed 461 business leaders across the nation in 1989 and 1990. Here, the major findings of the survey are summarized and discussed.

Executives' Knowledge and Interest

Exhibit 4.1 indicates that the executives interviewed had neither thought about housing benefit nor had direct experience in administering housing benefits. Ninety-three percent of the firms represented in the total sample offer no housing benefits to nonmanagement employees and 90 percent of the firms have never considered doing so. Nonetheless, the data arrayed in Exhibit 4.1 show that 21 percent of the executives interviewed believe that their firms should consider offering one or more direct housing benefits to nonmanagement workers or that they should be working with their firms' credit unions to provide such a benefit.

Exhibit 4.1   Executives' Knowledge and Interest in Employer-Assisted Housing

	YES	NO
Firm Now Offers Housing Benefits	32 (7%)	429 (93%)
Firm Has Considered Housing Benefits	16 (3%)	415 (90%)
Executive Favors Consideration of a Direct Housing	96 (21%)	365 (79%)

Source of data: All exhibits in this chapter are taken from the 1990 American Affordable Housing Institute Survey.
Note: Benefit or a Benefit via Credit Union.

It is expected that strong growth will occur in the number and percentage of American executives who will want to consider housing benefits as familiarity with the issue grows. This expectation derives from both studies on the diffusion of innovations and from other studies of employer-assisted housing. Most research on organizations and individuals who implement an innovative product or idea finds that innovators and early adopters are only 15 percent to 20 percent of the total group that ultimately adopts the innovation; and that exposure to, and consideration of, an innovation preceeds selection and implementation. Exhibit 4.1 shows that 7 percent of firms represented in the sample have already adopted a housing benefit and that an additional 3 percent have considered such a benefit. Clearly many more American firms are likely to consider or adopt housing benefits in the future. The expectation of significant growth in employer-sponsored housing benefits also derive from other recent studies: national research by the International Foundation of Employee Benefit Plans recently found that 37 percent of interviewed executives expected to offer such housing benefits as information and referral by the year 2000.[3]

Research on northern Virginia employers found that 25 percent to 40 percent were likely to adopt employer-assisted housing programs in the foreseeable future; business surveys in California, Connecticut, Maryland, and New Jersey are finding 30 percent to 75 percent of surveyed firms are experiencing labor force recruitment and retention problems due to unaffordable housing. Again, it is estimated that 35 percent to 50 percent of American business firms are likely to consider or adopt housing benefits in the foreseeable future.[4]

Similarities in Executives' Perceptions

Exhibits 4.2, 4.3, and 4.4 present data on the interviewed executives' perceptions of current business problems, the types of employees they need, and the percentage of their firms that are unionized. These tables indicate that managers interested in having their firms consider or work toward housing benefits do not differ in their perceptions and priorities about current business problems, types of labor force needs, or degree of union involvement from those executives who do not presently favor exploration of housing benefits by their firms. These findings suggest that the growth of employer-assisted housing benefits will not be inhibited by having early business proponents perceived as ideologically different from most executives, or as more (or less) attentive to unions, or as motivated by unique labor force requirements.

It should be noted that there is broad geographic dispersion and considerable uniformity by region in the business locations of executives favorable to considering or working toward housing benefits.

**Exhibit 4.2   Executive Perceptions of the Importance, to Their Firms, of
Current Problems Facing American Employers
(Percentage)
Problem Importance (rated on 1–10 scale, 10 = most
important)**

PROBLEM	EXECUTIVES FAVORING HOUSING BENEFITS (21%)	EXECUTIVES NOT FAVORING HOUSING BENEFITS (79%)
	(PERCENT RATING 9 OR 10 IN PARENTHESIS)	
Cost of Health Insurance	9.1 (76%)	9.0 (67%)
Getting Wage and Benefit Concessions	4.8 (57%)	4.5 (11%)
Difficulty in Finding Qualified Employees	6.4 (19%)	5.9 (13%)
Providing Flexible Benefit Packages	6.3 (19%)	6.0 (20%)

Note: None of the percentage differences in Exhibit 4.2 achieve statistical significance
at .05 or greater.

**Exhibit 4.3   Executive Perceptions of the Types of Employees Most
Difficult for Their Firms to Recruit and/or Retain
(Percentage)**

TYPE	EXECUTIVES FAVORING HOUSING BENEFITS (21%)	EXECUTIVES NOT FAVORING HOUSING BENEFITS (79%)
All	5	5
None	11	15
Unskilled	20	16
Clerical	7	10
Sales	3	3
Skilled Crafts	26	33
Engineers/Programmers	13	15
Professional	6	4

Note: None of the percentage differences in Exhibit 4.3 achieve statistical significance
at .05 or greater.

Exhibit 4.4   Executive Interest in Employer-Assisted Housing (By percentage of firms unionized, geographic location of firms, and company size)

	EXECUTIVES FAVORING HOUSING BENEFITS (21%)	EXECUTIVES NOT FAVORING HOUSING BENEFITS (79%)
Unionized	36	30
Larger Firms in Urbanized Counties	25	17
Smaller Firms in Urbanized Counties	25	26
Firms in Rural Non-South	29	24
Firms in Rural South	18	26

Note: None of the percentage differences in Exhibit 4.4 achieve statistical significance at .05 level or greater.

Differences Among Executives

The most significant and consistent differences between executives who want to consider or to work toward housing benefits and those who do not center on attitudes toward, and business experience with, work force recruitment and retention. Executives favorably disposed toward offering housing benefits report more severe recruitment and retention problems (Exhibit 4.5); spend more money on recruitment and retention functions (Exhibit 4.6); offer a larger array of personnel benefits (Exhibit 4.7); perceive the costs of retention and of overall benefit packages as more important to their firms (Exhibit 4.8); and have a much greater conviction that housing benefits could help solve their recruitment and retention difficulties (Exhibit 4.9).

In addition to their greater concern with recruitment and retention, these executives differ from their counterparts on other attitudinal, business, and socioeconomic dimensions. Specifically, managers who want to consider housing benefits are more convinced that housing benefits will enhance a number of business functions other than recruitment and retention (Exhibit 4.10); are employed in industries that have greater historical experience with housing concerns or industries that require employees who may have special housing needs (Exhibit 4.11); are more convinced that their unionized employees would react favorably to housing benefits; and are more convinced that lengthy commutes constitute a productivity problem for their firms (Exhibit 4.12).

Recruitment and Retention Concerns

The data arrayed in Exhibit 4.5 indicate that executives interested in considering or working toward housing benefits report their firms to have experienced significantly greater and more frequent recruitment and retention problems. It is not surprising that a much higher percentage of managers favoring housing benefits perceive their firms to have had recruitment and retention problems due to the unavailability of affordable housing near their corporate facilities. But two conclusions warranted by the data arrayed in Exhibit 4.5 *are* surprising: (1) executives favoring consideration of housing benefits also report greater recruitment and retention problems attributable to *non-*

Exhibit 4.5   Labor Recruitment/Retention Problems of Firms Led by Interviewed Executives (Percentage)

REASON FOR RECRUITMENT/ RETENTION PROBLEM	EXECUTIVES FAVORING HOUSING BENEFITS REPORT DIFFICULTY (21%)	EXECUTIVES NOT FAVORING HOUSING BENEFITS REPORT DIFFICULTY (79%)
Transportation		
No Difficulty	65	80
Some Difficulty	31	18
Great Difficulty	4	2
Education		
No Difficulty	36	65
Some Difficulty	58	33
Great Difficulty	5	2
Unavailability of Nearby Affordable Housing		
No Difficulty	65	92
Some Difficulty	21	4
Great Difficulty	15	2
Absence of Appropriate Skill Levels		
No Difficulty	20	43
Some Difficulty	61	49
Great Difficulty	19	8

Note: All percentage differences achieve statistical significance at .05 or greater.

Exhibit 4.6 Average Recruitment and Training Expenditures for Firms Led by Interviewed Executives (Percentage)

AVERAGE EXPENDITURE	EXECUTIVES FAVORING HOUSING BENEFITS (21%)	EXECUTIVES NOT FAVORING HOUSING BENEFITS (79%)
Recruitment of Most-Needed Workers		
Under $1,000 per employee	39	64
$1,000 or more per employee	56	30
Don't know, other	6	6
Initial Training of Most-Needed Workers		
Under $1,000 per employee	26	48
$1,000 or more per employee	67	43
Don't know, other	6	9
Retaining Most-Needed Workers		
Under $1,000 per employee	36	54
$1,000 or more per employee	41	22
Don't know, other	23	23
Upgrading/Training Entry-Level Workers		
Under $1,000 per employee	32	49
$1,000 or more per employee	66	40
Don't know, other	2	11

Note: All percentage differences in Exhibit 4.6 achieve statistical significance at .05 or greater. Percentages are fractionally below or above 100 percent due to rounding.

Exhibit 4.7 Available Benefits for Nonmanagement Employees in Firms Led by Interviewed Executives (Percentage)

BENEFIT	EXECUTIVES FAVORING HOUSING BENEFITS (21%)	EXECUTIVES NOT FAVORING HOUSING BENEFITS (79%)
Comprehensive Health Plan	99	97
Retirement Pension Plan	89	80
Childcare	10	8
College Reimbursement*	76*	53*
Disability Coverage	83	82
Eye Care and/or Dental	78*	65*
Housing Benefit	8	4
Flexible Benefits	16	11
Credit Union*	78*	56*

*Note: Starred percentage differences achieve statistical significance at .05 or greater.

Exhibit 4.8   Executive Perception of the Importance, to Their Firms, of Certain Benefit Costs
Problem Importance (Rated 1–10 scale, 10 = most important)

PROBLEM	EXECUTIVES FAVORING HOUSING BENEFITS (21%)	EXECUTIVES NOT FAVORING HOUSING BENEFITS (79%)
	(average rating and percent rating 9 or 10 in parentheses)	
Retention Costs of Training and Keeping Employees*	15* (6.3)	6* (5.2)
Total Costs of Benefits Package	56* (8.5)	42* (7.9)

---

*Note: Starred percentage differences achieve statistical significance at the .10 level or greater.

Exhibit 4.9   Importance of Recruitment and Retention Concerns Motivating Favorable Consideration of Housing Benefits (In Firms Offering or Likely to Offer Housing Benefits)

MOTIVATION	EXECUTIVES FAVORING HOUSING BENEFITS (21%)	EXECUTIVES NOT FAVORING HOUSING BENEFITS (79%)
To Recruit Qualified Workers		
Very Important Motivation	83	45
Somewhat Important	8	27
Not Important		27
Don't know, Other	8	
To Retain Qualified Workers		
Very Important Motivation	92	48
Somewhat Important		7
Not Important		4
Don't know, Other	8	

Note: All percentage differences in Exhibit 4.9 achieve statistical significance at .05 or greater. Percentages fractionally above or below 100 percent due to rounding.

Exhibit 4.10 Importance of Business Functions, Other Than Recruitment and Retention, As Motivating Favorable Consideration of Housing Benefits (Among Firms Offering or Likely to Offer Housing Benefits)

MOTIVATION	EXECUTIVES FAVORING HOUSING BENEFITS (21%)	EXECUTIVES NOT FAVORING HOUSING BENEFITS (79%)
Improve Community Relations		
Important	86	37
Not Important	14	63
Upgrade Neighborhoods Near Corporate Facility		
Important	64	42
Not Important	36	58
Generally Improve Labor Relations		
Important	90	69
Not Important	9	32
To Reduce Employee Drive Time		
Important	82	37
Not Important	14	61
Don't Know, Other	5	3

*Note: All percentage differences in Exhibit 4.10 achieve statistical significance at .05 or greater. Some data sets do not equal 100 percent due to rounding.

housing factors than do other executives; and (2) about two-thirds of the executives interested in employer-assisted housing report their organizations to have experienced no housing-related labor shortages. Clearly, the consideration of housing benefits is only part of the strategy these executives are employing, initiating, or planning to cope with real and pressing labor force problems.

One reason that certain executives might want to consider or actually implement housing benefits as part of their recruitment and retention strategy is that their firms are already spending more than other firms on recruitment and training. A housing benefit that helps to diminish labor turnover might save significant dollars and might even pay for itself. The data summarized in Exhibit 4.6 suggest that this reasoning makes sense for those interviewed executives who favor housing benefits—their firms are spending more on recruitment and training than are the other firms.

**Exhibit 4.11   Principal Line of Business and Special Recruitment
Needs of Firms Led by Interviewed Executives**

LINE OF BUSINESS	EXECUTIVES FAVORING HOUSING BENEFITS (21%)	EXECUTIVES NOT FAVORING HOUSING BENEFITS (79%)
Health Care*	29*	7*
Utilities*	13*	5*
Manufacturing	28	34
Agriculture	4	6
Retail	3	8
Construction	5	4
Other	18	31
Difficulty in Recruiting and/or Retaining Health Professionals*	23*	6*

*Note: Starred percentage differences achieve statistical significance at .05 or greater.

In the study, the firms of executives who favor movement toward a housing benefit program for nonmanagement workers are not only spending more on recruitment and training, they are offering a significantly broader (and probably more expensive) array of benefits than are the companies whose leaders are less favorable to employer-assisted housing. The data presented in Exhibit 4.7 show that a higher percentage of firms led by managers favorable to housing benefits had health care, pension, child care, college tuition reimbursement, eye care and dental

**Exhibit 4.12   Executive Perceptions of Housing Benefits as Positively
Valued by Union Members**

	EXECUTIVES FAVORING HOUSING BENEFITS (21%)	EXECUTIVES NOT FAVORING HOUSING BENEFITS (79%)
Perceive Housing Benefits Might Be Favorably Considered by Union Members*	10*	1*
Perceive Lengthy Commutes to be a Productivity Issue for Their Firm*	25*	17*

*Note: Starred percentage differences achieve statistical significance at .10 level or greater.

coverage, disability, flexible benefits, and credit unions. It is believed that the executives in the study who favor consideration of housing benefits tend to be located in corporate cultures that are sophisticated about (and obviously accepting of) new benefits.

But if executives favoring housing benefits are located in corporate cultures hospitable to the consideration of new benefits, this does *not* mean that they are in firms less interested in controlling benefit costs. On the contrary, the data presented in Exhibit 4.8 strongly suggest that executives interested in considering housing benefits are more concerned about costs than are other executives.

Perhaps the clearest, most dramatic evidence that recruitment and retention concerns are basic to the thinking of those executives who favor movement toward housing benefit programs in their firms is presented in Exhibit 4.9. It should be noted that the overwhelming majority of managers favorable to consideration of a housing benefit rated recruitment and retention as a very important motivation factor in any plans which their organization might have toward providing employer-assisted housing.

Other Factors

Beyond recruitment and retention concerns, managers favorable toward housing benefits are more convinced than other executives that adoption of such benefits will help their firms perform other business functions. Exhibit 4.10, for example, summarizes data showing that managers supporting consideration of employer-assisted housing are also motivated by concerns to improve community relations, to upgrade neighborhoods proximate to corporate facilities, to improve labor relations, and to reduce employee drive times (i.e., reduce employee tardiness).

The data arrayed in Exhibit 4.11 indicate that executives of hospitals and utilities are disproportionately likely to favor consideration of housing benefits for nonmanagement workers (and show, too, that firms needing to recruit and retain health care professionals tend to be led by executives favorably disposed toward employer-assisted housing). These data make sense in light of the historic interest of hospitals and utilities in housing—hospitals, because they have had long experience in providing some housing, particularly for nurses, interns, and residents for whom the prob-

lem of housing affordability proximate to work has become especially acute in recent years; and utilities, because their business is
so dependent on new housing starts.

Exhibit 4.12 summarizes data showing (1) that a small but
significant percentage of executives favoring housing benefits perceive that such benefits would be positively valued by labor union
members and (2) that a much larger percentage of executives who
want to consider or work toward housing benefits consider lengthy
commutes to be a productivity issue affecting their organizations.

The data presented thus far tend to show that there are good
business reasons why one in five interviewed executives want to
consider or work toward a housing benefit for their nonmanagement
workers—labor force recruitment and retention problems, productivity problems, improved labor relations, and enhanced community relations.

Another area that was explored was whether certain personal
characteristics of the interviewed executives made a significant
difference to their interest in employer-assisted housing. More
specifically, it was questioned if the gender and job title (i.e.,
responsibilities) of the respondents would impact on their willingness to consider or work toward housing benefits. Would men or
women executives, for example, be more sensitive to their employees' housing needs? Would personnel directors or human resource officers be more favorable to housing benefits than chief
executive officers or other corporate leaders? Exhibit 4.13 presents
data indicating that male executives tended to be more interested

Exhibit 4.13   Gender and Job Title of Executives Favorable and Not Favorable Toward Housing Benefits

	EXECUTIVES FAVORING HOUSING BENEFITS (21%)	EXECUTIVES NOT FAVORING HOUSING BENEFITS (79%)
Gender*		
Male	63*	54*
Female	38*	45*
Job Title		
Personnel Director, Human Resource Office	77	74
CEO, Comptroller, Other	22	25

*Note: Starred percentage differences achieve statistical significance at .10 level or greater.

in housing benefits than were female executives but that job title (as a surrogate measure for type of corporate responsibility) was not systematically related to an executive's orientation to housing benefits.

Types of Housing Benefits of Interest to Executives

Exhibit 4.14 indicates that each of the different housing benefits described in Chapter 2 have some appeal to some of the executives that were surveyed. Deferred downpayment loans and mortgage guarantees are attractive to about one-third of

Exhibit 4.14   Predisposition to Consider Various Types of Housing Benefits, Among Executives Who Want Their Firms to Consider or to Work Toward a Housing Benefit

TYPE OF HOUSING BENEFIT	PERCENTAGE THAT DEFINITELY OR PROBABLY CONSIDER AMONG EXECUTIVES WHO WANT FIRMS TO CONSIDER A DIRECT HOUSING BENEFIT (15%)	PERCENTAGE THAT DEFINITELY OR PROBABLY CONSIDER AMONG EXECUTIVES WHO WANT TO CONSIDER A HOUSING BENEFIT (21%)
$10,000 Forgivable Downpayment Loan	20	15
Deferred Payback Downpayment Loan	30	22
Deferred Payback Funded Out of Anticipated Growth in Extant Budgets	40	29
Mortgage Guarantee	32	23
Mortgage Insurance	27	20
Buy Below Market Rate Housing Bonds	26	19
Provide Flextime for Employees to Build Own Homes	61	44
Provide Child Care for Employees to Build Own Homes	26	19
Make $5,000 Grants to Employees to Build Own Homes	12	8
Make $5,000 Grants to Nonprofit for Housing	20	14

those managers who are interested in considering direct housing benefits, whereas flextime programs to help workers build their own homes appeals to about three-fifths. Not surprisingly, employer-assisted housing is more appealing to these executives if the benefits can be funded by redirecting anticipated growth in extant wage and benefit budgets. Child care programs and forgivable loans to employees to help employees build their own homes proved less appealing to executives who would consider direct housing benefits.

Company Size, Location, and Interest

Small versus Large Firms

The data reveal a modest but consistent tendency for executives in larger firms to be more interested in employer-assisted housing than are managers of smaller firms (larger firms are defined as those employing 1,000 or more workers). Exhibit 4.15, for example, indicates that executives in larger companies are more willing to consider direct housing benefits generally, and more willing to consider the purchase of housing bonds, and flextime and child care programs to help workers build their own

Exhibit 4.15   Executive's Interest in Considering Direct and Indirect Housing Benefits, by Size of Firm

PERCENTAGE WILLING TO CONSIDER	SMALL FIRMS	LARGER FIRMS
Any Direct Benefits*	14*	24*
Direct Benefit and/or to Work with Credit Union for Housing Benefit**	20**	28**
Purchase of Housing Bonds*	2*	12*
Flextime to Help Workers Build Homes*	7*	20*
Childcare to Help Workers Build Homes*	3*	11*
Downpayment Loans ($10,000)	3	2
Downpayment Loans ($5,000)	3	4
Deferred Payback Loans	5	4
Mortgage Guarantees	3	5
Mortgage Guarantees Benefit	3	9
$5,000 Grant for Workers to Build Homes	1	6
$5,000 Grant to Nonprofit Housing Corp.	3	4

Note: * Percentage difference achieving statistical significance at .05 level or greater.
** Those achieving significance at .10 level or greater.

Exhibit 4.16   Executive Interest in Targeted Versus Buy Anywhere Benefits, by Size of Firm

	SMALL FIRMS	LARGER FIRMS
Percentage Wanting to Restrict Benefits to Neighborhoods near Corporate Facilities*	43*	27*
Percentage Preferring "Buy Anywhere" Benefits*	35*	67*

*Note: All relationships in Exhibit 4.16 achieve statistical significance at .05 level or greater.

homes than are small firm managers. Exhibit 4.16 presents data suggesting that executives in smaller firms who favor consideration of housing benefits would want to target those benefits for use near corporate facilities, whereas managers in larger companies who want their firms to consider housing benefits lean more toward a "buy anywhere" program.

The motivations for wanting to consider direct housing benefits also vary by size of firm. The data indicate that executives in larger firms who favor such considerations are more motivated by recruitment, retention, and community development concerns whereas pro-housing managers in smaller firms are more motivated by the desire to enhance productivity via reduction of employee commute time. Exhibit 4.17 summarizes this data.

Underlying these motivational differences between executives in larger and those in smaller companies are some important

Exhibit 4.17   Executive Motivations for Wanting to Consider Housing Benefits, by Size of Firm

	SMALLER FIRMS	LARGER FIRMS
Percentage Wanting to Consider Housing Benefit, by Motivation		
Improve Community Relations	60	57
Upgrade Neighborhoods around Corporate Facilities*	45*	64*
Improve Labor Relations	80	86
Reduce Employee Drive Time	63	57
Recruit Qualified Workers*	76*	89*
Retain Qualified Workers*	76*	89*

*Note: Starred percentage differences achieve statistical significance at .05 level or greater.

differences in corporate experiences and practices. In this study, larger firms have more benefits, are more unionized, spend more on recruitment and retention, and have lost a significant number of workers due to housing unaffordability (see Exhibit 4.18). Interestingly, however, there are virtually no significant differences in perceptions of current business problems by size of firm (Exhibit 4.19).

Urban versus Rural Locations

It has been shown here that executives in larger businesses tend to be more interested in having their firms consider or work toward housing benefits than are their counterparts in smaller companies. Given the tendency in America today for larger firms to be headquartered in urban areas, it might have been expected that urban-located managers would be more interested in employer-assisted housing than rural-located executives. That is

Exhibit 4.18   Differences in Corporate Experiences by Size of Firm

PERCENTAGE OFFERING	SMALL FIRMS	LARGER FIRMS
Pension Plan*	77*	98*
Child Care Benefit	6	13
College Education Benefit*	53*	72*
Eye Care and/or Dental Benefit*	63*	86*
Disability	81	89
Flexible Benefits*	8*	26*
Cafeteria Benefit Plan	7	15
Comprehensive Health Benefit	97	99
Percentage Unionized*	28*	48*
Percentage Spending:		
under $1,000 to recruit most needed workers*	64*	39*
$1,000 or more to recruit most needed workers*	30*	49*
under $1,000 on training most needed workers*	45*	32*
$1,000 or more on training most needed workers	47	48
under $1,000 on retaining most needed workers*	54*	27*
$1,000 or more on retaining most needed workers	28	29
under $1,000 to upgrade the training of entry level workers	47	36
$1,000 or more to upgrade the training of entry level workers*	45*	56*
Percentage having lost significant numbers of workers due to unaffordable housing*	39*	50*

*Note: Starred percentage differences achieve statistical significance at .05 level or greater.

Exhibit 4.19 Perceived Importance of Current Business Problems to Executive's Employer, by Size of Firm

Note: Executives were asked to rate the degree of importance of each problem to their firm. Here, the percentage of executives ranking each problem as Very Important and, in parentheses, the Average Rating (10 = most important; 1 = least important) is reported.

PROBLEM	SMALL FIRMS	LARGER FIRMS
Cost of Health Insurance	69 (9.0)	64 (9.0)
Recruitment of Qualified Workers	16 (6.0)	13 (6.2)
Retention Costs	9 (5.5)	7 (5.7)
Costs of Overall Benefits Package	45 (8.0)	42 (8.2)
Providing Flexible Benefits	19 (6.0)	24 (6.0)
Getting Wage and Benefit Concessions	11 (4.6)	15 (4.6)

*Note: None of the percentage differences in Exhibit 4.19 achieve statistical significance at .05 level or greater.

not the case! Rural-located executives tend to be as interested in this issue as urban-located managers. Rural-located executives have different motivations to favor consideration of housing benefits, and they would prefer more targeted benefits, but the data indicate that very similar percentages of urban- and rural-located executives favor consideration of housing benefits.

Exhibit 4.20 shows no significant differences exist between the interests of urban- and rural-located executives on the 12 forms of employer-assisted housing. Exhibit 4.21, on the other hand, indicates that rural-located managers are more motivated to favor housing benefits for labor recruitment and retention concerns and general labor/community relations than are urban executives. Exhibit 4.22 summarizes data suggesting that rural-located managers tend to favor location-specific (i.e., targeted) benefits whereas urban executives disposed toward housing benefits favor a "buy anywhere" approach.

Some of the reasons that rural-located executives are about as equally interested in employer-assisted housing as urban managers can be seen in Exhibits 4.22, 4.23, and 4.24—where it is discovered that rural and urban corporate leaders tend to perceive the same business problems, to be experiencing about the same degree of difficulty in their recruitment efforts, and for the same reasons. A second set of reasons for urban/rural similarity in favorability toward housing benefits can be seen in Exhibits

Exhibit 4.20   Percentage of Executives Wanting Their Firms to Consider or Work Toward Housing Benefits, by Urban/Rural Location

PERCENTAGE OF:	RURAL	URBAN
Executives Wanting to Consider Any Direct Housing Benefit	13	19
Executives Wanting to Work with Credit Union to Provide Benefit	11	10
Executives Favoring Consideration of $10,000 Downpayment Loan	2	4
Executives Favoring Consideration of $5,000 Downpayment Loan	2	4
Executives Favoring Deferred Payback Loan	4	6
Executives Favoring Mortgage Guarantee	5	5
Executives Favoring Mortgage Insurance	3	9
Executives Favoring Buying Housing Bonds	1	7
Executives Favoring Flextime to Help Workers Build Their Own Homes	7	13
Executives Favoring Child Care to Help Workers Build Their Own Homes	3	4
Executives Favoring $5,000 Grant to Help Workers Build Their Own Homes	0	4
Executives Favoring $5,000 Grant to Nonprofits	4	4
Overall, Percent Executives Favoring Consideration of Workers Toward a Housing Benefit for Nonmanagement Workers	20	23

Note: None of the percentage differences in Exhibit 4.20 achieve statistical significance at .05 level or greater.

Exhibit 4.21   Motivation of Executives to Favor Consideration of Housing Benefits, by Urban/Rural Location

	RURAL	URBAN
To Improve Community Relations*	65*	55*
To Upgrade Community around Corporate Facilities	50	51
To Improve Labor Relations	76	69
To Reduce Employee Drive Time*	75*	52*
To Recruit Qualified Workers*	86*	75*
To Retain Qualified Workers*	85*	75*
Have Lost Significant Number of Workers Due to Unaffordable Housing*	50*	25*

*Note: Starred percentage differences achieve statistical significance at .05 level or greater. These data are limited to executives in firms offering or likely to offer housing benefits.

Exhibit 4.22 Executive Favorability toward Targeted or "Buy Anywhere" Housing Benefits, by Urban/Rural Location

PERCENTAGE OF EXECUTIVES FAVORING:	RURAL	URBAN
Housing Benefit Restricted to Neighborhoods Near Corporate Facilities*	50*	29*
"Buy Anywhere" Approach*	29*	57*

*Note: All percentage differences in Exhibit 4.22 achieve statistical significance at .05 level or greater.

Exhibit 4.23 Perceived Importance of Current Business Problems to Executive's Firm, by Urban/Rural Location

Note: Executives were asked to rate the importance to their firm of various current business problems. The percentage of executives rating each problem as Very Important and, in parentheses, the Average Rating (10 = most important; 1 = least important) is reported.

PROBLEM	RURAL	URBAN
Cost of Health Insurance	69 (8.9)	67 (9.0)
Difficulty in Recruiting Qualified Workers	17 (6.0)	14 (6.1)
Retention Costs	7 (5.4)	10 (5.6)
Providing Flexible Benefits	18 (6.1)	22 (5.9)
Getting Wage and Benefit Concessions	12 (4.7)	11 (4.6)

Note: None of the percentage differences in Exhibit 4.23 achieve statistical significance at .05 level or greater.

Exhibit 4.24 Recruitment/Retention Difficulties for Various Types of Workers, by Urban/Rural Location

	RURAL	URBAN
All Types	6	5
None	16	14
Unskilled	21	13
Clerical	4	13
Sales	2	4
Skilled Crafts*	37*	26*
Engineers, Programs	7*	22*
Professionals	3	3
Health Professionals	12	7
Average Percentage Indicating Difficulty in Recruitment/Retention (Deletes "None" Category)	11.5	11.6

*Note: Starred percentages achieve statistical significance at .05 level or greater.

4.25, 4.26, 4.27, and 4.28—where it is shown that urban executives are currently offering more benefits and spending more
money on recruitment and retention, but also tend to be more
concerned about the costs of their total benefits packages. The
data summarized in these tables, taken together, suggest broadly
similar potential for the growth in employer-assisted housing
across both urban and rural America.

Conclusion

Although modern concepts of employer-assisted housing are
very new and unfamiliar to American executives, one in five U.S.

**Exhibit 4.25   Reasons for Recruitment/Retention Difficulties, by Urban/
Rural Location**

PERCENTAGE OF EXECUTIVES PERCEIVING PROBLEM AS IMPORTANT:	RURAL	URBAN
Transportation	25	22
Education	45	41
Housing	10	14
Absence of Skill Levels	60	62

Note: None of the percentage differences in Exhibit 4.25 achieve statistical significance at .05 level or greater.

**Exhibit 4.26   Percentage of Firms Offering Various Benefits, by Urban/
Rural Location**

BENEFIT	RURAL	URBAN
Comprehensive Health Plan	98	98
Pension Plan*	74*	89*
Child Care	4	12
College Reimbursement*	49*	65*
Eye Care or Dental*	58*	78*
Disability	78	87
Flexible Benefits	10	14
Cafeteria Plan	9	8
Credit Union*	48*	71*

*Note: Starred percentage differences achieve statistical significance at .05 level or
greater.

Exhibit 4.27   Average Dollars Expended by Firms on Various Recruitment/Retention Functions, by Urban/Rural Location

PERCENTAGE SPENDING:	RURAL	URBAN
Less Than $1,000 to Recruit Most-Needed Workers*	66*	50*
More Than $1,000 to Recruit Most-Needed Workers*	26*	36*
Less Than $1,000 to Train Most-Needed Workers*	48*	37*
More Than $1,000 to Train Most-Needed Workers	44	52
Less Than $1,000 on Retaining Most-Needed Workers*	57*	40*
More Than $1,000 on Retaining Most-Needed Workers	24	31
Less Than $1,000 to Upgrade the Training of Entry-Level Workers	47	47
More Than $1,000 to Upgrade the Training of Entry-Level Workers	43	51

*Note: Starred percentage differences achieve statistical significance at .05 level or greater.

business managers interviewed reported themselves as wanting their firms to consider such a benefit or to work with their firms' credit unions to provide it. Overwhelmingly, the reasons for this level of interest—all across America—center on labor-related concerns, most notably on the recruitment and retention of the work force. It is especially important, therefore, to understand organized labor's role in employer-assisted housing: this is the focus of Chapter 5.

Exhibit 4.28   Perceived Importance of Total Benefit Costs to Executive's Firm, by Urban/Rural Location

	RURAL	URBAN
Percentage of Executives Rating Costs Very Important (in parentheses, Average Rating)	40* (7.8)	50* (8.2)

*Note: Percentage difference achieves statistical significance at .05 level or greater.

Notes

1. *See* E.M. Rogers, *Diffusion of Innovations,* as cited in T. Koebel, *The Potential of Employer-Assisted Housing in Northern Virginia* (Blacksburg: Virginia Center for Housing Research, 1990) 20 ff.
2. D.C. Schwartz, R. Ferlauto, and D. Hoffman, *A New Housing Policy for America* (Philadelphia: Temple University Press, 1988) 91 and *passim.*
3. "Nontraditional Benefits for the Workforce 2000: A Special Research Report" (Brookfield, Wisc.: International Foundation of Employee Benefit Plans, August 1990) 4.
4. T. Koebel, *The Potential of Employer-Assisted Housing in Northern Virginia, supra* note 1. *See also National Opinion Panels* (Brookfield, Wisc.: International Foundation of Employee Benefit Plans, 1990); D. Hoffman and D. Schwartz, *Employer-Assisted Housing: New Cost-Effective Management Benefit* (Englewood Cliffs, N.J.: Prentice-Hall, 1989) 185 ff.

Chapter 5

Labor and Housing Benefits

The affordable housing needs of American workers have been more directly and more comprehensively addressed by labor unions than by employers during the past 50 years. Recently, unions have dramatically expanded their activities in the housing field by investing their own funds, forging new partnerships with lenders, and creating their own nonprofit housing corporations. Now, an increasing number of labor unions are preparing to collectively bargain with America's major corporations for employer-assisted housing. What this means is that companies, chambers of commerce, and trade associations that are, or soon will be, considering the adoption of a housing benefit can and should look to the history and current programs of organized labor for models, partnerships, and sometimes, funding sources (as well, of course, as bargaining "opponents"). This chapter describes the history and the current activity of organized labor's role in providing affordable housing for workers.

Working men and women, and the labor unions that represent them, are increasingly concerned about housing availability and affordability. In part, this is a rekindling of a historic interest on the part of labor unions; housing has long been a central part of the relationship among workers, unions, and employers. The question of jobs was never far removed from concerns about where workers would live, the conditions of their housing tenure, and housing affordability. But there are also new reasons for labor's interest in housing—the increasingly unaffordable cost of housing in many regional economies is, today, generating demands that labor unions play a significant role in enhancing home ownership opportunities and affordable rentals for their members.

Housing costs are harder for workers to bear today than they were for workers in the past. In the years following World War II, millions of organized workers were able to buy the single-family suburban homes that characterized the "American dream," and came to expect that their children would have better housing than their own. Labor's power to influence government policies to promote home ownership was strong, and its negotiations for wage and benefit increases were successful. As a result, a substantial number of working families were propelled into home ownership. Further, owning a home marked and protected the rising status of the American worker.

In the current housing market, however, shelter is a persistent problem for many union members—younger workers find accumulating the downpayment necessary to purchase a home almost impossible; housing cost inflation has shut many people out of the towns they grew up in, and soaring rental costs have put many low-wage workers one paycheck away from homelessness. Even among people with relatively better paying union jobs, higher housing costs have precipitated a significant decline in real, spendable income, as wage gains made at the bargaining table continue to fall behind escalating housing costs.

Union members are acutely aware that the cost of housing—both home ownership and rental—is eroding their standard of living. Once, most working families (especially those with a union card) expected that one union wage job, together with savings and patience, would lead to home ownership after a reasonable number of years. But the social contract and economic conditions that drove those expectations—the essence of the "American dream" for many families—no longer exist. People who see owning a home as the definition of what it means to be middle-class find their status in America slowly slipping away.

The sons and daughters of working families, who had bought houses in the 1950s and 1960s, do not see that they have the same opportunities to buy affordable homes. These people perceive that they may fall out of the class position that their parents had achieved through unionization, increasing productivity, and sharing of the resources of the expanding economy. Given high rental costs, saving for a downpayment on one income is nearly impossible. The danger is even more apparent for low-skilled workers, single-parent workers, and others not already part of a generational housing equity safety net (i.e., where housing equity in the form of downpayments is often passed from parents or grandparents to their children). For these working people, not only is an affordable home beyond their reach, but decent and affordable shelter is increasingly difficult to find. In fact, millions of workers are so stretched by high housing costs and low savings that a layoff, an accident, or sickness threatens their housing tenure.

The attitudes and opinions of union member households (as surveyed in the employee poll) reflect the difficulty of the present housing conditions that they face. Eighty-three percent of union households who rent believe that it is impossible to buy a house with only one wage earner. But, *only 45 percent of union families have two wage earners*; 36 percent are either single or divorced; and 20 percent belong to traditional families in which only one spouse works. In part because of these changes in family structure and employment, *88 percent of union families think that it is harder to buy a house now than it was 20 years ago.*

Though union families in the survey believe that it is becoming more and more difficult to buy a home, their desire for home ownership remains strong. Eighty-three percent of union renters say that buying a home is either a very important financial priority or their top financial priority. While 63 percent fully expect to own a home at some point, *nearly one-third of those surveyed did not know or doubted that they would ever be able to afford to buy a home.* In fact, more than 40 percent of union families for whom housing was an important financial priority doubted that they could afford a home within the next five years. When queried about the major obstacle that prevented them from buying a home, 66 percent answered that the downpayment was the problem, 15 percent said that they could not meet the monthly payments, and 10 percent that they could afford neither the downpayment nor the monthly payments.

One of the most telling signs of the need to enhance housing affordability is the perceived lack of a supply of appropriately priced housing in the communities where working people live presently. Thirty-five percent of union respondents do not think that there is enough housing for people earning less than $30,000 per year within the 10-mile radius from where they live; this signals the severity of the housing problem since 45 percent of union families in the survey had family incomes under $25,000. Certainly, when the price of housing in working class neighborhoods is beyond the reach of a significant segment of working families, labor organizations will be and should be motivated to respond.

Changing Character of Families, Jobs, and Wages

The motivations of labor unions to get involved in housing for their members is very likely to grow stronger in the years ahead. As the 1990s continue, the growing diversity of the American work force and the restructuring of the national economy will make employer-assisted housing even more important to working people and to labor organizations interested in representing and servicing these workers. This is true because families are undergoing fundamental changes that are altering earning characteristics; the economy is shifting from an industrial to an information/service base that is creating new wage scales; new regional growth centers in finance, research, and high-technology are emerging that are influencing housing markets; and increased competition in the world economy has put a downward pressure on significant wage increases for American workers. All of these trends, as well as the absolute cost of housing units, impact negatively upon the ability of workers to find affordable housing opportunities (and thus the capacity of local economies and firms to grow).

Changes in Family

The changing character of the labor force is sparking new demands on employers for various benefits, and require innovative employer responses to attract and retain high quality workers. Four changes in the demographics of the family make work place housing benefits particularly important for, and of value to, the American worker: (1) increases in single, female-headed households; (2) increases in dual-income households; (3) mobility changes among workers; and (4) a new influx of an immigrant families in selected regions.

More than 15 percent of the American work force is now comprised of single-parent heads of households, predominately women, working in a variety of lower paying jobs. These working women face a large variety of work-related problems, including the need for day care services, job locations proximate to housing and child care, and increased training to boost earning potential. As a result of holding lower paying, "traditional jobs," these single-parent families are in the greatest need for appropriate types of housing to fit their locational and financial needs.

While the numbers of single working women are increasing, so are dual-income families, creating another set of work force needs and demands. In 1987, 57 percent of married couples had dual incomes; up from 45 percent of married couples in 1968.[1] Dual earner families are increasingly experiencing duplication in benefits, such as health care insurance, which one member may never have to (or be able to) use. Sixty-one percent of dual-income families with at least one union member have overlapping health care benefits. Benefits accounted for 17 percent in compensation costs in 1966, but rose to 27 percent in 1989.[2] Permitting employees to trade health care benefits for housing benefits could be a cost-effective way of dealing with redundant benefits— one that would be in the interest of employers and employees alike. Given the pressure to stretch family budgets, the workers interviewed show a strong preference for reprogramming overlapping benefits into a benefit that they could use.

The Joint Economic Committee of Congress calculates that family income would be 18 percent lower if women had not increased their participation in the work force. Often, that is the difference in affording the rent, a mortgage payment, or a down-payment and not affording these costs. A major influence on female work force participation is the desire to buy a house. Men and women surveyed in the 1981 General Mills American Family Report cited that the second most important reason for women seeking work was "helping to make ends meet" and "improving the standard of living."[3] Many dual-earner families face the dilemma of deciding between housing options made available by two incomes and maternity leave/child care/elder care often requiring the temporary loss of one income.[4] Exhibit 5.1 shows the dilemma graphically.

Mobility patterns, stimulated by job growth in regions with expanding economies, cause changes in the geographic distribution of housing that affect housing supply and cost. The national mobility rate declined fairly steadily in the 1960s and 1970s, leveling to 16.1 percent in 1983 and then increasing to 18.2 percent in 1988[5] (see Exhibit 5.2). About 35 percent of all moves are across county boundaries and from 13 percent to 17 percent are from one state to another. Mobility patterns vary by region—with people in the West moving nearly twice as often as those in the East. Over time, mobility rates have tracked inversely to home ownership levels— with mobility decreasing as people settled into homes and increasing in periods when housing was less affordable. Regional variations

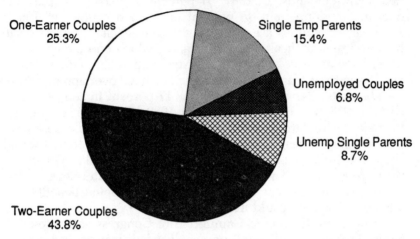

Exhibit 5.1
Family Employment and Earnings
Characteristics[6]

One-Earner Couples
25.3%

Single Emp Parents
15.4%

Unemployed Couples
6.8%

Unemp Single Parents
8.7%

Two-Earner Couples
43.8%

Source of data: J. Sweeney and K. Nussbaum. *Solutions for a New Work Force* (Cabin John, Md.: Seven Locks Press, 1989) 11.

in mobility rates also reflect greater numbers of renters and a larger population of younger people in the work force.[7]

The recent movement of foreign-born populations into the United States, particularly in Florida, Illinois, New Jersey, New York, and Texas is another demographic trend that impacts on housing (see Exhibit 5.3). In the 1980s, immigration from Asia, South America, and the Caribbean created new pools of low-wage/

Exhibit 5.2   Population Mobility Rates by Region, 1986–1987

REGION	PERCENT MOVING	PERCENT MOVING TO ANOTHER COUNTY	PERCENT MOVING TO ANOTHER STATE
Northeast	11.9	4.4	1.6
Midwest	16.7	6.0	2.4
South	20.3	7.4	3.4
West	22.4	7.9	3.4
Total	18.2	6.6	2.8

Source: U.S. Bureau of the Census, Current Population Reports, Series P-20, No. 430, *Geographical Mobility: March 1986 to March 1987*, p. 29.

Exhibit 5.3   Immigration by Major States of Destination, 1988

STATE	IMMIGRANTS PER 1,000 RESIDENTS	TOTAL POPULATION (MILLIONS)	TOTAL IMMIGRATION (THOUSANDS)
Virginia	2.0	6.0	11.9
Washington	2.1	4.6	9.9
Connecticut	2.2	3.2	7.2
Illinois	2.4	11.5	27.7
Rhode Island	2.4	1.0	2.4
Maryland	2.5	4.6	11.5
Nevada	2.6	1.1	2.7
Texas	2.6	16.8	43.3
Massachusetts	3.2	5.9	18.6
New Jersey	4.2	7.7	32.7
Florida	5.3	12.4	65.4
New York	6.1	17.9	109.3
Hawaii	6.1	1.1	6.6
California	6.7	28.2	188.7

Total Immigration to 14 states: 539,920
Total Immigration to U.S.:   643,025
14 States' Share of Total: 84.0 percent

Source: National Association of Realtors, *Demographics in the U.S.: The Segmenting of Housing Demand* (Washington, D.C.: November 1989) 70.

low-skill workers in selected urban areas that is stimulating the need for greater numbers of low-cost housing units. The effect of immigration on employment and the growth of regional economies has to be balanced by a continuing supply of affordable housing.

Changes in Jobs

The low-wage service sector is growing at the expense of manufacturing jobs, as part of the restructuring of the American economy. The average hourly service sector compensation in March 1990 was $13.97, while the average hourly compensation of a goods-producing job was $17.55.[8]

In 1988, 18 percent of workers were in manufacturing, down from 29 percent in 1968. Service producing industries rose in this same time period from 65 percent in 1968 to 76 percent in 1988.[9] Clerical and office workers have led service sector job growth, generating 7 million new jobs from 1970 to 1986. The fastest projected job growth will be in the low-wage service sector where 8 of the 10 jobs will pay less than the median income, and 5 in 10 will pay less than poverty-level wages (see Exhibit 5.4).

For both homeowners and renters, wages are not keeping pace with the cost of shelter. In 1959, a median-priced house cost 16 percent of the median income of the average 30-year-old worker; that figure jumped to 21 percent in 1973. By 1990, the median-priced house cost required over 45 percent of a 30-year-old's median income. According to a study of housing affordability for workers sponsored by the National Housing Institute, in 1989, the average annual wage in 74 out of 80 metropolitan areas was inadequate to afford the typical single-family home.[10]

The 1989 study calculated a "housing affordability ratio" by comparing home prices and average wages for 80 metropolitan areas. The housing affordability ratio was 4.1. Nationwide, the average full-time wage earner was paid $22,867. The median price for an existing single-family home that year was $93,100—4.1 times the typical wage.

For the typical wage earner to afford the median home, the housing affordability ratio should not exceed 2.7, which translates to 28 percent of household income, which is the traditional measure

Exhibit 5.4   Fastest Growing Jobs—Projected 1986–2000[11]

OCCUPATION	EMPLOYMENT 1986	EMPLOYMENT PROJECTED, 2000	CHANGE IN EMPLOYMENT, 1986–2000 NUMBER	CHANGE IN EMPLOYMENT, 1986–2000 PERCENT	AVERAGE WAGE 1987
Salespersons, retail	3,579	4,780	1,201	33.5	$11,544
Waiters and waitresses	1,702	2,454	752	44.2	$9,880
Registered nurses	1,406	2,018	612	43.6	$25,064
Janitors and cleaners, including maids and housekeeping cleaners	2,676	3,280	604	22.6	$13,416
General managers and top executives	2,383	2,965	582	24.4	$27,560
Cashiers	2,165	2,740	575	26.5	$9,828
Truck drivers, light and heavy	2,211	2,736	525	23.8	$17,810
General office clerks	2,361	2,824	462	19.6	$15,184
Food counter, fountain and related workers	1,500	1,949	449	29.9	$8,008
Nursing aides, orderlies, and attendants	1,224	1,658	433	35.4	$11,232

Source: G. T. Silvestri and J. Lukaasiewicz, *Monthly Labor Review*, September 1987, and Sweeney and Nussbaum, *Solutions for a New Work Force*, (Cabin John, Md.: Seven Locks Press, 1989) 11.

of housing affordability used by mortgage underwriters. In other words, an income of $34,450 was needed to afford the purchase of a median-priced home.

In only 6 out of the 80 metropolitan areas studied—Detroit, Houston, Lansing, Oklahoma City, Peoria, and Toledo—could the typical single wage earner afford the median-priced home. In 13 of the 80 metropolitan areas, the combination of two average wages was insufficient to afford the typical existing single-family home. These areas include Anaheim, Boston, Hartford, Honolulu, Los Angeles, New Haven, New York City, Providence (RI), Riverside/San Bernadino(Calif.), San Diego, San Francisco, Springfield (Mass.), and Worcester (Mass.). (See Appendix 3.)

The National Governors Association has reported that, from 1976 to 1986, families with annual incomes under $10,000 experienced a 4 percent decline in real income and an increase in rental costs from 48 percent to 58 percent of income. The impact of these changes have been felt throughout the nation, but are especially pronounced in the New England, Mid-Atlantic, and West Coast states. There, housing costs have outpaced the nation's highest wages (see Exhibit 5.5). From 1982 to 1987 in the New York City metropolitan area, housing prices doubled while wages rose only 27 percent. In San Francisco, according to a report by the Bay Area Council, a business-oriented policy group, 71 percent of households are unable to rent median-priced units and 87 percent cannot buy the median-priced house.[12] In Boston, where wages are 28 percent above the national average, the cost of buying a house is approximately double that in the rest of the nation.[13] Across the nation, union wage increases have not kept pace with the cost of buying and maintaining a home.

The spread of service-oriented economies across the nation also impacts on regional wage scales and housing costs. A bi-modal wage scale is developing in service economies—people who compete in the national wage/salary market (highly skilled service workers in finance, research, etc.), and local entry-level workers who are employed at lower regional wage rates (clericals, maintenance, etc.). This bi-modal wage pattern has created a competition for housing between people in the national high-wage labor pool and people in the local labor pool. As the price of housing gets bid up to meet the demand of the high-wage workers, low-wage workers are forced to allocate more of their income to housing, or to commute farther and farther to job centers. In the end, economies may suffer when the labor force shrinks as workers leave to take jobs

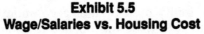

Exhibit 5.5
Wage/Salaries vs. Housing Cost

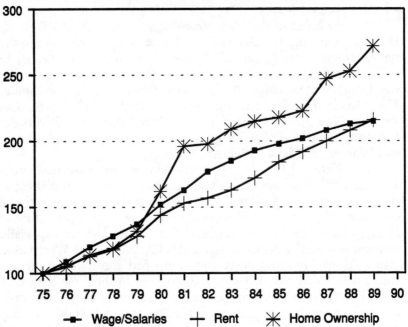

Source of data: Bureau of Labor Statistics, *Wage and Earnings Bulletins 1975-90*, and
National Association of Homebuilders, Research department, *Monthly Labor Review
Bulletins 1975-90*.

closer to more affordable housing opportunities, or as a larger portion of the population incurs a reduced living standard as more
household income is used to pay for housing expenses, leaving less
income for other expenses.

New Conditions for Unions

Unions have entered a period that challenges their strength
and demands new solutions to deal with the turbulence of economic
change. The effects of international and regional economic competition, productivity demands, and the mobility of capital and
investment tend to thwart labor's ability to negotiate substantial
wage increases. During the past decade, union strength has been
declining—union membership is down from 35 percent of the entire work force in 1954 to about 17 percent in 1990. As a result of

declining strength, many unions have been forced into concessionary bargaining stances. New bargaining strategies may be emerging to replace labor's difficult current bargaining position, however. These strategies seek to create a "new contract" between labor and management in which each group benefits and the economy is strengthened. For example, in the 1980s some businesses sought a bifrication of union wages, as documented by the growth of two-tier wage contracts. According to the Bureau of National Affairs, 28 percent of all wage contracts negotiated in 1989 included two-tier wage clauses (which pay newly hired employees on a reduced scale from workers hired previously).[14] These new employees, usually people just entering the work force, are predominantly younger workers and renters. These second tier workers are at a distinct disadvantage as they try to save for a downpayment with lower wages, while at the same time they are the group most likely to be prospective homebuyers. Unions that find themselves settling for two-tier contracts may detect a strong membership interest in obtaining housing assistance for lower-wage employees. Similarly, some unions in mature manufacturing industries are negotiating contracts that trade wages or work rules for job guarantees. Companies willing to guarantee employment presumably have made a commitment to keep their facilities in the region and therefore may be interested in participating in housing-related relationships with workers that stabilize communities.

History of Labor and Housing

A chronicle of the American work force evidences the important link between worker housing and economic development. From the advent of company housing to worker-funded cooperatives and the creation of federal housing legislation, the availability of affordable worker housing has been essential to the employment options of working men and women. Employer-assisted housing has long been part of the American system of industrial relations.

Employer-provided housing represented a substantial portion of worker housing in the United States during the first two decades of the century. Although much invective has been associated with the term "company town," a review of the literature on housing built by employers in that time period shows varying levels of social and economic control over the lives of workers. Most urban areas and industrial villages contained some amount of housing built for workers by their employers. In some cases, particularly in isolated areas, the modern image of paternalism, employer domination, and union busting existed in the extreme, in others it was almost non-existent.[15]

As early as 1914 at the annual convention of the American Federation of Labor, labor unions called for government action to provide low-cost housing loans to American workers.[16] While other important social welfare benefits such as life and medical insurance would evolve so that they were paid either entirely or partly by employer contributions, housing, after the decline of company-provided housing, remained out of the benefit equation.

In 1925, the Amalgamated Clothing and Textile Workers Union established a cooperative subsidiary to deal with the housing shortage being felt by the needle trades workers.[17] The Amalgamated efforts became the model for thousands of cooperative units built in New York in the 1930s, 1940s, and 1950s.[18] Outside of New York City, other efforts were underway to increase the affordability of housing for workers. A number of labor organizations began to finance their members' single-family homes through labor banks and building and loan societies, particularly as suburban detached housing became the housing ideal for working men and women seeking to escape the bleakness of working class urban life.[19]

The stock market crash of 1929 and the Depression restructured the federal role in all aspects of American life including the system of providing housing for working people. During 1930 and 1931, 1,000 homes a day were foreclosed on by banks and thrift institutions, thousands of lenders became insolvent, and 5 million members of the building trades were thrown out of work. By 1933, 49 percent of the $20 billion in home mortgage was in default. Housing starts fell from over 900,000 in 1924 to 93,000 in 1933.

The New Deal established a number of programs for workers' housing, producing housing for lower- to middle-income workers, but not the most destitute as public housing would later become. A provision for housing was included in the National Industrial Recovery Act. A housing division within the Public Works Administration was established that made loans to limited dividend corporations and cooperatives. These cooperatives needed to contribute 30 percent of the equity in a project to receive support. Ultimately the program helped finance 3,123 housing units in seven projects. Labor unions tapped this new source of government finance to expand their cooperative housing agenda. John Edelman, president of the American Federation of Hosiery Workers, used the program to fund 284 cooperative units now known as the Carl Mackley Houses.

The Subsistence Homesteads Division of the Public Works Administration financed 99 new worker communities. Although the program was oriented towards resettling farmers displaced from the Dust Bowl, nearly half of the newly established communities were for industrial workers in urban or suburban settings. Under this program, Jersey Homestead outside of Hightstown, New Jersey, was founded by Jewish needle trades workers seeking better housing conditions and employment opportunities in a cooperatively run factory. But by the end of World War II most of the new communities established by Homestead Division failed as workers sought higher pay and "suburban" housing conditions promised by the post-war economic boom.

The Labor Housing Conference

Organization of the Labor Housing Conference

In 1934, the Labor Housing Committee was established. Under the leadership of John Edelman, president of the American Federation of Hosiery Workers, Boris Shisken of the American Federation of Labor (AFL), and Catherine Bauer, a noted housing activist and author, the committee sought "to organize and promote a powerful, intelligent demand for workers' housing." The Labor Housing Committee was particularly effective in mobilizing support for federal housing initiatives from the building trade unions who were interested in promoting increased employment opportunities. The Labor Housing Conference coordinated the work of local labor housing committees that were set up by labor organizations in communities across the country.

CIO Demands Worker Housing

The Congress of Industrial Organizations also established a Committee on Housing in 1935 to press for a large scale public housing programs to meet the growing demands of their industrial membership for affordable housing. In its pamphlet "Labor's Program for Better Housing" the CIO demanded legislation that would create local housing authorities in every city on which at least one labor representative would serve. The CIO committee also called for "a program of public construction of perhaps a million units a year for the next ten years . . . to come closer to satisfying the housing needs of the American people."

The Housing Act of 1937

At the 1935 Convention of AFL in Atlantic City a resolution on housing was unanimously adopted, calling for the construction of sufficient numbers of rental housing to meet current needs, that public housing authorities be created and funded, that labor should lead the way promoting workers' housing as a public responsibility, and an AFL housing committee be established to complement the work of the Labor Housing Committee.

Organized labor is credited with the passage of the Wagner-Steagall Housing Bill of 1937, which became the first piece of national housing legislation to stipulate that the national goal was to provide decent, safe, and sanitary housing for low-income workers. The AFL helped draft the legislation and lobbied it through the legislative process. The CIO continued to press demands for a million new government-sponsored units of housing for workers.

The absence of available housing near defense sites motivated a strong federal response during World War II. By 1940, 2 million defense workers who did not have convenient housing options caused turnover rates to approach 500 percent.[20] As a result, 1.6 million affordable housing units were built by the government in new population centers across the country as part of the effort to deal with the problem.

In the early 1950s, labor leadership galvanized the efforts of existing housing cooperatives in the New York area by forming the United Housing Foundation to promote the creation and expansion of moderate-income housing cooperatives for increasingly affluent union wage workers. The Foundation directed its energies toward labor organization sponsorship and financial support for housing development, and advocated the use of pension funds for low-interest loans and equity investment to spur their memberships' involvement in cooperative housing ventures.[21] The most renowned success of the United Housing Foundation was the cooperative housing program of the International Ladies Garment Workers Union.

Throughout the 1960s and 1970s, unions supported nonprofit housing programs such as Section 202 Housing for the Elderly and Handicapped program, Section 221(d) 3, and the Section 8 New Construction programs. The American Federation of State, County, and Municipal Employees; the Communication Workers, Building Service Employees, Teamsters; and International Brotherhood of Electrical Workers were all nonprofit sponsors for these programs. Under these government-financed programs, unions built and managed properties for retirees and low- and moderate-income people, but invested little of their own money. The cost to the unions for sponsoring the projects was limited to predevelopment costs that were recovered upon project financing. The principal return to participating unions was job creation in the construction and maintenance trades and the income that pension funds received. The housing itself was not specifically targeted with the needs of union households. In recent years, union sponsorship of this housing has declined, corresponding to the U.S. Department of Housing and Urban Development's (HUD) 80 percent cut-back in funding since 1980.

In 1981, the Housing Investment Trust was organized by the Executive Committee of the AFL-CIO, which expanded labor's commitment to real estate investment activities.[22] The trust continues to grow, with assets in 1991 totaling more than $350 million. The trust, which returned 17.05 percent in 1989, has a portfolio consisting of 55 percent Government National Mortgage Association securities, 14 percent Federal Home Administration–backed mortgages, 18 percent construction loans, and 13 percent cash.[23] The Trust invests in single- and multi-family residences, retirement facilities, and nursing homes. It is considering increasing investments in mortgage-backed securities, working more with state and local governments, and providing bridge loans to facilitate low-income housing tax credit projects.

Union Housing Programs

As unions enter the 1990s, with the problems of declining membership, a changing work force, and new economic structures, they have begun to respond to the needs of their membership for more affordable housing opportunities. Labor unions are providing new sources of housing finance through pension investments, supporting such traditional union housing concepts as cooperatives and mutual housing associations, and exploring new ideas—including negotiating with employers for housing benefits. Many of the programs described in this chapter are viewed as models by the leadership of organized labor and are likely to become more widespread as other unions learn about the successes of these new approaches.

Collectively Bargained Benefits

Labor unions are beginning to collectively bargain for housing benefits in contract negotiations with employers. Historically, benefits have spread when employers see that they gain some advantage from the offering of a benefit, the government mandates a benefit (such as social security or unemployment insurance), or unions are successful in collectively bargaining for them to improve the welfare of their members. Given the declining housing conditions that American workers are now facing, labor organizations may promote the widespread institution of employer-assisted housing benefits by seeking housing affordability enhancements as it has done in collective bargaining negotiations with health insurance, pension plans, group life insurance, dental care, and, most recently, child care.

The National Labor Relations Act requires that employers and unions bargain collectively over "wages, hours, and conditions of employment."[24] The Act does not define these terms, but the National Labor Relations Board and court precedent indicate that housing falls within its jurisdiction as a bargainable benefit.[25]

In recent reports, the leadership of the AFL-CIO welcomes the expansion of collective bargaining to cover new contract subjects. The AFL-CIO Committee on the Future of Work, responding to the changing economic conditions confronting organized labor, recommended in 1985 that collective bargaining should seek to adapt to the changing times and changing needs of the work force:

> Collective bargaining is not, and should not be, confined by any rigid and narrow formula: the bargaining process is shaped by the times, and circumstances and the interplay between particular employers and employees. It is the special responsibility of individual unions that make up the labor movement to make creative use of the collective bargaining concept and adapt bargaining to these times and to the present circumstances.[26]

A national precedent for successfully negotiating a housing benefit was set by Local 26 of Boston's Hotel and Restaurant Workers' Union. On December 1, 1988, the 5,000 member union signed a three-year contract with 13 area hotels establishing the first collectively bargained for joint labor/management–administered housing trust fund in the nation. The three-year contract established an employer contribution of 5 cents per hour per worker to a Taft-Hartley trust fund jointly administered by union and management representatives. The fund will accumulate more than $1.5 million during the life of the contract to be used toward various affordable housing programs. Local union pension funds will be combined with trust fund dollars in order to further expand housing opportunities for Local 26 members.

The effort to establish the housing trust fund began in 1985 after the Local had bargained for a legal services benefit plan for its members in contract negotiations. Given the rapidly escalating cost of housing in Boston, Local 26's president Domenic Bozzotto surveyed the membership on the desirability of establishing a similar trust fund for housing. The membership (made up of low-wage chamber maids, bus boys, and "back of the house" service employees, as well as better-paid gratuity workers) responded positively and overwhelmingly to the suggestion, mobilizing to win what they understood to be a new opportunity for them to improve their limited housing options. The contract between the union and the Boston Hotel Association included Hyatt, Sheraton, Marriott, ARA, and Saunders Hotels as signatories.

A negotiating committee of 165 members, representing all the job sites and classifications, attended every negotiation session, indicating the broad support for a housing program among the membership. A contract establishing the housing fund was negotiated without a strike and prior to the union's bargaining deadline. In negotiating the contract, the Local did not trade away other significant benefits won over the years.

Peter Van Kleek, president of the Saunders Hotel Company, sees the housing trust fund as helping to solve the hotels' problems with labor availability and worker turnover. "The 5 cents for housing compared to the 86 cents we pay for health benefits is not a tremendous amount to solve what is recognized as a national problem that employees cannot afford to live in cities where they work."[27]

When the contract was signed in December 1988, housing trust funds were not permissible under Taft-Hartley law. To deal with this legal roadblock, the contract language read:

Effective December 4, 1988, $.05 per hour computed as in Health & Welfare program be accrued to each employer for a minimum of eighteen months. If a change in Sec. 302(c) of the Taft-Hartley Act to permit a housing joint trust is enacted on or before May 31, 1990, the money so accrued shall be transferred to such a trust. If no such change is made in the law, money will be added to Health and Welfare Fund for the remainder of the contract.

No union local had ever attempted to change the Taft-Hartley Act, which had not been amended in 17 years. But union leaders undertook the task because the unavailability of affordable housing was such a fundamental issue for the members. A survey of the Local's membership found that 98 percent of the members could not afford to buy a median-priced Boston home and 78 percent could not afford to rent the median-priced Boston apartment. The membership had a median family income of less than $20,000, only 55 percent of the area median. The average member could only afford a $75,000 house, while the median-priced Boston house sells for $190,000. Nearly three-quarters of the survey respondents cited some type of problem with their current housing tenure. When asked to rank negotiating priorities for the contact, affordable housing was ranked first, selected as being of higher importance than wages, health care and retirement benefits, and day care.[28]

In September 1989, more than 200 hotel workers spent five days in Washington, D.C., lobbying Congress to make housing a legal benefit at the bargaining table. Since Local 26 is primarily an immigrant union, lobbying to legalize their contract was for many their first direct participation in the political process. Small delegations of workers impressed upon Senators and Congressmen the importance of housing benefits for working people and asked only that Congress clarify the law to allow labor unions and employers, working together, the opportunity to make housing more affordable.

Democrats and Republicans in Congress, and the Bush Administration, responded to the message. On November 22, 1989, the United States Senate unanimously passed S-1949, co-sponsored by Senators Edward Kennedy and Orin Hatch, with the support and approval of the Department of Labor. The bill amended Taft-Hartley to permit labor and management to bargain for a labor–employer co-managed housing trust fund. With the aggressive support of Representative William Clay of Missouri, Chairman of the House Labor-Management Subcommittee, the required legislation passed the house in April 1990. On April 29, 1990, President Bush signed the changes into law, beating the contract-imposed deadline of May 31, 1990 that would have voided the new benefit.

The legislative language change adds an additional exemption to Section 302(c) of the Taft-Hartley Act. Subsection 7 of Title 29-186, which constitutes Section 302(c), now reads:

> (7) with respect to money or other thing of value paid by an employer to a pooled or individual trust fund established by such representative for the purpose of (A) educational assistance (B) childcare (C) housing assistance for the benefit of employees. . . .
> Provided that no labor organization or employer shall be required to bargain on the establishment of any such trust, and refusal to do so shall not be constituted an unfair labor practice; further provided . . . employees and employers are equally represented in the administration of such fund.[29]

The legislative provisions establish that housing benefits via Taft-Hartley trust funds is a permissive subject of bargaining; it can only be negotiated if both sides agree to include it in the collective bargaining process. Further, the benefit allowed by the legislation does not redefine housing as a non-taxable employee fringe benefit like contributions to health care and welfare plans.

The trust fund is essentially a private sector initiative for affordable housing, one that creates a true union/management partnership for affordable housing. Three representatives from union and management sit on the board of trustees, which administers the fund. The Department of Labor reviews the rules governing the fund and the programs it will provide for Taft-Hartley compliance. The $1.5 million raised by the trust over the span of the contract will be used in direct assistance programs for the lowest-income union members and to leverage more favorable financing for home ownership programs when combined with investment from the Local 26 and International Hotel and Restaurant Employees pension fund for higher-income members. The direct assistance programs include a tenant security guarantee program fund, a downpayment loan program that matches member down payment savings, a mortgage buy down program, a master lease program for affordable apartments, and a low-interest housing renovation fund.[30]

In 1988, the union created the Union Neighborhood Assistance Corporation (UNAC), a Section 501c(3) nonprofit corporation, which administers a number of housing services and advocates and organizes for better housing in the Boston neighborhoods where Local 26 members live. The 13-member staff speak the five major languages that predominate the union. Current programs provide housing and credit counseling to members interested in buying a home, and organizing to pressure absentee slum landlords to make deteriorating apartments conform to building and health codes. UNAC, in combination with the Trust, will service the wide variety of housing needs that face the low- and moderate-income hotel work force in one of the highest housing cost regions in the country.

Labor unions wanting to negotiate housing benefits in new contracts are not limited to Taft-Hartley trusts that are similar in structure to the Local 26 agreement. Alternative bargaining positions could create non–Taft-Hartley trust funds or seek defined housing benefit programs. Such programs include paying the premiums on group mortgage insurance and co-insurance programs, group mortgage guarantees, the marketing of a variety of bank/community reinvestment agreements by employers, or other programs. The ultimate choice in benefit selection must be determined by an analysis of the housing needs of union membership; the wage, recruitment, and turnover characteristics of the particular job and industry; and the financial position of the employer. In most cases, labor and management should be able to organize housing benefits in a way that serves the needs of the union, the union members, and the employer.

Because of the high priority that union members place on home ownership, work place housing benefits—even though they are not yet widely available (and, therefore, people are not yet familiar with how they would function)—ranked as the third most preferred employee fringe benefit, behind medical and retirement benefits, in the AAHI survey, ahead of educational and child care benefits. Indeed, 70 percent of union members see a role for employers providing some kind of housing assistance. Fifty-five percent believe that employers should become involved in arms-length financial aid and an additional 15 percent believe that employers should become involved in every aspect of the provision of housing. Only 25 percent say that employers should have no role at all. The largest objection made by some union members to employer provision of housing benefits is the potential for the invasion of their financial privacy. Programs that remove the employer's direct involvement in program administration, therefore, are perceived most positively. The most highly regarded programs for housing assistance are based on the third-party provider approach, similar to health insurance programs.

The need that union members have for reducing housing costs is so great that 44 percent would definitely, or most likely, be willing to move into an apartment building owned by their employer to save $50 per month in rent. If it means getting a house, more than 70 percent of union members were willing to trade a one year's wage increase for an employer guarantee that would substantially reduce downpayment requirements. About half of all union members were willing to give up an average wage increase to get a 1 in 15 chance at obtaining an employer-guaranteed mortgage in which no downpayment was needed.

As a result of strong member interest, unions will be interested in seeking more expansive benefits that help union members with particularly serious housing problems. For example, contracts containing provisions that set aside small pool funds to make emergency loans to prevent eviction from mortgage default or nonpayment of rent for members, pay for strike insurance that covers housing payments in case of layoffs or authorized strikes, cover displaced workers offered jobs in other regions of the country to receive some type of help in selling their home or sales guarantee from the employer similar to those offered in executive compensation packages, and workers covered by two-tier wage contracts to help toward saving for a home to compensate for the lower wages they receive.

The amendments to the Taft-Hartley Act authorizing housing trust funds and the Local 26 contract have attracted the attention of an increasing number of labor organizations. The inclusion of housing benefits in the collective bargaining contracts of public employees could be especially significant. Many municipal and state governments in high-cost housing areas have residency requirements for teachers, fire fighters, police, and other public employees. A housing benefit provides a "carrot" approach, enabling public workers to live in the communities in which they work rather than the currently used regulatory "stick" of simply requiring residency. Further, in those jurisdictions that cannot *require* residency, housing benefits can be an *incentive* for residency.

In action that could set the stage for labor agreements across the nation, the United Auto Workers 1990 National Collective Bargaining Convention adopted a resolution seeking housing benefits in their contract talks with U.S. automakers that year. In part, the resolution reads:

> We intend to seek an assistance program that enhances housing affordability for all workers. Using their enormous financial clout, the larger UAW employers could negotiate volume discounts on mortgage interest rates with lending institutions, or sell bonds to the

public with the proceeds earmarked for below-market mortgage loans
to their workers. These and other loan, grant and subsidiary arrangements can be used to make home ownership more accessible.[31]

Although housing benefits were not adopted during 1990 contract negotiations with the automakers, it is clearly on the future
agenda. As the large automakers move into the financial services
industries with Ford's purchase of First Nationwide Savings, and
the growth of GMAC, investment in employee mortgages either
to meet contract agreements or to fulfill Community Reinvestment
Act obligations seem to be in the offing.

AFL-CIO Programs

A 1985 report by the AFL-CIO Committee on the Evolution
of Work, "The Changing Situation of Workers and Their Unions,"
recommended that the AFL-CIO should begin programs that offer
direct benefits and services to workers and their families outside
of those provided by work place collective bargaining. The report
argued that by providing work place financial services and other
benefits, the AFL-CIO could increase the attraction of unions by
meeting a large range of worker needs, and could also reach out
to a new category of associate membership interested in union
benefits, but not employed in a work place with union represen-
tation.

The Union Privilege membership program was born in May
1989 from those recommendations. "Union Privilege's ultimate ob-
jective in developing a program of benefits is to find ways of using
those benefits to attract new members to unions either as full
members, or where full membership is not possible, as associate
members," the executive council of the federation said in its 1989
convention report.[32]

Today, Union Privilege offers a menu of financial services to
AFL-CIO members who belong to unions affiliated with the program. Union Privilege uses the massive clout of the bargaining
power of a 14 million member organization to negotiate considerable volume discounts. The negotiating ability that Union Privilege has in the market is setting new standards for lending. For
example, Union Privilege's largest program, an AFL-CIO credit
card, is offered by a majority of the 89 affiliated Federation unions,
covering more than 1.5 million participants. Based on this volume,
the AFL-CIO card has become the market leader with interest
rates 5 percent to 7 percent lower than most other cards. The
newly conceived UnionRATE savings program had 22 unions and

4 million participants in its first two months of operation. The plan is guaranteed to meet or surpass the yield of the average rate of money market accounts in the nation's 100 largest banks.

It is clear that the role of Union Privilege will continue to expand within the AFL-CIO. A 1989 resolution at the AFL-CIO national convention reiterates "support of Union Privilege and its goal of serving the needs of union members at home as well as in the workplace. . . . Union Privilege is therefore directed to continue to develop a full menu of services and benefits. . . ."[33] In the Spring of 1991, Union Privilege in conjunction with PHH/US Mortgage unveiled a group mortgage plan for union members of the AFL-CIO that are affiliated with the program. In June 1991, the program was expanded to include special affordability features designed to meet the needs of low- and moderate-income homeowners, who lacked down payment necessary to qualify for a mortgage. Within a three-week period, 1,700 households had sought mortgages and 100 loans were closed.

This new program—the Union Mortgage Program—brought Federal Home Loan Mortgage Corporation (Freddie Mac), GE Capital Mortgage Insurance Corporation, and the Amalgamated Bank of New York into partnership with Union Privilege and PHH/ U.S. Mortgage. The programs allow union families to buy homes with lower than traditional payment requirements, while establishing a secondary market for the loans originated by the program. The program includes the following features:[34]

- **Low Downpayments.** Mortgage downpayments for qualified members are reduced to 5 percent, of which only 3 percent must come from the borrower. The remaining 2 percent may be in the form of a gift from a relative or an unsecured loan from Amalgamated Bank of New York.
- **Downpayment Loans.** Qualified union members can obtain this downpayment loan at the same interest rate and term as their mortgage.
- **Reduced Closing Costs.** Union members may elect a "no-points" mortgage (although the interest rate may be higher if the member does not pay the points). The initial cost of private mortgage insurance is reduced by about 40 percent, and the usual requirement that a borrower have a two-month cash reserve is waived.
- **More Flexible Underwriting Criteria.** Borrowers' debts can be as much as 38 percent of their incomes. Ordinarily, debts can only total 36 percent of income.

With this program, first-time homebuyers are required to pay a 3 percent downpayment. The remaining 2 percent of the downpayment is borrowed from the Amalgamated Bank as an unsecured loan for the term of the mortgage. Over two years, Freddie Mac is committed to purchasing $50 million in mortgages and GE Capital Mortgage Insurance Corporation will provide mortgage insurance. Members in good standing with a participating AFL-CIO union for three years can apply for the downpayment loan from the Amalgamated Bank. The program is available to families whose income does not exceed 115 percent of the median area income.

Thomas Donahue, secretary-treasurer of the AFL-CIO, explains that "the program keeps organized labor in the forefront of finding ways to make housing more affordable for working men and women in this country. The program shows what is possible when the resources of the labor movement, including our own Amalgamated Bank of New York, are harnessed along with the commitment of the financial community to address the housing affordability crisis in this country."

Union Privilege intends to use a mortgage program to expand their membership and associate membership programs among service workers and white collar middle class employees—two diverse groups traditionally reluctant to join unions.

Based on the growing interest in employer-assisted housing programs generally, and a renewed interest in housing on the part of labor specifically, Union Privilege is planning to expand its group mortgage discount program so that it integrates its program with housing benefits that are derived from either contract agreements with employers or contributions from an affiliate or local. In this way, unions can leverage their housing benefit plans with the plan created by Union Privilege. The existence of the Union Privilege plan can also be an incentive for local unions or internationals to seek contracts establishing mortgage guarantees, or group mortgage insurance programs or co-insurance programs, while in other cases individual unions or locals could utilize their pension funds—with the appropriate guarantees and yields— to capitalize downpayment loan pools or co-insurance pools for plan participants. In other words, rather than viewing the Union Privilege program as entirely separate and distinct from union collective bargaining ability or innovations in pension investment strategies, it could evolve into a program that compliments other union activities.

IBEW Local 3

Spearheading worker and management affordable housing initiatives, the International Brotherhood of Electrical Workers (IBEW) Local 3 and the Joint Industry Board of the Electrical Industry in New York offers three financial assistance programs that enhance the ability of members to buy a home. The Local 3 Credit Union will write an interest-free loan of up to $2,000 for use as a downpayment loan or to pay the closing costs associated with financing a home or cooperative unit. The loans are repaid at a rate of $25 per week through a payroll deduction plan. In the late 1970s, the Local instituted a plan to help members who were laid off temporarily. The union offers a low-interest loan of up to $10,000 that can be used by union members to pay off an existing mortgage. The union suspends collection on the loan during periods of layoff or unemployment. In 1985, the Local initiated a group mortgage origination plan in conjunction with Metropolitan Life Insurance. Union members can obtain a 30-year fixed rate mortgage with no points down at ½ percent below prevailing mortgage lending rates.

Iron Equity

The Iron Workers locals of New York City offer a reduced rate mortgage program to its pension plan participants in conjunction with the Amalgamated Bank of New York, which is owned by the Amalgamated Clothing and Textile Workers Union. The Amalgamated Bank manages over $3.2 billion in pension fund assets of area unions. This lending program, Iron Equity, provides $18 million in mortgage financing for members of Iron Worker Locals 40, 361, and 417, who are vested in their multi-employer pension plan. Since the programs' inception in 1987, 157 loans have been made, totalling $14.2 million. Amalgamated Bank has a service agreement with the Iron Worker locals that governs the collection process for loans, including foreclosure. The pension investment is further secured by a $90 million annuity fund, separate from the pension fund, that collatoralizes mortgages in addition to the lien against the home.

First mortgages are made for up to $150,000 on primary residential units of one to four families within 200 miles of New York City. The program requires a 25 percent downpayment and standard underwriting criteria. Mortgages are pegged below current bank rates. Union members achieve additional savings because no points or origination fees are charged other than an initial application fee.

According to John Delaney, pension fund administrator, the program was attractive to pension trustees in two ways, "First, they felt that it would be of great benefit to a lot of members in today's market. . . . Second, they get a decent rate of return for the pension fund."[35] The Department of Labor has issued an opinion that the bank/pension program meets the Employment Retirement Income Security Act of 1974 (ERISA) criteria for a prudent investment, earning a rate of return commensurate with investment in treasury securities and short-term notes.

Construction trade unions in Toledo, Ohio, have recently begun a mortgage program for pension plan participants. The Roofers, Sheet Metal Workers and Carpenters retirement plan leverages preferable financing for home mortgages and home equity loans through major purchases of Certificates of Deposits from a local bank. In return for the deposit, the bank provides mortgage financing at 95 percent of loan-to-value ratio with no closing costs or points, and no private mortgage insurance.

Most of the programs reviewed throughout this book go beyond the concept of a group mortgage discount. Union group mortgage arrangements do exist, but they are typically leveraged by other relationships that provide additional affordability enhancements or discounts. Leveraging is usually accomplished by linked deposit programs, the use of economically targeted pension fund investment, the creation of mortgage pools capitalized by pension investment, and by Taft-Hartley trust funds.

Pension Funds

In the United States, more than 450,000 pension funds, with assets exceeding $2.9 trillion, provide retirement benefits for 41 million workers. Since 1978, pension fund assets have ballooned by 500 percent, and these assets are expected to double again in the 1990s.[36] Pension funds invested in affordable housing programs for plan participants, or for moderate-income workers, could provide retirement plans with acceptable returns and long-term stability for participants. Pension investment in housing may well become more important and economically desirable as the traditional sources of mortgage financing, the thrift institutions, shrink and related problems within the banking system continue to grow.

Prior to bank deregulation in the 1980s, consumer savings were largely contained in passbook accounts of thrift institutions. While the return on these funds was low, government regulation of the industry and certain tax code incentives enabled the savings and loan industry to develop a stable financial base that was able to lend long term to provide home mortgage loans to millions of families. Regulated savings and loans provided the vast bulk of low-interest mortgage money for moderate-income working people. In today's deregulated environment, however, thrifts provide a smaller percentage of their mortgages to low- and moderate-income working people than either commercial or mortgage banks and, as is clear from declining levels of home ownership, a new source of mortgage capital capable of meeting the needs of aspiring home-owners must be found.[37]

Some public pension funds have taken the lead in "economically targeted investing" (ETI), investing funds in housing and other community development activities that earn a market rate of return and also provide a social benefit. Linked development deposits, state mortgage–backed investment pools for housing, individual mortgage lending to pension plan participants, pension-funded secondary markets for affordable housing, and capitalization of nontraditional labor and community lending institutions are growing as new ways of providing home ownership opportunities at affordable terms to moderate-income families. California and New York public pension funds are the most aggressive users of this approach. Since the early 1980s, the California Public Employee Retirement System and the California State Teachers Retirement system have made nearly $1.5 billion in mortgage money available to plan participants at below prevailing market rates, while achieving a return at least equal to its other fixed income investments. In addition, the California funds have committed $100 million to the AFL- CIO Housing Investment Trust to be used for union-built affordable housing initiatives. New York state and city public pension funds have committed about $400 million in an urban housing rehabilitation program for New York City.

Unfortunately, billions of additional dollars in pension funds, which could finance housing at a lower cost than current capital markets, have largely gone untapped due to ERISA, which defines the fiduciary responsibilities of private pension fund managers in ways that restrict the ability of pension managers to service the housing needs of those whose money is being managed.

Pension fund managers, constrained by ERISA requirements, stress diversification of assets, strong allegiance to enrolled participants, and the prudent expert rule for investing. The Department of Labor, charged with administering the Act, holds that standards for investment should be based solely on return to the fund and not on other advantages that accrue to plan participants. Such regulation-driven investment patterns do not fulfill the needs of individual workers to access their own pension savings for mortgage loans or fund low- and moderate-income housing construction needed by lower-income workers. Home ownership could be made affordable to millions of working people if pension plan participants could gain access to their retirement savings for mortgages at rates below those made available by traditional lenders.

As discussed in Chapter 6, Congress should re-evaluate ERISA regulations mandating investment at prevailing rates. Pension fund trustees have been required by the Department of Labor's present interpretation of ERISA to use the terms offered by banks, and securitized by the secondary market, as a benchmark return. But these rates often exceed the average rate of return achieved by pension fund managers. Further, pension funds and banks do not have comparable costs of funds. The cost of funds to a pension plan is the opportunity cost of not funding the plan on an accelerated schedule. Banks, however, do have a real cost of funds: they pay interest or deposits, have tax liabilities, and they pay a premium to obtain liquidity or sell mortgages in the secondary markets. The prevailing return on treasury bills provides a better target for the appropriate yields to pension funds. Moreover, mortgages made from pension funds could have longer terms than traditional mortgages to reflect actuarial factors that govern fund investment strategies, further reducing the income requirements for plan participants seeking mortgages. For example, increasing the amortization of a standard 25-year mortgage to a 40-year mortgage would reduce the annual income needed for a homebuyer by about $3,000.[38]

Even with the present restrictions imposed by ERISA and the Department of Labor, other new investment techniques being promoted by some AFL-CIO unions and public pension funds—such as economically targeted investments—offer the possibility of new sources of capital for work place–oriented housing benefits. Linked development deposits, state mortgage–backed investment pools for housing, individual mortgage lending to pension plan participants, pension-funded secondary markets for affordable housing, and capitalization of nontraditional labor and community lending institutions have become important models for how labor organizations could make their resources available for affordable housing activities.

Linked Deposits

The Bricklayers and Masons Union and the Laborers' Union in Boston have gained considerable recognition for their affordable housing projects funded by the leveraged use of pension fund assets. This model of linked deposits has served the dual purposes of creating construction trades jobs at prevailing wages and financing low- and moderate-income affordable housing development, while proving to be a prudent investment for their retirees.

The Bricklayers and Laborers' Nonprofit Housing Company, Inc., the union-owned nonprofit company that does the development, has completed construction of 250 units. Their first project produced a 17-unit development of 1,200 square foot, two-bedroom townhouses that sold for an average of $70,000 in a Boston market where comparable market-rate units sell for more than $140,000. Contributing to the affordability of the units was the acquisition of the site, a vacant public school lot, for $1 and the waiving of development fees charged by the city of Boston, a standard no-frills architectural design, and below market 9.9 percent mortgage financing from the Massachusetts Housing Finance Authority (at the time, about 200 basis points below prevailing mortgage lending rates). Buyers of the housing, selected by lottery, had family incomes averaging less than $27,000.

Key to the project was a linked deposit agreement between the union pension fund and the United States Trust Company, the union's local bank in Boston. The union invested $1.2 million in the bank's certificates of deposit, earning a return of 7 percent interest. This investment leveraged a construction loan of an equal amount at 8 percent interest, about 4 percent less than prevailing construction loans.

Based on their initial success, the Bricklayers and Laborers' Nonprofit used the same formula to construct and finance 48 units in Charlestown, where more than 1,700 families signed up for a housing lottery to get a chance at buying a house. In Boston's Mission Hill district, the Bricklayers completed another 160 townhouses. Deed restrictions guarantee the long-term affordability of the units.

By establishing the nonprofit development program, the Bricklayers showed how pension funds could leverage favorable lending agreements with local banks, and enhanced labor's image of concern regarding housing affordability for low- and moderate-income families. Most importantly, union members received new employment opportunities at union wages. While the benefit to their membership is job creation at prevailing wages and an enhanced public image, the Bricklayers now have a model with which they can approach other unions whose membership seeks affordable housing. Other unions could leverage their pension funds for construction loans to union nonprofit developers, providing both jobs and housing for union members.

A similar approach is being used by the New York State Pension Investment Policy Group to direct pension monies into low- and moderate-income housing production. The New York State AFL-CIO founded the Pension Investment Policy Group in 1984 to increase the social benefits of the vast amount of investment from their pension plan resources. Using $23 million in pension fund assets from the International Brotherhood of Electrical Workers, the Amalgamated Clothing and Textile Workers Union, the Amalgamated Life Insurance Employees, and the Hotel Employees and Restaurant Employees International Union, a $6.5 million construction loan was leveraged for the New Communities Housing Development in Brooklyn, New York.

The pension fund investment policy group invests in Federal Deposit Insurance Corporation (FDIC)–insured certificates of deposit issued by the Crossland Savings Bank. The project has rehabilitated more than 100 housing units, including 34 moderate-income condominiums financed by the New York State Mortgage Authority, and 31 low-income cooperatives, additionally subsidized by the state Housing Trust Fund. Unionized construction workers are employed for all projects.

Public Pension Investment

While a majority of states use private mortgage investment firms to invest their public employee retirement funds, a growing number of state governments have tapped their public employee retirement systems for investment in affordable housing programs.

Five states—Colorado, Connecticut, Hawaii, Michigan, and North Carolina—have operated programs for the investment of these public funds in housing opportunities for moderate-income state residents and pension plan participants.

Between 1980 to 1986, the Connecticut Pooled Mortgage Investment Program (YankeeMac) targeted $475 million in mortgages to about 8,000 plan participants. YankeeMac offered fixed-rate 20- to 30-year mortgages with 5 percent to 10 percent downpayment requirements at mortgage rates 100 to 150 basis points below conventional financing sources. The state sold AA rated bonds at 13.75 percent, a rate substantially lower than that available at lenders. The State Employees' Retirement Fund, Municipal Employees' Retirement Fund, and Teachers' Retirement Fund purchased the bonds, enabling the pension funds to yield a return commensurate with other portfolio investments.

Similarly, Colorado, North Carolina, and Oregon, securitize mortgage pools for sale to their pension systems. The Pennsylvania State Employers' Retirement System buys individual home mortgages at discounts of 30 to 50 basis points below equivalent (Fannie Mae) securities. Hawaii makes below market rate mortgages available to public employees enrolled in their state pension system.

In 1984, the New York City's Employees Retirement System and the Police Pension Fund became the first public employee pension funds in the nation to finance urban housing rehabilitation. They initially made a $50 million commitment to the Community Preservation Corporation (CPC), formed in 1974 by local banks to finance housing rehabilitation loans. The program has invested more than $200 million. The program invests pension funds at market rates in combination with 1 percent loans from the City housing agency to provide developers with a blended interest rate that is lower than available through a conventional mortgage. The investments yields returns are slightly greater than that offered by the federally chartered Government National Mortgage Association (Ginnie Mae). The program has rehabilitated 9,000 apartment units in "changing neighborhoods" and increased their useful life by 30 to 40 years.[39]

In the fall of 1990, the New York City Retirement System bought $100 million in Federal National Mortgage Association (Fannie Mae) securities with special provisions that allow moderate-income homebuyers to qualify for home mortgages with 5 percent downpayments rather than traditional 20 percent downpayments. The

New York City fund earns a return comparable to standard Fannie Mae securities at a rate that is about 125 basis points more than long-term treasury bonds.[40]

A program established by the Pennsylvania Treasurer and the Pennsylvania Housing Finance Agency provides affordability enhancements in a $100 million mortgage-backed security packaged by Fannie Mae. The program has made mortgages at about 15 basis points below market rates to 1,500 middle-income homebuyers. The investment yields about 20 basis points more than short-term treasury securities and is regarded as an investment superior to other short-term investments by the fund.

James W. White, general council to the Pennsylvania Department of Treasury, describes the program as "the first private placement between a state housing agency, a state treasury and Fannie Mae . . . this deal is capable of replication across the country."[41]

New techniques are also being developed to steer the pension funds of municipal workers into affordable housing programs. Although no program presently exists in which municipal pension funds are used to directly support low-cost mortgages for municipal employees, a recent initiative undertaken in Connecticut by the City of Hartford Municipal Employees Retirement Fund (MERF), the City of Hartford, and the Local Initiatives Support Corporation (LISC) could provide a model for such a program.

The Land Acquisition for Neighborhood Development program is a $1.25 million property acquisition pool for Hartford's community development corporation. The municipal pension fund capitalized the pool with a $1 million loan to the Local Initiative Support Corporation (LISC), a national nonprofit development financing intermediary, at 7.25 percent for six years. The city of Hartford contributes $72,000 per year from its Community Development Block Grant funds to reduce the effective interest rate on the pension fund's loan to LISC to zero. LISC fully guarantees the loan. The community development corporations qualifying for the program borrow from the pool managed by LISC at 1 percent interest.

Since property acquisition without development financing is more speculative than other types of lending, LISC has established a system of management and technical support to help mitigate risk. A review committee composed of public and private sector lenders of permanent financing must approve each application, and LISC requires a strategic business plan before projects are accepted for LAND assistance. Repayment of loans is due upon receipt of permanent financing. Lending to any developer is limited to $500,000.

Similar programs in other cities could be targeted to pension plan participants. While there may be some political umbrage at using Community Development Block Grant (CDBG) funds for public workers, if loans were designated for declining neighborhoods and for lower-income public workers, it could be explained as a low-cost neighborhood revitalization plan. Rather than providing interest subsidy from block grant funds, interest could be subsidized from other sources such as a housing trust fund established in contract negotiations or from over-funded municipal bond reserves.

Individual Mortgages via Pensions

In 1978, the Operating Engineers Local 675 established a below-market mortgage program for its membership using union pension funds.[42] The mortgages were offered at below-market rates because the risk of the investment was reduced by securing the loans with a separate union-controlled annuity fund. The Operating Engineers provided $3 million in mortgage loans to members at 212 basis points lower than market loans for single-family homes.

The offer of a below-market return by the Operating Engineers investment plan was challenged by the Department of Labor in a 1986 suit that claimed the investment strategy violated standards established by ERISA. In *Brock v. Walton*, 794 F.2d 586 (11th Cir 1986) the 11th U.S. Circuit Court of Appeals upheld Local 675's mortgage plan, ruling that the lower interest rate offered by the fund was prudent and reasonable due to increased protection from risk. However, the Department of Labor continued to maintain that "reasonable return" meant the "prevailing" interest rate, and that this is the standard that must be applied to the fiduciary conduct of pension investments. In 1989, the U.S. Department of Labor rewrote the language of the ERISA regulations, requiring that the return on pension plan investments to commensurate with prevailing interest rates offered by financial institutions, and capped permissible mortgage loans at $50,000. Based on the new regulation, Local 675 has placed a moratorium on the program until further clarifications to ERISA are made through the courts or Congress.

In addition to the membership mortgage program, Local 675 has successfully used its pension fund to invest in a wide variety of real estate holdings that have greatly enhanced the earnings of the fund and provided financing of construction projects that employ many hundreds of unionized workers. The Operating Engineers fund has leveraged more than $400 million of development for local trade union members accounting for more than seven million hours of work. Since the early 1980s, the pension fund has grown four-fold to more than $65 million.

In an extension of this type of pension investment strategy, the Florida Building Trades council organized the Florida Affirmative Investment Roundtable (FAIR). FAIR invests construction union multi-employer retirement plans in union construction projects. In the early 1980s, construction trade multi-employer pension plans established 11 regional construction foundations that invested in all union-contracted housing and real estate ventures (see Exhibit 5-6). These real estate ventures met with varying degrees of success, but established for the unions a track record of real estate involvement and a strong understanding of the significant impact that the control of pension capital can give unions institutionally.

Bank Capitalization

Pension funds have also been used to create and capitalize a variety of alternative financial institutions that respond to the needs of union members and other moderate-income workers without access to conventional lending sources. These new lenders offer a number of programs that promote home ownership and the construction of multi-family dwellings.

In Massachusetts, the Massachusetts State Carpenters Union has contributed $25 million from the Carpenters Pension and Annuity Fund to capitalize the First Trade Union Savings Bank. Chartered in 1987, the bank provides a full range of financial services and actively participates with the public sector and nonprofit developers in affordable housing programs. The bank is also the trustee for the recently organized Taft-Hartley housing trust of Hotel and Restaurant Employees Union, Local 26.

The Community Capital Bank in Brooklyn is being capitalized from a variety of nontraditional sources, including labor pension funds from the Joint Board of Electrical Workers. Modeled after the South Shore Bank in Chicago, the bank hopes to originate more than $100 million in loans to developers of low-income housing and small businesses. Similar community development banks could be capitalized with labor funds in numerous places in the United States with concentrations of union members. These banks could build-in labor par-

Exhibit 5.6 Multi-Employer Housing Foundations

NO.	YEAR FORMED	NAME	AMOUNT INVESTED* (MILLIONS OF $)
1	1980	Development Foundation of Southern California	125
2	1980	Northern California Pension Investment Foundation	15
3	1980	Massachusetts Construction Industry Development Finance Foundation	12
4	1980	Syracuse Building Trades Investment Group	6
5	1981	Buffalo and Western New York Building Trades Investment Foundation	20
6	1982	Florida Affirmative Investment Roundtable (includes Palm Coast Affirmative Investment Roundtable)	20
7	1983	Pacific Northwest Construction Financing Forum	12
8	1983	Minnesota Construction Industry Foundation	30
9	1984	Tri-State Investment Foundation	0
10	Pending	Northwest Ohio Building and Construction Industry Foundation	—
11	Pending	Baton Rouge Building and Construction Industry Foundation	—

*Approximations provided by the foundations.
Source: AFL-CIO Industrial Union Department, *Labor and Investments* 5, no. 4 (1985).

ticipation on its boards, operate joint ventures with union affiliated developers for housing production, or offer special mortgage products to union members through work place housing assistance programs.

The New York City Employee Retirement System and Police Pension Funds have been used by the Community Preservation Corporation (CPC) in New York City to create a secondary market in the city for the purchase of single and multi-family mortgages originated by area lenders. The Housing Partnership Mortgage Corporation, begun in 1986 by the CPC, uses $50 million in pension money to buy 30-year, fixed-rate loans on conventional and subsidized projects. Local lenders, knowing that they can sell loans, have a greater interest in community lending in areas of the city in which they have been traditionally reluctant to invest.

Challenge for Labor

Changes in the American economy are making it more difficult for working men and women to buy homes or find affordable rental units. Inflation in housing costs, as well as the increases in health care and education, have contributed to a real drop in disposable income among workers. When combined with changes in the composition of the work force—more dual earner families, more single women heads of households, more immigrants, and changes in the structure of the work force; more service than manufacturing jobs, and bifurcated pay scales—the link between housing opportunities and jobs becomes more evident for working people and their union representatives. Similar to employers, unions are beginning to understand that by helping to create and promote affordable housing for workers, they will directly impact on the principal problems facing working people today, while strengthening their own ability to survive and grow.

Survey research indicates that labor union members view housing programs, whether union-sponsored or directly employer-assisted, as something that they want and in which they would participate. Service workers and white-collar, middle-class employees, who traditionally have been harder to organize, have a particular need for housing assistance, which may yield organizing opportunities for unions.

Recently, a variety of programs that enhance home ownership opportunities for union members via use of union resources have come into existence. Some unions have designed housing programs as a members-only benefit, others are negotiating directly with employers to create new types of fringe benefits. Based on these initial activities it can be expected that housing benefits of all kinds will be the new bargaining position of the 1990s. These new programs will work for the benefit of both labor and management by providing a highly leveraged benefit that saves employers money (and leverages value), but also is more valuable than cash to many union members. In other cases, individual unions or locals will try to utilize their pension funds—with the appropriate guarantees and yields—to capitalize downpayment loan pools for plan participants replacing, in part, the role that thrift institutions once played in the provision of mortgage capital.

In Chapter 6, changes in federal pension and tax law, as well as other federal policy initiatives that could be taken to encourage business and labor to become involved in work site–related housing benefit programs will be identified and discussed. By the removal of obsolete barriers to the offering of housing benefits, unions will be better able to hark back to their long and significant involvement in housing issues and in the coming decade play a decisive role in the provision of housing for working people.

Notes

1. "Flexible Benefit Plans: Employees Who Have a Choice," *Monthly Labor Review*, December 1989, 18.
2. Employee Compensation in the Private Non-farm E, 1974 Bulletin 1963 (BLS) and Employment Costs Indexes and Levels, 1975–89.
3. J.P. Fernandez, *Child Care and Corporate Productivity* (Lexington, Mass.: D.C. Heath and Company, 1986) 8.
4. Ibid, 14–16.
5. P. Osterman, *Employment Futures* (New York: Oxford University Press, 1988) 56.
6. J.J. Sweeney and K. Nussbaum, *Solutions for a New Work Force* (Cabin John, Md.: Seven Locks Press, 1989) 11.
7. *Demographics in the U.S. the Segmenting of Housing Demand* (Washington, D.C.: The National Association of Realtors, 1989) 63–65.
8. "Employer Costs for Employee Compensation—March, "*Bureau of Labor Statistics News*, U.S. Department of Labor 90-317, released June 19, 1990.
9. "Flexible Benefit Plans," note 1, above.
10. "Working Paper for Affordable Housing," (Orange, N.J.: National Housing Institute, 1990).
11. G.T. Silvestri and J. Lukasiewicz, "A Look at Occupational Employment Trends to the Year 2000," *Monthly Labor Review*, September 1987 and Sweeney and Nussbaum, *Solutions*, note 5, above.
12. P. Dreier, D.C. Schwartz, and A. Griener, "What Every Business Can Do About Housing", *Harvard Business Review* (Boston, Mass.: Harvard Business School), Reprint No. 88505, September–October 1988, 3.
13. R. Ferlauto and D. Hoffman, "Organizing for Housing Benefits", *Social Policy*, (New York: The Institute) Vol. 19 No. 3, Winter 1989, 39.
14. *Basic Patterns in Union Contracts-12th Edition*, The Bureau of National Affairs, (Washington, D.C.: BNA Books), 117.
15. For more information on social control in company housing see S.D. Brandes, *American Welfare Capitalism, 1880–1940*, (Chicago: University of Chicago Press).
16. Speech by Joseph Keenan, Chairman of the AFL-CIO Housing Committee at the AFL-CIO Housing Conference, April 11, 1972.
17. M. Joesephson, *Sidney Hillman: Statesman of Labor* (New York: 1952) 316.

18. See "Thirty Years in Cooperative Housing—The United Housing Foundation," A.E. Kazan in *Housing the Cooperative Way*, Jerome Liblit, ed. (New York: 1974) 222.
19. D. Bok and J. Dunlap, *Labor and the American Community* (New York: Simon and Schuster, 1970) 377.
20. G.S. Fish, ed., *The Story of Housing* (New York: MacMillian, 1979) 247.
21. Ibid., 253.
22. "The AFL-CIO Investment Program: 25 Years of Service to Labor," *Housing Investment Trust* (Washington, D.C.: AFL-CIO, 1989) 14.
23. "Funds on Move to House America," *Pensions and Investments*, November 12, 1990, 1.
24. NLRA, Sections 8(d).
25. *WW Cross & Co. v. NLRB*, 174 F.2d 875 (1st Cir. 1949).
26. "The Changing Situation of Workers and Their Unions," AFL-CIO Committee on The Evolution of Work (Washington, D.C.: AFL-CIO, 1985) 19.
27. "A Union Employer Housing Fund," *New York Times*, June 24, 1990, F5.
28. J. Kluver, "Labor and Housing in Boston," Massachusetts Institute of Technology, unpublished thesis, 1988.
29. P.L. 273, 101st Congress.
30. *A Dream Come True*, Brochure; Union Neighborhood Assistance Corporation, 62 Berkeley St., Boston, Mass. 02116, July 1991.
31. "United Auto Workers 1990 Special Convention Collective Bargaining Program," United Auto Workers, May 21–23, 1990, Kansas City Convention Center, Kansas City, Missouri.
32. "Unions Are Expanding their Role in the 90's," *New York Times*, Aug. 19, 1990, F12.
33. AFL-CIO National Convention Resolution, 1989.
34. From Union Privilege Benefits Program Press release: "Freddie Mac and AFL-CIO Pair Up to Make Housing Affordable for Union members," June 25, 1991.
35. L. Smith, ed., "Our Monies Worth: The Report of the Governor's Task Force on Pension Fund Investment" (New York State Industrial Cooperation Council, 1989) 1.
36. "S&L's Shun Lower Income Neighborhoods," *CRA Reporter*, (Washington, D.C.: Center for Community Change) August 1989, 6.
37. "A Pension Fund Reinvestment Program to Finance Affordable Housing," New York City Housing Partnership, to the U.S. Department of Labor.
38. *Competitive Plus*, New York State Industrial Cooperation Council, February 1990, 15.
39. "Funds on Move to House America," Pensions and Investments, November 12, 1990, 1.
40. Ibid.
41. See A.R. Banks, "Dennis Walton's Capital Wars," *Labor Research Review* (Midwest Labor Research Institute, Fall 1988) Vol. VII, No.2.
42. "Few Better Investment Options Than This," 42. *Crain's New York Business*," April 27, 1987.

Chapter 6

The Role of Federal Policy

The public policies of the past 15 years have not lead to an expansion of affordable housing opportunities, and business and labor are increasingly recognizing the negative consequences to employees and business operations. As a result of increased levels of philanthropic and employer-assisted housing activity, the private sector is likely to become even more acutely aware of the shortcomings of current governmental housing policies and the effect of those policies upon employee turnover rates, wage rate distortions, business productivity, and worker alienation as the goal of home ownership recedes against the tide of stable wages and increasing home prices. If federal policy will not return to the expansive level of activity of the 1937–1977 period (and it could be argued that a policy of "back to the future" is neither wholly useful or desirable, even if fiscally achievable), then a national policy that encourages new levels and types of participation by business and labor is essential.

This chapter identifies federal statutory or regulatory impediments to employer-assisted housing and suggests some ways that these barriers can be overcome. This chapter also suggests some public sector technical assistance programs and fiscal policies that would facilitate and encourage employer involvement in housing benefit programs.

Tax Consequences of Housing Benefit Programs

An *employee benefit* is virtually any form of compensation other than the provision of wages, that is paid for in whole or in part by the employer, even if the benefit is delivered by a third-party provider such as a government entity or insurance company. Because employee benefits affect the employee's total level of compensation, employee benefits, as they relate to employee earnings, are regulated by the tax code. Within the overall benefit definition, benefits are considered either mandatory (e.g., Social Security, unemployment compensation, and workers' compensation) or nonmandatory. Nonmandatory benefits can be further categorized as taxable, tax-exempt, or tax-deferred. A taxable benefit is one that is offered to an employee without regard to hours actually employed. A paid holiday or a vacation is an example of a taxable benefit.

A tax-exempt benefit is one in which the cost of the benefit is not counted as income to the employee. Three benefits fall into this special category: health insurance, life insurance (up to $50,000 of coverage), and dependent care costs (up to $5,000 annually). In each instance, the cost of the benefit (such as the premium payment for insurance) is received by the employee on a tax-exempt basis. Of less importance, but also received on a tax-exempt basis, are those benefits often referred to as "fringe benefits" such as subsidized company cafeterias, van pools, or parking privileges. These benefits are judged to be tax-exempt because the benefit is intended to meet an employer need, even though these programs may be helpful to the employee. In certain very specific instances a housing benefit may be tax-exempt because it meets an employer need. For example, emergency personnel who must live near a hospital or fire station may be eligible to receive a tax-exempt housing benefit.

A tax-deferred benefit is one that is not taxed when the employer pays for the benefit, but is taxed when the employee uses the service. Pension programs are an example of a deferred benefit—employees are not taxed when the employer contributes to the pension plan, but tax liability is incurred when the employee withdraws funds from the pension.

With the exception of those relatively few employees who can plausibly receive a tax-exempt housing benefit, housing benefits are classified as taxable. Of course, for the employer all benefits are a tax deductible cost of doing business, as are wages, equipment, and other operating costs.

That housing benefits are taxable does not make them valueless, particularly to lower-income employees in the 15 percent income tax bracket. For example, to an employee who is able to participate in a group mortgage insurance program, requiring an employer payment of perhaps $900 to a co-insurance fund, the additional tax liability of $135 is indeed a trivial price to pay to get into a home. Even an employee receiving a several thousand dollar downpayment grant may well find that the tax advantages of home ownership (principally the mortgage interest deduction) more than offsets the temporary additional tax liability caused by the grant.

Loans, of course, are not income and thus have no tax implications; though below-market interest rate loans may result in tax liability for the imputed value of the difference between a market-rate loan and the below-market interest rate charged by the employer. Forgivable loans that, in effect, convert to grants, do increase income, but by forgiving loans over a period of time (which coincides with corporate retention strategies) the tax impact of the grant can be distributed over several years.

Notwithstanding housing benefits being classified as taxable, some employers have discovered that some valuable housing benefits have a structure that results in no tax consequences to the employee, although these benefits are not technically tax-exempt. For example, group mortgage origination programs, mortgage guarantee programs, and purchase guarantee programs are among the housing benefits that require no employer payment to the employee or third-party provider. Because no cash changes hands, the discounts offered by lenders or builders are viewed by the IRS as market discounts rather than employee benefits. Employees are not taxed for receiving services from the market at discount prices.

Congress created the category of tax-exempt benefits because it wished to encourage certain types of activity, such as the provision of health and child care benefits. Housing is arguably as important as the other tax-exempt benefits. Indeed, when asked to choose from a menu of possible benefits, surveyed non-home-owners chose a housing benefit 50 percent more frequently than a child care benefit. As part of the reshaping of national housing policy to permit the active participation of business and labor, Congress should add housing benefits to the list of tax-exempt benefits. In so doing, Congress will clearly send the message that housing is an important family need and that business and labor can and should play a role in meeting this need. If authorized as a tax-exempt benefit, employers will feel legally comfortable offering housing benefits. In response to this authorization there would be additional incentive for insurers, financial institutions, and the building industries to create new housing benefit products and services. As a tax-exempt benefit, housing assistance would be even more desired by employees.

Of course, in an era in which domestic policy decisions have been dominated by the federal deficit, some view the creation of a new tax-exempt benefit as unaffordable, even if desirable. A new tax-exempt benefit is seen as increasing the deficit as employees receive new untaxed services, perhaps even in exchange for previously taxed income. But this need not be the case. Some revenue loss can be prevented by prohibiting tax-exempt status for those benefits that simply substitute a tax-exempt employer-paid housing voucher for taxable wages. This would prevent monthly housing voucher and "lump sum" programs from being initiated that do not increase employee access to better housing, but simply place a larger portion of compensation in the tax-exempt category.

Benefit programs that would gain from the adoption of tax-exempt status include those benefits that are already de facto tax-exempt, in that employers would be more aware and more comfortable offering a benefit that is explicitly tax-exempt. There would, of course, be no increased revenue loss to the Treasury in that these benefit program structures are already nontaxable. Other benefit programs that would gain from tax-exempt status are those programs requiring direct cash expenditures, such as below market rate downpayment loans, downpayment grants, closing cost subsidy programs, and group mortgage insurance premiums. To the extent that these programs grow at the expense of taxable wage growth, these programs would cost the Treasury money (although revenue from the housing activity encouraged might more than make up for this loss), but there are ways of limiting these losses.

One way that the federal government could limit the cost of an additional tax-exempt benefit is by "capping" the maximum amount of housing benefit that could be received on a tax-exempt basis. Capping is already applied to life insurance benefits, with the tax-exemption restricted to $50,000 worth of coverage. Employees who receive life insurance coverage in excess of $50,000 are taxed on the sum that pays for the cost of the additional coverage. A tax-exempt housing benefit might be limited to 10 percent of the cost of a median-priced home. In 1988, the national median was $112,500 for a newly constructed single-family home,[1] thus, the total benefit might be limited to $11,250. The benefit might further be limited by permitting its receipt as a tax-exempt benefit on a one-time per address basis. This would permit employees who relocate, or move from assisted rental dwellings to units that they own, to continue receiving a benefit, but ongoing wage supplement programs would be prohibited. A cap would also tend to add progressivity to the benefit, making the benefit more valuable to lower-income workers purchasing lower-priced homes and less valuable to those workers purchasing higher-priced homes.

A second way that the federal government could limit the cost of a tax-exempt housing benefit is by limiting the overall amount of tax-exempt benefits an employee or household could receive. In return for capping the total amount of tax-exempt benefits, households would be permitted wider descretion in how a household's tax-exempt dollars are allocated, although a requirement that a minimal level of health care coverage be retained would be needed to prevent households from voluntarily uninsuring themselves and transfering emergency care expenses, should they occur, to the taxpayers.

The changing nature of the American family makes greater employee discretion in the use of tax-exempt income beneficial to many families, as survey data indicate that 30 percent of renter households having working age members are households with two incomes, and two-thirds of these households have dual health care coverage. By permitting the trading of spousal health care coverage that is not being used (but for which employers are paying) for a housing benefit, millions of households would be advantaged.

Although a tax-exempt benefit that all employers were capable of offering would result in more employers participating in housing benefit programs, less expansive legislation could provide a limited number of employers with the ability to offer tax-exempt housing benefits. For example, some benefits received by unionized workers and funded through Taft-Hartley trusts are on a tax-exempt basis. This concept could be expanded to permit employers offering Internal Revenue Code Section 125 "cafeteria benefit" plans to include housing as a qualified benefit.

In general, a cafeteria plan must offer employees a choice between cash and qualified benefits. Section 125 of the Internal Revenue Code defines a *qualified benefit* as any benefit that is excludable from gross income or wages under an express provision of the code, benefits such as health care and life insurance are among the benefits that fall into this category. In addition to these typical benefits, 401(k) deferred compensation plans can also be offered as part of a cafeteria plan. Because housing is not a qualified benefit, if offered, it would be considered as a benefit purchased

with after-tax cash contributions, thus eliminating the value of receiving the benefit via the cafeteria plan, which permits the purchase of services with pre-tax income. A housing benefit could be
classified as a qualified benefit when offered as part of a Section
125 plan, however. The effect of this would be to encourage the
trading of duplicative spousal health care and child care programs
for housing benefits. If a cafeteria plan includes a 401(k) plan, and
if 401(k) programs are amended to facilitate withdrawals for the
purchase of a home (which will be discussed later in this chapter),
an added incentive will be gained for having a qualified housing
benefit within a Section 125 cafeteria benefit program.

By giving housing benefits tax-exempt status, Congress will
confirm that housing is an important family need, on a par with
health care and dependent care. Congress will also be declaring
that corporate, public, and institutional employers have a role in
meeting the housing needs of working families. However, by limiting the kinds of housing benefits that may be received on a tax-
exempt basis, or the cost of tax-exempt housing or other benefits,
or the types of benefit plans that can offer a housing plan, Congress
will also be ensuring that this new tax-exempt benefit is offered in
a way that is fiscally responsible for both the employer and the
national treasury.

Pension Programs

Pension funds in the United States have assets of $2.9 trillion,
but less than 1 percent of this sum is invested in home mortgages.[2]
An amount far smaller still is invested in the housing of those whose
money is being managed.

A supportive federal employer-assisted housing policy would
encourage pension fund investment in housing owned or rented
by pension plan participants. The Employment Retirement Income
Security Act of 1974 (ERISA) system has gone awry in that the
interest of the fund (or the fund managers) has become too removed
from the interests of the individuals whose money is being invested.
Under the guise of fiduciary management, a system has been permitted to evolve that allows pension funds to be invested in junk
bonds and foreign debt rather than in the homes of the individuals
whose deferred wages capitalized that pension fund. Investing in
the home of a pension plan participant is in the long-term, or
retirement, interest of pensioners, for owning a home is the prin-

cipal way in which millions of Americans save money. It is clear that ERISA needs legislative, or regulatory, amending to correct the present situtation that finds marginally below market rate investment in the home of the plan participant to be a violation of fiducuary standards, but finds junk bond investment to be proper.

One way that ERISA might be amended is by redefining "reasonable" rate of return, which has come to be mean "prevailing" rate of return. The Department of Labor, which is charged with writing and interpreting ERISA regulations, has adopted a standard that requires pension funds to lend at rates that are at least what any other lender making a similar investment would charge. Thus, if the current mortgage industry standard for a 30-year fixed rate mortgage is 10 percent, a pension fund must charge 10 percent. But a mortgage lender charging 10 percent is not making a 10 percent return. The lender has to pay investors or depositors for the use of the money (cost of funds) that is then lent as a mortgage. A pension fund, however, does not pay fees or interest to acquire funds; funds are deposited in the pension plan as a matter of contractual obligation. As a result, a pension fund earning 10 percent on a mortgage has a much higher *net* yield than the conventional mortgage lender. ERISA regulations should be amended to recognize the fact that pension funds acquire capital differently than banks and as a result can lend at rates that differ from banks. Continuing to require pension fund returns to equal or exceed bank gross rates of return is to perpetuate a substantially meaningless comparision. ERISA regulations should require that the prevailing rate of return be judged based upon a comparision of net rates of return rather than gross rates of return. If a prevailing net rate of return on investment standard was adopted, pensions funds would be able to make all kinds of investments at rates below that which conventional lenders ordinarily make. The purpose of ERISA regulations should not be to protect lenders from competition; the mission of ERISA is to ensure that pension funds are managed in a way that ensures the accumulation of sufficient capital so as to be able to pay future pension outlays.

As recently as November 1990, U.S. Department of Housing and Urban Development (HUD) Secretary Jack Kemp requested that the Department of Labor (DOL) permit several New York pension funds to invest in below-market mortgage-backed securities to assist in financing affordable housing in New York City. Kemp, in a letter to then Labor Secretary Elizabeth Dole said, "the implications of such an effort nationwide . . . would result in a dramatic increase in affordable housing for families."³ However, less than one month later, HUD's request was denied by the DOL.⁴

If Congress or the DOL were to adopt the net rate of return standard, pension plans could lend money to participants at rates below those of other mortgage lenders. Of course, all types of other borrowers, none of whom were associated in any way with the fund, might also be able to obtain lower-cost pension financing. This was the thrust of Secretary Kemp's request to the DOL.

A more limited alternative to overturning the prevailing gross rate of return standard would be for Congress or the DOL to specifically authorize below market rate lending for the purpose of financing plan participant owned or rented housing. As discussed in Chapter 5, Operating Engineers Local 675 in Fort Lauderdale, Florida attempted to do just this, offering members a 30-year, fixed-rate mortgage at 212.5 basis points below the prevailing market rate. The DOL opposed this program and challenged Local 675 in court. In this case, *Brock v. Walton*,⁵ the United States Court of Appeals for the 11th Circuit ruled that Local 675 was charging a "reasonable" rate of return, as ERISA regulations then required, and upheld the Local 675 program. Subsequently, the DOL redefined "reasonable" rate of return to mean "prevailing" rate of return, based upon the gross rate of return standard. This regulation forced Local 675 to discontinue its below market mortgage lending program.

Congress could reverse this DOL regulation by amending ERISA Sections 404 and 408(b)(1) (which establishes fiduciary standards and set standards for loans to plan participants) to specifically authorize below market housing loans to pension plan participants and to developers of housing for pension plan participants.

Coupled with this statutory law change, pension managers should be required to offer plan participants housing investment programs to the extent that such programs do not violate fiduciary responsibilities for portfolio diversification or otherwise imprudently jeopardize the pension fund's overall rate of return. This regulation is needed because pension managers are more familiar and interested in large multi-million dollar investment vehicles; consequently, left to their own preferences, pension managers may not automatically offer mortgages to plan participants. Ultimately, pension managers should want to offer a variety of investment vehicles including mortgages, second mortgage downpayment loans, shared appreciation loans, and group mortgage co-insurance trust funds. The ability to offer one benefit, the cost of which is paid for, or facilitated by, another benefit should prove very attractive to business and as a result both business and labor, together, should seek to change ERISA to make it more responsive to their mutual needs.

Brock v. Walton, and the subsequent redefinition of what constitutes a reasonable rate of return, triggered regulatory comment regarding how this regulation would affect defined benefit programs (traditional pension programs, such as Local 675's pension fund), but changes are also needed in the regulation of defined contribution programs. While *Brock v. Walton* was being litigated and DOL was rewriting the regulations, members of Congress were publicly discussing creation of Individual Housing Accounts, patterned after Individual Retirement Accounts (IRAs), or permitting early withdrawal of IRA assets (the largest defined contribution program) in order to purchase a home (and implicitly recognizing the linkage between home ownership and retirement security). Proposals to permit IRA withdrawals for the purchase of a first home continue to percolate in Congress.

While there is nothing wrong with permitting IRA withdrawals for the purchase of a first home, the utility of doing so has been greatly diminished by the Tax Reform Act of 1986, which made contributing to an IRA less attractive, and by the fact that contributions of not more than $2,000 annually mean that it will take years, in many of the nation's most expensive housing markets, for households to accrue the money needed for a downpayment, even assuming that housing prices will not appreciate more rapidly than contributions are made. A more supportive federal employer-assisted housing policy would permit plan participants housing investment by all defined contribution plans, principally 401(k) deferred compensation plans.

Employees currently participating in 401(k) programs are able to place up to $8,728 (1992 dollars) of income in a 401(k) retirement plan. By doing so, they shift the time when this income is taxed from the current year to the year when the income is drawn upon (when the participant is at least 59½ years old). 401(k) programs are structured in several ways, including plans that have only employee contributions or only employer contributions. In some programs, employee and employer contributions are made with employer contributions based on a matching formula or on profit sharing. Because 401(k) programs permit larger contributions than IRA programs, the potential exists for employees to accrue funds more rapidly than IRA programs allow.

In proposing to permit penalty free use of 401(k) savings for the purchase of housing, it is not proposed that a new tax advantaged savings program for prospective homebuyers be created. Rather, it is proposed that a home be considered an eligible investment vehicle, just as stocks or bonds are. As such, 401(k) housing investment must be structured so as to permit the benefit to be taxed at age 59½, as are other 401(k) investments (other 401(k) benefits are taxed when drawn upon, in this case the beneficiary is living in the home, in essence drawing upon the benefit). This might be accomplished by establishing a 10-year tax schedule based upon the original 401(k) contribution and some imputed level of return on the housing investment.

By structuring 401(k) housing investment in this way, those who choose a housing investment will be neither any better off, nor worse off, from a tax perspective, than those who choose alternate investment vehicles. Further, by treating housing as just another investment vehicle, no additional federal revenue will be lost by this proposal.

Employee Stock Ownership Plans (ESOPs)

In Chapter 2 it was described how ESOPs might participate in an employer-assisted housing program, but in practice few ESOPs have considered a housing benefit for employees.

One way in which federal policy might encourage ESOP housing benefit programs is by permitting ESOP trusts to guarantee a portion of a mortgage based upon the employee's personal stock holding in the ESOP firm. By using the employee's stock as collateral, the ESOP can provide a lender with additional loan security, thus enabling the lender to reduce downpayment and mortgage insurance requirements.

A more expansive policy would enable employers to assign their stock holdings back to the ESOP trust and then have the trust make a below market rate loan to the employee. The interest rate of this loan would be based upon the interest rate available to the ESOP if it was to borrow money and purchase stock from the employer. This rate is below market because loans to ESOPs are tax advantaged, in that lenders are able to deduct half of the interest charged on loans to ESOPs from their tax liability. In response to this tax advantage, lenders offer loans to ESOPs at a 15 percent to

20 percent discount from rates charged the employer. In this instance, the trust is not borrowing to acquire stock, but issuing a loan against stock acquired by the ESOP. Should the employee default on the loan, the ESOP would be entitled to the employee's pledged stock.

Using this stock as collateral, an employee wanting to buy a $90,000 home might seek a mortgage of $70,000 from a conventional lender and obtain a loan from the ESOP for the $20,000 balance.[6] This is feasible because the ESOP trust has a lien on the stock, not on the home, while at the same time the primary mortgage is for less than 80 percent of the loan-to-value ratio and thus needs no mortgage insurance. The result is a no downpayment mortgage and no mortgage insurance costs. Although of less financial significance, it is also worth noting that the effect of the tax advantaged loan is to create a blended mortgage rate, further reducing monthly housing expenses and lowering the annual income needed to support the amortization of a $90,000 loan.

While these modest changes in law would encourage ESOPs to offer housing benefits, admittedly all of these changes have a certain "Rube Goldberg" quality about them. This is because incremental changes in housing or personnel benefit law are suggested, while trying to graft new solutions to new problems facing business and labor onto existing programs. But Congress is not required to take an incremental approach to facilitating the provision of housing benefits by ESOPs.

Congress could authorize the creation of Employee Home Ownership Plans (EHOPs), which would use ESOP financing methods, but for the express purpose of providing employee housing benefits. In comparison to an ESOP, an EHOP trust would consist entirely of debt and equity positions in employee housing, including individual mortgages, pools of mortgages, mortgage bonds, co-insurance funds, and new construction investment. An EHOP trust would be capitalized through the same tax advantaged mechanism as an ESOP, except that firms would transfer stock that could be converted to cash or retained as collateral. The incentives for employers to participate would be similar to those that exist for ESOPs, principally the ability to deduct ESOP loan principal and income from corporate tax liability. The goal of an EHOP trust would be to provide for the financial and residential security of employees through investment in employee owned and leased housing.

Low-Income Housing Tax Credits

With the demise of direct federal financial support for low-income housing during the 1980s, the principal form of federal support for the construction of new or rehabilitated low-income rental housing has become the Low-Income Housing Tax Credit program, which was created as part of the Tax Reform Act of 1986.

The tax credit program provides investors with a dollar-for-dollar reduction in tax liability for each dollar invested in low-income housing projects, but tax credit investment opportunities are limited. Congress sets the total volume of tax credits available nationally for eligible projects and allocates the credits to the states. The states then allocate credits to various eligible projects.

Corporate investors have purchased millions of dollars in tax credits since the program was enacted. Some firms have quietly purchased credits as part of corporate investment strategies, while others have used their purchases as an opportunity to work with local and national nonprofit housing developers and advocates and as a way of calling public attention to national housing problems. No corporation has initiated a project on behalf of its own employees, however; and indeed, federal law prohibits corporate or union investors in tax credits (unions would want to resell the tax credits as unions typically do not have tax liability) from giving priority to its own employees or members, respectively. The reason for this prohibition is that Congress, in seeking to prohibit housing discrimination, mandated that tax credit–assisted housing would have to be available for "general public use."[7] To ensure general public availability, religious, fraternal, social, and civic organizations, along with unions and employers, were prohibited from sponsoring projects on behalf of their memberships.

While it is certainly not proposed to weaken the federal fair housing laws, it is believed that Congress could exempt business and labor from this requirement without weakening fair housing efforts. Federal fair employment law prohibits discrimination in the work place, and the protected classes under employment law are substantially similar to those classes protected by the nation's fair housing laws; consequently, the pool of employees from which tenants in the tax credit assisted project will be drawn will be a pool that was established subject to anti-discrimination statutes. It should also be required that employers or unions file a plan detailing how they will select tenants for approval from among eligible workers by the state agency that allocates tax credits. This plan would additionally ensure that all eligible employees (those meeting federal targeting requirements) have an equal opportunity to obtain a tax credit–assisted unit. This proposal is analogous to permissible local government "set aside" requirements that permit local governments to offer publicly assisted units to current income-eligible residents of the municipality prior to offering units to residents of other communities.

Congress might want to make this change on an experimental basis to see if, by removing the prohibitions on employer and union involvement in tax credit–financed projects for workers or members, employer or union sponsors of projects would come forward. One way of conducting this experiment would be by limiting this exemption to projects located in federal Urban Enterprise Zones, should this proposed legislation be adopted. By linking employer or union housing involvement to economic development in distressed communities, these groups will have the opportunity to address the housing as well as the economic needs of these neighborhoods, and in so doing will be able to further meet the neighborhood stabilization and security needs of employers locating in the enterprise zones.

Some have suggested that the effect of this policy would be to subsidize employers who are paying low wages (a policy already established in various job training and sub-minimum wage programs), arguing that employers should simply pay higher wages. While this might be true, the setting of wage rates is a complex matter and such a critique does not represent the actual continuum of employer choice. While there is evidence that employers do raise wages in markets where the cost of living (including housing) is higher, the capacity to offer wage increases or absorb wage rate distortions in comparision to other regions is not unlimited. At some point, employers respond to the need for a lower-paid work force by either relocating to a place (foreign or domestic) where wages are lower, or by absorbing a reduced level of productivity that results from their inability to hire suitable personnel at low wages. There is no evidence to suggest that if employers are not permitted to offer tax credit–financed units to employees, employers will respond by significantly raising wages. Rather, by permitting employers and unions to develop projects for low-income employees or members, the federal government will be taking advantage of new employers coming into a neighborhood with new economic resources and giving these companies the opportunity to bring jobs and housing to a neighborhood in need. In sum, therefore, while some employers may use this program to hold down wages, the positive effects of having employers with the capacity to assist in the redevelopment of housing in a distressed neighborhood more than outweigh this consideration.

Other Federal Efforts

This chapter has focused on ways in which the federal government might remove obstacles to employer-assisted housing benefits. In addition to removing impediments, there are affirmative policies that the federal government might initiate to encourage the growth of employer-assisted housing.

One action that might be taken is for Congress to fund already authorized sections of the National Affordable Housing Act of 1990, which authorizes HUD to conduct research regarding employer-assisted housing and permits states and local governments to provide technical assistance to employers and labor organizations so as to inform them of how they can offer or facilitate employer-assisted housing programs.

HUD could also initiate an employer-assisted housing demonstration program. This program would provide matching loans or grants to employers offering various types of housing assistance programs. Although matching grant programs are clearly not necessary for the establishment of housing benefit programs, the federal government has often attracted additional interest to a program by authorizing a demonstration program and appropriating some money. In a modest form, the program could be as simple as explicitly making employer-assisted housing an eligible Community Development Block Grant activity, provided the program is assisting low- or moderate-income workers. A more expansive program would provide a new source of funding that could be structured as a revolving fund.

Finally, the federal government could set an example by offering a housing benefit program to the civil service (housing for civilian defense workers and military dependents is already a multibillion dollar program). By providing a housing benefit, the federal government could demonstrate to other employers how programs could be implemented and gauge the reactions of employees to such programs. By initiating a federal housing benefit program, many private employers will be encouraged to offer their own housing benefit programs.

The federal housing policy toward employer-assisted housing that is advocated here is one that for the most part, can be characterized as supportive, but limited, in that the goal of federal policy would principally be to remove existing obstacles in federal law that act to discourage employers from offering and workers from seeking housing benefit programs. Taken together, the proposals made may prove to be a comprehensive federal employer-assisted housing policy, and enacting all of these proposals might well result in an expansion of housing benefit programs. But the policy agenda for business and labor should not be the passage of a comprehensive federal employer-assisted housing bill. It must be stressed that employer-assisted housing is not an idea waiting for an act of Congress, it is something that business and labor can initiate today in order to better respond to the work force problems that they face today. With this point being clear, Chapter 7 of this book examines national housing policy beyond employer-assisted housing and suggests why business not only has a stake in housing policy and in housing employees, but also has a stake in having a comprehensive national housing policy.

Notes

1. *Demographics in the U.S: The Segmenting of Housing Demand* (Washington, D.C.: The National Association of Realtors, November 1989) 116.
2. New York City Housing Partnership, "Proposal to Establish A Pension Fund Reinvestment Program to Finance Affordable Housing" (unpublished) April 30, 1990.
3. "Ease ERISA Rules for Housing: Kemp," *Pensions and Investments*, November 26, 1990, 2.
4. "Labor Rejects Call for Housing Help," *Pensions and Investments*, December 10, 1990, 6.
5. *Brock v. Walton*, 794 F.2d 586 (11th Cir. 1986).
6. The ESOP Association reports that the average account balance of employees participating in ESOP programs is $16,629, down nearly $2,000 from the previous year as there has been a recent spurt of new ESOP programs that have relatively low balances. Twenty-one percent of all ESOPs reported payouts in excess of $100,000 in 1988. Source: "1989 ESOP Association Survey Results," *ESOP Report* (Washington, D.C.: The ESOP Association, January 1990) 4.
7. *Report of the Mitchell-Danforth Task Force on the Low-Income Housing Tax Credit* (Washington, D.C.: 1989) 4.

Chapter 7

Building on Employer-Assisted Housing: Benefits for the Business Community

Case for Employer-Assisted Housing: A Summary

The case studies, survey data, and trend analyses that have been presented in previous chapters warrant the following short list of conclusions:

1. There was a significant increase in the number of individual businesses, all across America, that began in the 1980s, to offer housing benefits to their nonmanagement workers.
2. Those companies that made the decision to offer housing benefits in the 1980s did so for good, "bottom line" business reasons (i.e., primarily to achieve cost-effective labor recruitment, retention, and productivity objectives).
3. More companies, chambers of commerce, and trade associations are likely to offer or to facilitate the offering of housing benefits in the 1990s, because:
   a. workers want and need these benefits;
   b. existing housing benefits programs can be readily adapted to match the cash, risk, and debt preferences of many companies;
   c. new methods and programs are coming into the marketplace that will be still more cost-effective and that will assist smaller employers to pool their resources and to share the advantages and risks of offering housing benefits;

   d. a sizeable (and apparently growing) percentage of busi-
      ness executives want to consider or work toward offering
      housing benefits for their nonmanagement employees;
   e. those demographic and economic trends that encour-
      aged companies to offer employer-assisted housing in
      the 1980s (i.e., trends in the labor force needs of em-
      ployers, the unaffordability of housing for workers, and
      the cost-effectiveness of housing benefits compared to
      labor shortages and turnover) will continue, and most
      likely accelerate, in the 1990s;
   f. the historic housing interests of organized labor are fast
      being rekindled in the 1990s; and
   g. governmental facilitation of employer-assisted housing
      has already begun and is likely to continue and expand
      in the 1990s.

For all these reasons, and because employer-assisted housing
has the potential to meet a significant portion of the housing needs
of the American people, the authors believe that business executives in individual corporations, chambers of commerce, and trade
associations should move *now* to consider and adopt housing benefit
programs for their nonmanagement workers. Companies, workers,
and all of the major regional economies of the United States will
be significantly advantaged by the widespread adoption of such
benefits.

Why Business Should Advocate Affordable Housing

As more individual businesses, chambers of commerce, and
trade associations adopt housing benefits for nonmanagement workers, some portion of the nation's moderate-income housing needs
will be met. Therefore, some of the resources that governments
(and churches and community-based nonprofit groups) devote to
housing will be enhanced or freed up to meet still more of America's
housing needs. The business community has very strong reasons
to involve itself in the housing policies and programs that governments and nonprofits adopt in the 1990s—more specifically, business ought to speak and act forcefully to ensure that American
housing policies and programs are adopted that will be appropriately stimulative of the economy and that avoid or reduce large

and unnecessary social costs imposed by the unaffordability of housing in much of the United States.

Stimulation of Economic Activity[1]

An effective housing policy that permitted the nation to meet its major housing needs in the 1990s could also generate, during this decade, millions of new jobs, an additional $.5 trillion in private sector economic activity, and billions of dollars for the federal treasury in corporate and personal income tax revenues.

It is appropriate to be specific and conservative in estimating the jobs, economic development, and governmental benefits likely to derive from meeting current housing needs. Accordingly, consider a housing policy that is targeted only on the three housing problems that emerged in the 1980s, that will grow more pressing in the 1990s, and that warrant governmental response because they concern large numbers of people whose needs are unlikely to be met by the unaided market—the housing requirements of young families, the frail elderly, and the poor. These groups did not have their housing needs adequately met in the 1980s, their numbers and their likely housing difficulties will grow in the 1990s, and their below-average incomes suggest that the private housing market is unlikely to be fully responsive to their needs. To house each of these population sectors adequately, it will be necessary to adopt governmental policies encouraging the construction of new housing units for these families and/or to assist these families directly, through loans or grants, so that they can afford existing dwelling units.

Based on demographic trends,[2] there would seem to be a need in the 1990s to encourage the supply or affordability of starter homes for about 3.3 million young families; of new or substantially rehabilitated units suited to the life needs of 1.7 million frail elderly people; and of 3.4 million new or substantially rehabilitated units for low- and moderate-income families. Of this need for 8.4 million new, rehabilitated, or affordability-enhanced units in the decade of the 1990s, at least 6.8 million will have to be newly constructed or substantially rehabilitated. More specifically, the national need in the 1990s will be to facilitate 1.7 million newly constructed starter homes for young families (i.e., about 170,000 per year), 1.7 million new or moderately rehabilitated units for the frail elderly (about 170,000 per year), and 3.4 million new units for the poor (almost 340,000 per year).

To assess the jobs, economic development, and governmental benefits of meeting these housing goals in a specific and conservative manner, consider only these 6.8 million housing units as the decade-long target of new federal governmental activity. For the purpose of this analysis, hypothesize a housing policy that aims at encouraging the supply and/or affordability of these specific 680,000 units each year for 10 years.

A 1980 study by the Bureau of Labor Statistics (BLS) on the economic multiplier effects of single and multi-family housing construction, cited in the December 1981 *Monthly Labor Review*,[3] found that, for each billion dollars of multi-family construction contract expenditures, 25,400 jobs were created. Similarly, for each billion dollars of single-family construction activity, 22,000 jobs were created. Using BLS formulas, and assuming a construction cost of $60,000 for each rental unit to be produced by the hypothesized housing policy, a cost of $90,000 for each home ownership unit, and a cost of $15,000 for each unit rehabilitated for the frail elderly, some 920,000 new jobs would be created each year, or 9.2 million for the decade.

A correction factor deriving from a 1984 University of Maryland study[4] on the economic multiplier effect of housing construction applied to the target numbers in the hypothesized housing policy suggests an additional 276,000 jobs would be generated by multiplier effects. Adding multiplier-effect jobs to the previous "basic jobs generated" total yields an estimate of 11.96 million jobs created over the decade of the 1990s. Using BLS formulas and the Maryland multiplier yields a very conservative estimate of $3.3 billion in individual federal income and wage tax revenues annually, or $33 billion for the decade.

If housing equals new jobs, it also equals new economic activity—that is, the wages, profits, and commerce directly associated with the construction of new dwelling units, plus the additional indirect impact of spending the dollars resulting from housing construction in other areas of the economy. In 1979, the National Association of Home Builders (NAHB) provided an exceedingly conservative estimate of this economic activity.[5] Excluding all the spinoff purchases encouraged by new construction (furniture, draperies, garden supplies, etc.), the NAHB gauged the overall economic impact of 1,000 new, single-family homes at $110 million, and the economic activity generated by 1,000 new multi-family units at more that $50 million.

Using these conservative estimates, the hypothetical level of housing activity considered would result in economic activity worth about $440 billion in the decade. Utilizing an updating correction factor (derived largely from computing wage differentials in housing construction from the 1979 NAHB data to the 1987 BLS indices) yields a conservative estimate of economic activity for the decade-long period of about $600 billion (unadjusted upward for inflation).

Reduction of Social Costs

If the federal government is unable to adopt a new, more effective housing policy soon, profoundly negative consequences are likely to be visited upon millions of American families, on the American economy, and on many American communities. Acceptance of lowered home ownership levels, inattention to the needs of the frail elderly, continued failure to prevent homelessness, neglect of both urban and rural housing requirements, underfunding of needed housing construction programs for the poor—these characteristics of recent and present policy do not just hurt individuals and families, they hurt the economy; they truncate the middle class; they reduce equality of opportunity; they sap the vibrancy of efforts to revitalize cities or restore farm communities; they create new ghettos while reinforcing a culture of poverty and violence in urban centers. A national governmental decision to accept or continue these policies, or a non-decision (which has the same effect), will accelerate these hurtful trends and diminish the quality of life, the moral stature, and perhaps the social peace of the nation. Business is already paying much of the costs of the affordable housing shortage, (and of policy failures to cope with that shortage) and business will pay a high percentage of increasing costs if more effective policies are not adopted.

Consider, first, the social costs of diminished home ownership. If the millions of young families who have been priced out of the housing market in the 1980s, and the millions more who are coming of first-home buying age in the 1990s, cannot be helped to attain home ownership, a substantial truncation of the American middle class is likely to result—a phenomenon of considerable and troublesome significance. Remember that housing equity is a major tool for, as well as a symbol of, achieving and maintaining middle-class status. In a 1989 report the National Association of Realtors indicated that "home equity contributes over 50 percent of the typical baby-boom household's (defined as those between 22 and 40 years of age in 1986) net worth and about two-thirds of net worth for pre-baby boom and elderly households."[6] Obviously, if the post-baby boom generation is unable to move into the ranks of home ownership (and home ownership rates have declined the most for this segment of the population), this generation will look forward to a significantly poorer lifestyle. A continued diminution in home ownership will mean diminished opportunity for families to pay the costs of college education for their children, the costs of health care and retirement for themselves, the costs of caring for their elderly parents. Lower home ownership levels effect a downward spiral of opportunity with probable detrimental impact on the nation's economy and societal structure. The result is unlikely to be a better-educated, healthier, more prosperous, politically stable America. For millions of young families, a lost opportunity to attain home ownership could mean the failure to achieve or maintain middle-class status. Home ownership and the equity reserve that builds in an appreciating home is now as important as, or even more important than, second incomes as a basic tool that Americans use to acquire and maintain middle-class status. Home equity is increasingly the only fixed financial asset that most people have that rises in value as fast as health care, college education, nursing home care, or retirement costs.

Between 1980 and 1989, median family income rose but 10.9 percent, (or less than 1.1 percent annually)[7] and savings rate increases have been in the single digits, too small to cope with double-digit price increases of many major life expenses. For the average American family, absent home equity, the savings curve tends never to cross the major expense curve. In the 1980s, without home equity, the average American family was unable to save enough, and has been hard pressed to borrow enough, to meet the rising costs of major life expenses. The 1990s look like more of the same.

But add only one factor: home equity. The median price of a new home rose 130 percent from 1977 to 1989 (from $48,800 to $112,500)[8] the median price of existing homes escalated 117 percent (from $42,900 to $93,100).[9] Home ownership brought a return, an appreciation, of more than 40 percent in constant dollars, over the 1977 to 1989 period. Families purchasing the average American home in 1975 would have the financial base, the ability to accrue or borrow the money, to meet many of the emergency expenses that they are likely to face some day.

If the nation cannot or will not adopt a better national housing policy, enhancing home ownership, America's future seems likely to have a somewhat smaller middle class comprised mostly of those whose parents have already made it, and a somewhat larger worker class, dispossessed of the "American dream" and disadvantaged in their efforts to educate their children, nurture aged parents, or meet their major life expenses.

Business will pay for continued housing policy failures on home ownership primarily by foregone opportunities. But business will pay for other housing policy failures in far more direct, expensive, and perhaps dangerous ways. Consider, for example housing policy and the nation's cities.

In the 1980s, there were more poor people in America with less money, seeking fewer apartments, at sharply rising rents.[10] In the 1990s, there will be still more poor families, increasingly concentrated in central cities. A continuation of present federal policies (limited new construction, inadequate levels of rental assistance for low-income housing, and no emergency homelessness prevention program) and of current housing trends (most new construction in suburbs, loss of lower-income urban rental stock to gentrification and abandonment) will make the present crisis even worse. The Neighborhood Reinvestment Corporation found, in 1987, that continuation of present policy will lead to a homeless and hidden homeless population of 18 million people by 2003.[11] This is not an assessment that can make anyone sanguine about American societal peace in the 1990s or the 21st century, or about the future of urban areas.

Continuation of the present housing policy will negatively impact both the nation's cities and its class structure. America's older cities declined (and parts of them burned) in the 1960s, then stood poised between renaissance and further decline in the 1970s. During the 1980s many cities experienced, simultaneously, large-scale commercial revitalization of some areas and rapid retrogression of other neighborhoods. Absent a new, urban-targeted housing policy, these cities may become glittering Babylons of business culture downtown, but they will have far too many deteriorated neighborhoods where most city residents actually live.

A continuation of the present national housing policy will mean a continuation, if not exacerbation, of urban decline and a certain increase in social costs.

The business community (and everyone else) will also be asked to pay still more societal costs if the country continues the failed housing policies of the 1980s. Continued inattention to the housing needs of elderly people in general and the frail elderly in particular—a hallmark of current policy—will mean an increase in home accidents and injuries, some number of them fatal, and an increase in the incidence of premature, needless institutionalization. Americans will pay more for health care and nursing home care and lose the economy-expanding, and community-enhancing, participation of many senior citizens. It began to happen in the 1980s. It will happen with much greater frequency, at much greater expense, in the 1990s, because there will be so many more "old elderly" in the population in this decade and the costs of health care and nursing home care will rise. It does not have to be that way; it would surely be cheaper, wiser, and more compassionate to have home equity and housing rehabilitation loan programs to help senior citizens remain in the community. The continuation of present public policy will have the effect of causing avoidable hurt to some senior citizens and of driving others out from their homes.

Continued inattention to the housing needs of single-parent, female-headed households, in combination with the feminization of poverty, will consign more children to bad living environments, mostly in deteriorating apartments. It does not have to be that way—their mothers (the vast majority of them working) could be provided with long-term deferred-payback loans to purchase larger homes and convert or rehabilitate them to several smaller units, the rental income from which would facilitate loan repayment; homesharing and housing with child care could be encouraged. The continuation of current public policy will have the effect of causing or tolerating avoidable hurt to a generation of children in an America where 60 percent of the children born today can expect to live in a one-parent family before they reach 18 years of age.[12]

A Call for Enhanced Business Advocacy

The business community as a whole, and most organizations that represent large sectors of that community, have been relatively uninformed and silent on the subject of a national housing policy. Industries that are directly impacted (builders, realtors, mortgage bankers, etc.), of course, regularly monitor and seek to influence these policies; but the U.S. Chamber of Commerce, the Business Roundtable, the National Association of Manufacturers, the Conference Board, and most other business organizations have taken little (or, at most, infrequent and episodic) interest.

The American business community as a whole has a real stake in, and a real contribution to make concerning, a national housing policy. National business associations must get interested, get sophisticated, and get involved in national housing policy. Indeed, it may well be time to create a national business committee on affordable housing.

Actions Beyond Employer-Assisted Housing

"Think globally, act locally" is a maxim that might usefully guide business leaders in their efforts to get interested, sophisticated, and involved in housing. Corporate executives who want to initiate or expand philanthropic gifts to expand affordable housing programs could found a National Business Foundation for Affordable Housing for example; but, we think, they would do better to target their gifts and grants to existing nonprofit housing groups in the communities which are home to corporate facilities. These local groups could also benefit from the services of loaned executives and from business support for local zoning and land use policies which facilitate affordable housing. Business people who take these actions are likely to find that their efforts are rewarding to them, their companies, and their communities. They are likely to discover, too, that a business-led coalition or partnership for affordable housing is needed at national and state levels and in every city and town across America.

Keeping the Emphasis Where It Belongs— On Employer-Assisted Housing

In the end, business executives—like all people—will do first what they perceive to be in their direct interest to do. For a sizable and growing proportion of America's business executives, that means adopting housing benefit programs for their non-management workers in a manner which best meets the needs and preferences of the employer, workers, and the community. Happily, the self-interest of employers manifested in the offering of employer-assisted housing programs is likely to serve the broader interest of the nation and its communities by meeting a significant part of the country's housing needs.

Notes

1. Much of the material presented in this section derives from work previously published in D.C. Schwartz, R.C. Ferlauto and D.N. Hoffman, *A New Housing Policy for America* (Philadelphia: Temple University Press, 1988) 42–47 and *passim*. The authors gratefully acknowledge the permission of Temple University to reprint portions of that work.
2. Ibid.
3. R. Ball, "Employment Created Construction Expenditures," *Monthly Labor Review*, December 1981, 39.
4. *See* discussion of this subject in Chapter 3.
5. Material made available to the authors by the National Association of Home Builders, July 1987.
6. National Association of Realtors, *Demographics in the U.S.: The Segmenting of Housing Demand* (Washington, D.C.: National Association of Realtors, 1989) 74.
7. *State of the Nation's Housing—1991*, Joint Center for Housing Studies of Harvard University (Cambridge, Mass., 1991) 29.
8. *See* note 5, above.
9. Ibid.
10. *See* Schwartz *et al, A New Housing Policy*, 287.
11. P.L. Clay, *At Risk of Loss: The Endangered Future of Low-Income Rental Housing Resources* (Washington, D.C.: Neighborhood Reinvestment Corporation, 1987).
12. *See* Schwartz *et al, A New Housing Policy*, 228.

Appendixes

Appendix 1

Employee Study

A. Sample

1. The sample for this survey was developed on a national probability basis.
2. The Employee study was based on a standard probability sample of all households in the 48 contiguous states. A description of the procedure for selecting primary sampling units for that base sample follows. These primary sampling units were then grouped or stratified into two basic strata:
   a. Urban counties defined as all counties located within a metropolitan area with a population of 150,000 or more.
   b. Rural counties defined as all other counties in the 48 states utilizing the national sample's primary sampling units for each of the two strata. Separate projectable probability samples of all telephone households in that stratum were then drawn. This was done to oversample the rural counties. In particular, the total number of interviews eventually conducted in each stratum were
   Urban Stratum—511 interviews
   Rural Stratum—689 interviews
3. The individuals contacted using the two probability samples (i.e., the samples of urban and rural counties) were then screened for eligibility for the study. An eligible individual was defined as someone meeting *all* of the following three criteria:
   a. Non-owner of a house, condominium, or other residence;
   b. 18 to 44 years of age; and
   c. either currently employed full-time, or had a spouse currently employed full-time (or both).

209

B. Interviewing

Pre-test interviews were conducted by full-time professional staff of RL Associates. All regular interviews were conducted by trained professional interviewers who had been fully briefed and trained for this particular interview.

C. Questionnaire

1. The same basic questionnaire was conducted over the telephone with all eligible employee households. However, on a number of questions the employee questionnaire was split-sampled to permit
   a. covering a somewhat wider range of material, and
   b. to allow testing of the effect of limited variations in the details of a particular housing program.
2. Two examples should clarify.
   a. Half the respondents were asked if they agreed or disagreed with the statement, "It is *easier* for young couples to buy their first house then it was 20 years ago," and the other half were asked if they agreed or disagreed with the statement, "It is *harder* for young couples to buy their first house then it was 20 years ago."
   b. Half the respondents were asked about their interest in "Another program an employer could have is one where banks would not charge certain closing costs, saving the employee about $400 to $900 depending on the price of the home. . . ." while the other half were asked about their interest in "Another program an employer could have is one where banks would not charge certain closing costs, saving the employee about $1,000 to $1,500 depending on the price of the home. . . .".

D. Coding and Processing

All coding and data processing was carried out by the full-time professional staff of RL Associates.

E. Design of a Probability Sample

The national sample design is a two-stage, stratified, internally replicated national probability sample. The first stage of stratification is the nine census regions in the contiguous United States, omitting Hawaii and Alaska. The second stage is Areas of Dominant Influence (ADIs) within each of the census regions.

To construct the sample, the entire country is first divided into the nine regions defined by the U.S. Bureau of Census, except that Hawaii and Alaska are deleted from the Pacific region. Within each region, the ADIs, as defined by Arbitron, are arrayed in terms of population. These ADIs form the primary sampling units.

Within each ADI, counties are arrayed by population, and within each county, minor civil divisions (MCDs) are arrayed in terms of population. Using this listing for each region, systematic random sampling is used to select a sample of MCDs.

A total of 500 sampling units was chosen overall. This actually consists of eight separate matched samples, each consisting of 62 or 63 sampling units. Each of these eight matched samples is itself a national probability sample. The use of eight matched samples of internal replicates allows data-based estimates of sampling to be obtained.

For each of the 500 MCDs selected, the actual sampling point is defined as the largest telephone book containing the MCD. Since each MCD in the United States has a chance of selection proportional to its population, and since each MCD is associated with one and only one telephone book, each telephone book has a probability of selection proportional to the number of people living in the area, and *not* to the number of telephones, whether listed or unlisted.

An equal number of telephone numbers is selected from each telephone book in such a way that every number listed in the book has an equal chance of being selected. These numbers form a base for the sample, but since they are all listed numbers, they are not used for actual calling. Rather, a random digit is systematically added to the listed numbers selected so as to give a random sample of both listed and nonlisted numbers. This takes advantage of the fact that unlisted numbers are randomly distributed over all telephone numbers.

The procedure gives every telephone household a known (and approximately equal) chance of selection into the sample. To extend the sampling procedure to individuals, systematic random respondent selection will be used as defined in the main body of the proposal.

In projecting results, an unequal probability of selection of individuals is corrected by weighting all respondents, where the weight given each individual is inversely proportional to the probability of selection of the individual. Weighting is also done when necessary by demographic factors to compensate for any random variation in response.

Appendix 2

Employer Study

A. Sample

1. The employer sample was developed from three national probability samples of different groups of employers: hospitals, colleges and universities, and for-profit industrial corporations. Each of these was in turn stratified into a total of 10 sub-strata as follows:

    a. Hospitals. A total of 50 interviews were completed in four strata:
    - 15 interviews among hospitals with between 125 and 400 beds in rural areas in the southern census region.
    - 15 interviews among hospitals with between 125 and 400 beds in rural areas in the balance of the country.
    - 10 interviews among hospitals with between 125 and 400 beds in urban areas throughout the country.
    - 10 interviews among hospitals with over 400 beds.

    b. Colleges and universities. A total of 27 interviews were completed in two strata:
    - 17 interviews with colleges having between 1,000 and 3,000 students.
    - 10 interviews with colleges having over 3,000 students.

    c. For-profit industrial corporations. A total of 384 interviews were completed in four strata:
    - 111 interviews among for-profit industrial corporations with between 250 and 1,000 employees in rural areas in the southern census region.
    - 117 interviews among for-profit industrial corporations with between 250 and 1,000 employees in rural areas in the balance of the country.

- 120 interviews among for-profit industrial corporations with between 250 and 1,000 employees in urban areas throughout the country.
- 85 interviews among for-profit industrial corporations with over 1,000 employees.

2. Within each of the 10 sub-strata systematic random sampling of available lists of employers were used to produce probability samples for telephone contact. The lists used were
   a. The American Hospital Association list of all accredited hospitals in the United States
   b. Barron's Guide to colleges and universities.
   c. Dun and Bradstreet's list of U.S. corporations.

Respondents were either the Human Resource Director (or equivalent title) or the President/CEO of the organization.

B. Interviewing

Pre-test interviews were conducted by full-time professional staff of RL Associates. All regular interviews were conducted by trained professional interviewers who had been fully briefed and trained for this particular interview. The employer interviews were carried out by interviewers with previous experience in "executive" interviewing.

C. Questionnaire

1. Employer Questionnaire. The employer questionnaire was modified subsequent to the first 151 interviews. This was done to allow extending the questioning on certain issues. The need for these modifications had become evident from the comments and responses to open-ended questions of the first 151 respondents. In a sense, the survey can be considered as having two components.
   a. A main body of material that remained fixed for all 461 interviews
   b. An additional body of material for which the first 151 interviews can be conceived of as a very extended pretest followed by a 310-interview survey.

D. Coding and Processing

All coding and data processing was carried out by the full-time professional staff of RL Associates.

E. Design of a Probability Sample

The national sample design is a two-stage, stratified, internally replicated national probability sample. The first stage of stratification is the nine census regions in the contiguous United States, omitting Hawaii and Alaska. The second stage is Areas of Dominant Influence (ADIs) within each of the census regions.

To construct the sample, the entire country is first divided into the nine regions defined by the U.S. Bureau of Census, except that Hawaii and Alaska are deleted from the Pacific region. Within each region, the ADIs, as defined by Arbitron, are arrayed in terms of population. These ADIs form the primary sampling units.

Within each ADI, counties are arrayed by population, and within each county, minor civil divisions (MCDs) are arrayed in terms of population. Using this listing for each region, systematic random sampling is used to select a sample of MCDs.

A total of 500 sampling units was chosen overall. This actually consists of eight separate matched samples, each consisting of 62 or 63 sampling units. Each of these eight matched samples is itself a national probability sample. The use of eight matched samples of internal replicates allows data-based estimates of sampling to be obtained.

For each of the 500 MCDs selected, the actual sampling point is defined as the largest telephone book containing the MCD. Since each MCD in the United States has a chance of selection proportional to its population, and since each MCD is associated with one and only one telephone book, each telephone book has a probability of selection proportional to the number of people living in the area, and *not* to the number of telephones, whether listed or unlisted.

An equal number of telephone numbers is selected from each telephone book in such a way that every number listed in the book has an equal chance of being selected. These numbers form a base for the sample, but since they are all listed numbers, they are not used for actual calling. Rather, a random digit is systematically added to the listed numbers selected so as to give a random sample of both listed and nonlisted numbers. This takes advantage of the fact that unlisted numbers are randomly distributed over all telephone numbers.

The procedure gives every telephone household a known (and approximately equal) chance of selection into the sample. To extend the sampling procedure to individuals, systematic random respondent selection will be used as defined in the main body of the proposal.

In projecting results, an unequal probability of selection of individuals is corrected by weighting all respondents, where the weight given each individual is inversely proportional to the probability of selection of the individual. Weighting is also done when necessary by demographic factors to compensate for any random variation in response.

Appendix 3

Single-Family Home Prices, Wages, and Home Price/Wage Ratios for Selected Metropolitan Areas, 1989

By Home Price/Wage Ratio

METROPOLITAN STATISTICAL AREA	MEDIAN HOME PRICE (000)(1)	AVERAGE ANNUAL WAGE (2)	HOUSING AFFORDABILITY RATIO (HOME PRICE/WAGE)	INCOME NEEDED TO AFFORD HOME PRICE (3)
Honolulu	267.6	21,875	12.2	99,020
Anaheim	245.3	25,041	9.8	90,768
San Francisco	260.6	28,751	9.1	96,429
Los Angeles	215.5	26,844	8.0	79,741
San Diego	175.2	22,893	7.7	64,829
Boston	182.8	27,528	6.6	67,641
New Haven	163.5	25,413	6.4	60,500
Worcester	141.5	23,061	6.1	52,359
Providence	130.2	21,492	6.1	48,178
Riverside/San Ber	124.1	20,863	5.9	45,921
Hartford	159.9	27,588	5.8	59,168
Springfield	127.1	22,036	5.8	47,031
New York	183.4	32,714	5.6	67,863
Washington, DC	144.4	27,677	5.2	53,432
Sacramento	112.6	22,639	5.0	41,665
Raleigh/Durham	103.6	21,922	4.7	38,335
West Palm Beach	102.6	22,465	4.6	37,965
Albany	104.9	23,300	4.5	38,816
Baltimore	96.3	22,988	4.2	35,634
Charlotte	88.7	21,390	4.1	32,822
Las Vegas	85.7	21,020	4.1	31,711

METROPOLITAN STATISTICAL AREA	MEDIAN HOME PRICE (000)(1)	AVERAGE ANNUAL WAGE (2)	HOUSING AFFORDABILITY RATIO (HOME PRICE/WAGE)	INCOME NEEDED TO AFFORD HOME PRICE (3)
Philadelphia	103.9	25,564	4.1	38,446
Charleston	74.5	18,528	4.0	27,567
Albuquerque	49.7	20,350	3.9	29,491
Lexington	77.0	19,703	3.9	28,492
Orlando	79.8	20,599	3.9	29,528
Ft. Lauderdale	83.9	21,678	3.9	31,045
Miami	86.9	22,596	3.8	32,155
Columbia	73.8	19,474	3.8	27,308
Daytona	63.4	16,775	3.8	23,460
Nashville	79.9	21,156	3.8	29,565
Memphis	78.1	21,054	3.7	28,899
Tampa	71.6	19,341	3.7	26,494
Birmingham	78.5	21,472	3.7	29,047
Dallas	92.3	25,284	3.7	34,154
El Paso	63.1	17,292	3.6	23,349
Madison	76.5	20,967	3.6	28,307
Ft. Worth	79.8	21,907	3.6	29,528
Montgomery	68.8	19,147	3.6	25,458
Minneapolis	87.2	24,451	3.6	32,266
Phoenix	78.8	22,125	3.6	29,158
Milwaukee	79.6	22,569	3.5	29,454
Denver	85.5	24,398	3.5	31,637
Salt Lake City	69.9	20,122	3.5	25,865
Atlanta	84.0	24,226	3.5	31,082
Greenville	68.6	19,879	3.4	25,384
Chicago	91.5	26,594	3.4	33,858
Syracuse	79.3	23,114	3.3	29,343
Buffalo	72.5	21,738	3.3	26,827
New Orleans	70.0	21,073	3.3	25,902
St. Louis	76.9	23,537	3.2	28,455
Corpus Christi	64.9	20,025	3.2	24,015
Jacksonville	66.5	20,657	3.2	24,607
San Antonio	64.1	19,973	3.2	23,719
Chattanooga	65.4	20,392	3.2	24,200
Kansas City	71.6	22,360	3.2	26,494
Little Rock	63.6	19,931	3.2	23,534
Portland	70.1	22,131	3.2	25,939
Indianapolis	71.2	22,648	3.1	26,346
Columbus	69.3	22,052	3.1	25,643
Baton Rouge	63.8	20,569	3.1	23,608
Omaha	60.6	19,850	3.1	22,424
Dayton	68.7	22,753	3.0	25,421
Cincinnati	68.2	22,751	3.0	25,236
Mobile	56.7	19,073	3.0	20,981
Louisville	58.4	20,101	2.9	21,610
Rochester	72.6	25,108	2.9	26,864
Grand Rapids	64.2	22,581	2.8	23,756
Tulsa	62.6	22,061	2.8	23,164
Akron	64.5	22,786	2.8	23,867
Cleveland	67.4	23,864	2.8	24,940

METROPOLITAN STATISTICAL AREA	MEDIAN HOME PRICE (000)(1)	AVERAGE ANNUAL WAGE (2)	HOUSING AFFORDABILITY RATIO (HOME PRICE/WAGE)	INCOME NEEDED TO AFFORD HOME PRICE (3)
Spokane	52.4	18,586	2.8	19,389
Pittsburgh	65.5	23,478	2.8	24,237
Wichita	62.0	22,307	2.8	22,942
Des Moines	57.9	21,018	2.8	21,425
Detroit	73.7	27,540	2.7	27.271
Toledo	60.8	22,759	2.7	22,498
Houston	66.7	25,229	2.6	24,681
Oklahoma City	53.5	20,669	2.6	19,797
Lansing	59.8	23,868	2.5	22,128
Peoria	46.8	23,514	2.0	17,317
UNITED STATES	93.1	22,867	4.1	34,450

1. Existing single-family homes, preliminary 1989.
2. 1989 wages are 1989 wages adjusted using the Bureau of Labor Statistics September 1989 Employment Cost Index.
3. Assumptions: that the household is spending 30% of its income on a 30-year mortgage for 90% of the value of the home (10% down payment) at a 10.69% interest rate (average for June—fixed-rate) and 1% property tax on sale value of the home.
Source: National Association of Realtors; U.S. Department of Labor, Bureau of Labor Statistics, 1989.

Index

National Low Income Housing Information Service 24
Neighborhood Housing Services (NHS) 48–49, 53–54
Neighborhood Reinvestment Corporation 7, 19, 203
New Jersey Business and Industry Association 11, 120
New Jersey Housing and Mortgage Finance Agency (HMFA) 44–46
New York City Employees Retirement System and Police Pension Funds 173–74, 177
New York State Mortgage Authority 172
New York State Pension Investment
Policy Group 172
Nonprofit developer 64, 70, 77–78

O

Operating Engineers Local 675 175, 188–89
Organized labor *See* Union(s)

P

Payroll deduction programs 50, 52–53, 111
PC Connection 68–69
Pennsylvania Housing Finance Agency 174
Pennsylvania State Employee Retirement System 173
Pension programs 168–78, 186–90
Peterson Industries 69–70
PHH/US Mortgage 165
Port Authority of New York and New Jersey 10–11

Pride Container Corp. 54
Private mortgage insurers 41, 47
Public pension investment 172–78
Public Works Administration 154, 155
Purchase guarantee program 36, 53, 65–67, 183
Purchase of securities programs 35, 58–59

R

Recruitment of employees *See* Employees, recruitment and training
Regional Plan Association 10–11
Relocation compensation 5, 7
Rent security deposit program 52
Rental housing 70–71
affordability 23–25
employer-sponsored benefits 116
RL Associates 122
Roofers, Sheet Metal Workers and Carpenters 168
Ryerson, Laurie 53

S

St. Joseph Hospital 36, 50–52
Saunders Hotel Company 159
Second mortgage
downpayment loan 49, 52
programs 54–55
Secondary market 42
Section 125 cafeteria benefit program 186
Section 202 Housing for the Elderly and Handicapped Program 156

About the Authors

David C. Schwartz is Professor of Political Science and Director of the American Affordable Housing Institute at Rutgers University. He is Chairman of the Board of the National Housing Institute and a Vice President of the National Housing Conference. In addition to his interest in employer-assisted housing, David has been a leading advocate of homelessness prevention programs, one of which was awarded a United Nations International Year of Shelter citation.

Daniel N. Hoffman is Research Director of the American Affordable Housing Institute. Prior to joining the Institute in 1988, Dan spent a decade planning and implementing housing and economic development projects in settings ranging from Sioux communities in southern Minnesota to New Jersey's most urbanized cities. Dan holds a Masters degree from the Hubert Humphrey Institute of Public Affairs, University of Minnesota.

Richard C. Ferlauto works for the Center for Policy Alternatives located in Washington, D.C., where he coordinates the Public Capital Program which provides policy guidance for state and local governments in the areas of economic revitalization, housing, pension fund investments, community-based development and community lending programs. Prior to joining CPA, Rich was Special Projects Director at the American Affordable Housing Institute where he worked closely with Local 26 Hotel Employees/Restaurant Employees of Boston to design and implement the nation's first Taft-Hartley Housing Trust Fund. In addition to his work as a policy analyst, he has extensive experience building community/labor coalitions around housing and economic issues.

Schwartz, Hoffman, and Ferlauto have written together extensively on a variety of housing issues including as co-authors of

New Housing Policy for America: Recapturing the American Dream (Temple University Press 1988). The authors are principals of Housing Benefit Strategies, Inc., which provides housing benefit design and implementation services to business, labor, and public agencies.

They can be contacted at:

American Affordable Housing Institute
P.O. Box 118
New Brunswick, NJ 08903

Housing Benefit Strategies
41 North 7th Avenue
Highland Park, NJ 08904